card & pocket
in Back

D1557680

Connectivity, Complexity, and
Catastrophe in Large-Scale Systems

Wiley IIASA International Series on Applied Systems Analysis

1  CONFLICTING OBJECTIVES IN DECISIONS
   Edited by David E. Bell, *University of Cambridge,*
   Ralph L. Keeney, *Woodward-Clyde Consultants, San Francisco,*
   and Howard Raiffa, *Harvard University.*

2  MATERIAL ACCOUNTABILITY
   Rudolf Avenhaus, *Nuclear Research Center Karlsruhe,*
   and *University of Mannheim.*

3  ADAPTIVE ENVIRONMENTAL ASSESSMENT AND
   MANAGEMENT
   Edited by C. S. Holling, *University of British Columbia.*

4  ORGANIZATION FOR FORECASTING AND
   PLANNING: EXPERIENCE IN THE SOVIET UNION AND
   THE UNITED STATES
   Edited by W. R. Dill, *New York University,*
   and G. Kh. Popov, *Moscow State University.*

5  MANAGEMENT OF ENERGY/ENVIRONMENT
   SYSTEMS
   Edited by Wesley K. Foell, *International
   Institute for Applied Systems Analysis,*
   and *University of Wisconsin—Madison.*

6  SYSTEMS ANALYSIS BY MULTILEVEL
   METHODS
   Yvo M. I. Dirickx, *University of Louvain,*
   and L. Peter Jennergren, *Odense University.*

7  CONNECTIVITY, COMPLEXITY, AND
   CATASTROPHE IN LARGE-SCALE SYSTEMS
   John Casti, *New York University.*

7 International Series on
Applied Systems Analysis

# Connectivity, Complexity, and Catastrophe in Large-Scale Systems

John Casti
*New York University*

*A Wiley—Interscience Publication*
*International Institute for Applied Systems Analysis*

JOHN WILEY & SONS
Chichester – New York – Brisbane – Toronto

QA
402
.C 36

**British Library Cataloguing in Publication Data:**

Casti, John
  Connectivity, complexity and catastrophe in
  large-scale systems.—(International series
  on applied systems analysis).
  1. System theory   2. Catastrophes (Mathematics)
  I. Title   II. Series
  003           Q295           79-40818

  ISBN 0 471 27661 8

  Typeset in Northern Ireland at The Universities Press (Belfast) Ltd.
  and printed by The Pitman Press, Bath.

To Rudolf Kalman,
who transformed systems theory
from a mystical art
into a mathematical discipline

# Preface

Connectivity, complexity, catastrophe: these are loaded words in the system theory lexicon. At one level the words connote an intuitively satisfying characterization of important aspects of processes that pervade modern life. How often does one see descriptions such as "a tightly connected system," "a large, complex system," "a catastrophic outcome," and so on? Upon more careful examination, though, the "three C's" appear as the smile of the Cheshire cat rather than as a useful characterization of system-theoretic properties. The problem is one of translation of intuition into operational terms. Until the words are given a definite operational meaning within the context of a given mathematical model of a particular problem, they mean whatever one wants them to mean, a normal situation in philosophy but one with obvious defects as a model for policy making or control.

In the pages that follow, we attempt a somewhat eclectic overview of some of the recent work aimed at mathematically coming to grips with connectivity, complexity, and catastrophe (ccc). In some sense, this book can be regarded as an extended outline, as the goal has been more to range over a wide variety of approaches to ccc, rather than to provide in-depth coverage of a few particular approaches. Since there is by no means consensus about how the basic concepts should actually be viewed, we feel that our approach is at least defensible. Nonetheless, many readers may wish for more details. For this reason, we have attempted to provide a balanced reading list at the end of each chapter for those who wish to dig deeper. Consequently, the book should be regarded as a high-altitude flight over some of the mountaintops of the system theory world, not paying too much attention to the fine points found only in the valleys. It is to be hoped that this approach will make the basic ideas accessible to a wider range of readers than would a purely technical treatment devoted to detailed excursions down into the valleys. For the same reason, we have also provided numerous applications of the CCC ideas from a wide variety of fields. At worst, these applications should assist the reader by providing motivation for some of the more esoteric mathematics. At best, some of the applications may justify the entire book; the reader himself must be the final judge.

As system theory is an intellectually alive, rapidly developing activity, it is clearly impossible in a volume of such modest proportions to do justice to all of the important work done in CCC. The choice of subject and selection of results has been motivated by the author's personal prejudices and view of the field. The reader will note an emphasis on tools and techniques based in algebra and topology, as opposed to analysis. This is no accident: it is our firm belief that the methodological future of large systems lies in the development and extension of those areas of algebra and geometry that characterize the global features of mathematical objects. Once the overall landscape is identified, the *local* tools of analysis may be employed to sharpen our knowledge of detailed behavior.

In overall outline, the book's structure is shown by the following dependency diagram:

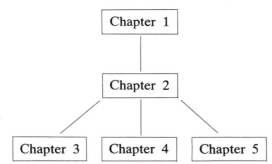

Chapters 1 and 2 are devoted to a presentation of background philosophy of systems and modeling. In particular, the vital point that the mathematical form of the system description dictates the type of questions that can be asked is addressed in the first chapter. There we are concerned with a presentation of several alternative mathematical descriptions of a process and a discussion of how each description possesses characteristic features useful for analyzing certain subclasses of questions.

Chapter 2 is devoted to a rapid survey of several important system-theoretic ideas that *do not* form the main topics of the book but that, nonetheless, are critically important to keep in mind in any analysis—among these ideas are such concepts as identification, stochastic effects, constraints, and optimization. A very brief introduction to CCC is also given in this chapter in order to provide a backdrop for the more detailed treatment given in the remainder of the book.

In Chapter 3 we turn to the main topics of the book, beginning with connectivity. A fairly detailed discussion of elementary simplicial homology theory is given as the underlying basis of the $q$-analysis methodology of R. H. Atkin. This technique for exploring connective structure is then systematically exploited in a number of diverse areas. We also discuss the connectivity question from the viewpoint of the algebraic theory of modules and machines in this chapter and relate it to other state-variable approaches.

The complexity of a system is our leitmotiv for Chapter 4. Beginning with a discussion of various features that a reasonable mathematical definition of complexity should possess, we develop an axiomatic definition having its basis in semigroup theory. This definition is explored in several applications and is contrasted with alternative approaches from information theory and topology.

The final chapter is devoted to a thorough discussion of stability theory in all of its mathematical manifestations. After a rapid treatment of classical notions involving input–output and Lyapunov stability, the chapter turns to a more detailed discussion of qualitative ideas centering upon structural stability. In particular, we present an extended account of catastrophe theory and its relations to bifurcation analysis. In addition, several sections are devoted to the topic of the "resilience" of a dynamic process. This notion, originally motivated by ecological considerations, involves the ability of a system to persist in the face of unknown (and possibly unknowable) external disturbances. Details of several approaches to mathematically characterizing resilience are given, along with an extended economic example.

It is patently clear that a book with such a wide array of topics and techniques could not possibly be put together without the generous advice and assistance of many people. I have been luckier than most authors in having had the opportunity to "dry-run" the material past scientists from many disciplines in an attempt to strike some suitable balance between general comprehensibility and mathematical content. For their help in this regard, I particularly wish to thank A. Casti, C. S. Holling, R. Dennis, D. Ludwig, C. Muses, G. Leitmann, M. Shakun, D. Sahal, J. Dathe, and M. Peschel.

*New York City*
*October 1978*

# Contents

1  *System Concepts and Descriptions*   1

Intuitive Notions   1
Mathematical Descriptions   6
Notes and References   21

2  *Basic Questions and Perspectives on System Theory*   23

Controlled versus Free Dynamics   23
Identification   25
Constraints   27
Stochastic Effects   30
Optimization   31
Global Perspectives   32
Connectivity and Graphs   35
Connectivity and Simplicial Complexes   37
Complexity   40
Stability   45
Catastrophes and Resilience   49
Notes and References   53

3  *Connectivity*   57

Complexes and Connections   58
Eccentricity   60
Holes and Obstructions   61
Betti Numbers and Torsion   66
$p$-Holes   66
Cochains and Coboundaries   68

xi

xii

Predator–Prey Relations: A Homological Example   70
Hierarchical Systems and Covers   74
Applications of $q$-Connectivity to Chess and Shakespearean Drama   76
Algebraic Connectivity   81
Linear Systems   82
Nonlinear Problems   88
Semigroups and Wreath Products   88
Krohn–Rhodes Decomposition Theorem   90
Decomposition of Analytic Systems   92
Notes and References   93

4   *Complexity*   97

Static Complexity   98
Dynamic Complexity   102
Computational Complexity   105
Axioms of System Complexity   106
Complexity of Finite-State Machines   108
Evolution Complexity and Evolving Structures   110
Choice Processes and Complexity   113
Design versus Control Complexity   115
A Program for Practical Applications of Complexity   116
Polyhedral Dynamics and Complexity   116
Algebraic System Theory and Complexity   117
Nonlinear, Finite-Dimensional Processes   119
Complexity and Information Theory   120
Notes and References   122

5   *Stability, Catastrophes, and Resilience*   126

External Descriptions   127
Internal Descriptions   127
Structural Stability   129
Connective Stability and Resilience   130
Graphs and Pulse Processes   131
Input–Output Stability   133
Internal Models and Stability   135
Connective Stability   141
Hopf Bifurcations   144
Structurally Stable Dynamics   147
Catastrophe Theory   151
Some Catastrophe-Theoretic Examples   156
The Cusp Catastrophe and the Logistic Equation   162
Pulse and Value Stability   163

Resilience of Dynamical Processes   166
Resilience and Catastrophes   169
Morse–Smale Systems and Resilience   173
Stability, Control, and Feedback Decisions   181
Lyapunov Stability and Pole-Shifting   183
Bifurcation Control   187
Controlled Resilience   189
Observations   193
Notes and References   193

Index   201

# 1 System Concepts and Descriptions

The mystery of their profession lies only in their terms.
THOMAS VAUGHAN

Sometimes he thought sadly to himself, "Why?" and sometimes he
thought, "Wherefore?" and sometimes he thought, "Inasmuch or
which?"—and sometimes he didn't quite know what he was thinking
about.
A. A. MILNE, *Winnie the Pooh*

## INTUITIVE NOTIONS

One of the most pervasive and least well-defined concepts in modern
intellectual thought is the notion of a "system." In a vague, personal sort of
way, almost everyone who thinks about the matter for a moment can
visualize his own image of what constitutes a system. Sometimes it is even
possible to verbalize these fleeting images to describe hazy pictures of many
"elements" interacting in a "complicated" manner in order to achieve some
fuzzy "objective." Occasionally, the private system conceptualizations of
two individuals will overlap to a sufficient degree that a true meeting of the
minds can take place followed by meaningful discussion or collaboration.
More often, intellectual, professional, and cultural gaps are too great, and
communication breakdowns occur despite the good intentions and desires
for interaction of the parties involved. One of the primary goals of this
monograph is to provide a basis for common discussion of system-theoretic
issues by presenting numerous examples of system problems from many
disciplines and showing how they all may be described and analyzed by
means of a rather small number of abstract paradigms.

Of necessity, our treatment of the main topics in this book will involve a
certain amount of mathematics. This is to be expected, as the implications of
existing knowledge in fields such as biology, sociology, psychology,
economics, not to mention the "harder" sciences such as physics and
chemistry, are far too great to digest without abstractions, i.e., without
mathematics. However, it is a pleasant surprise to discover that understanding most of the fundamental system concepts does not require much beyond
ordinary calculus, geometry, and elementary algebra. (In a few places, we
must employ somewat more sophisticated mathematics, such as semigroup

1

2

theory and homology theory. However, when these occasions arise, every attempt will be made to motivate the formal mathematics with system-theoretic considerations and examples to ease the burden on the reader.) Consequently, as we go along, we shall endeavor to illustrate the main points more by examples than by exotic theorems, hoping thereby to convey the essence of the matter without becoming too entangled in fine details.

Probably the simplest way to begin our exposition is to examine some prototypical situations universally conceded to be "system" problems and then to analyze these cases to uncover some of the unifying themes which will be discussed in detail in Chapter 2. After the four examples of system problems, we shall examine several possible mathematical structures that may be employed to study system problems, our objective being to emphasize the point that there is no such thing as the model of a system: there are many models, each with its own characteristic mathematical features and each capable of addressing a certain subset of important questions about the system and its operation. What is important is that the analyst have as many mathematical tools at his disposal as possible, tools that he can use to probe the workings of the system at hand.

EXAMPLE 1   MACROECONOMICS

We consider an economic complex consisting of $n$ sectors with output rates $x_1, x_2, \ldots, x_n$, respectively. Let us assume for the sake of definiteness that the outputs are measured in dollars per year. The output of each sector is used by itself, by the other sectors, and by the rest of the world—the consumers.

Let $a_{ij}$ represent the value of output $i$ required as input to produce 1 dollar's worth of output $j$; $i, j = 1, 2, \ldots, n$. Further, let $y_i$ represent the rate at which consumers absorb the output of sector $i$. On the basis of these definitions, we have the relations

$$x_i = \sum_{j=1}^{n} a_{ij}x_j + y_i, \qquad i = 1, 2, \ldots, n.$$

This elementary model may be used to determine the amount of production required to meet a given consumer demand, given the currently available "technology" (represented by the coefficients $a_{ij}$). Obvious extensions and generalizations are possible, forming the basis of what has come to be called input–output economics. The matrix $A = [a_{ij}]$ of technological coefficients is often called a Leontief matrix, in honor of the founder of this branch of mathematical economics.

EXAMPLE 2   WATER RESERVOIR DYNAMICS

A simplified version of a water reservoir system is depicted in Figure 1.1. Here the states of surface storage at time $t$ at locations 1–3 are denoted by

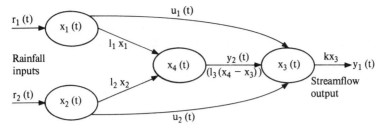

FIGURE 1.1 Water reservoir network.

$x_1(t)$, $x_2(t)$, $x_3(t)$, respectively, while the state of groundwater storage (including infiltration) is given by $x_4(t)$. The constant $k$ is for surface water flow, while $l_1$ and $l_2$ are for infiltration. The expression $l_3(x_4-x_3)$ signifies the exchange between streamflow and groundwater. The outputs $y_1$ and $y_2$ are the streamflow output and the contribution of groundwater to the streamflow, respectively, while the external inputs $r_1$ and $r_2$ represent the rainfall. The quantities $u_1$ and $u_2$ denote the water release.

The continuity relations for the problem immediately yield the dynamical equations

$$x_1(t+1)=-l_1x_1(t)-u_1(t)+r_1(t),$$
$$x_2(t+1)=-l_2x_2(t)-u_2(t)+r_2(t),$$
$$x_3(t+1)=l_3(x_4-x_3)-kx_3(t)+u_1(t)+u_2(t),$$
$$x_4(t+1)=l_1x_1(t)+l_2x_2(t)-l_3(x_4-x_3).$$

The measured system outputs are

$$y_1(t)=kx_3(t),$$
$$y_2(t)=l_3(x_4-x_3).$$

A number of crucial questions involving the feasibility of flood control, optimal release strategies, accurate determination of groundwater levels, and so on may now be approached using the above description of the system.

EXAMPLE 3   PREDATOR–PREY RELATIONS

A favorite problem of biologists and ecologists is the study of interactions and interrelations among a collection of predators and their prey in a localized spatial environment.

For clarity of exposition, we consider a single-trophic-level ecosystem in which the predator and prey have been divided into disjoint sets. As an example, let the predator set be given by

$$Y=\{\text{man, lions, elephants, birds, fish, horses}\},$$

while the prey are the elements of the set

$$X=\{\text{antelopes, grains, pigs, cattle, grass, leaves, insects, reptiles}\}.$$

A problem of some delicacy and subtlety is the determination of precise quantitative dynamic relationships between the predators and their prey. Most often, all that can be asserted with confidence is that certain predators feed on certain prey. In such instances, a surprising amount of information concerning the underlying structure of the ecosystem may be obtained by describing the system in terms of an incidence relation. That is, we formulate a relation $\lambda$ between the sets $X$ and $Y$ defined as

"Predator $y$ is $\lambda$-related to prey $x$ if and only if $y$ feeds upon $x$."

A convenient way to represent $\lambda$ is by means of the incidence matrix $\Lambda$:

|   | $\lambda$ | Antelopes | Grains | Pigs | Cattle | Grass | Leaves | Insects | Reptiles |
|---|---|---|---|---|---|---|---|---|---|
|   | Man | 1 | 1 | 1 | 1 | 0 | 0 | 0 | 0 |
|   | Lions | 1 | 0 | 1 | 0 | 0 | 0 | 0 | 0 |
| $Y$ | Elephants | 0 | 0 | 0 | 0 | 1 | 1 | 0 | 0 |
|   | Birds | 0 | 1 | 0 | 0 | 1 | 0 | 1 | 1 |
|   | Fish | 0 | 0 | 0 | 0 | 0 | 0 | 1 | 0 |
|   | Horses | 0 | 1 | 0 | 0 | 1 | 0 | 0 | 0 |

Here we have constructed a plausible incidence relation $\lambda$, where a 1 is present if predator $y$ feeds upon prey $x$, a 0 otherwise.

In later chapters, we shall indicate some of the rather nonintuitive structure that can be obtained about the above predator–prey system from properties of the incidence matrix $\Lambda$. The main point to note for now, however, is that even in situations for which obvious dynamical equations are not available, it may still be possible to formulate meaningful (and tractable) mathematical representations of a given situation.

EXAMPLE 4   BINARY CHOICE

In many problems of practical interest, it is reasonable to assume that the system operates so as to seek the minimum of some, possibly unknown, potential function. In other words, in the absence of external perturbations the dynamical motion of the system moves toward an equilibrium corresponding to the minimum of a "force" field, where the force may be physical, social, economic, psychological, or "force X," depending upon the context.

To illustrate this notion, suppose we have a situation in which two choices are possible, governed by a utility function $U(x, a, b)$. Here $x$ is the choice variable and $a$ and $b$ are external parameters that influence the choice. We can then define a function $E(x, a, b) = -U$ to be disutility and construct a model in which the function $E$ is minimized.

A concrete example of the above idea can be given. For a particular journey of a given individual we assume there are two different modes of travel $A$ or $B$. The associated costs are $C_A$ and $C_B$, respectively. We let $AC = C_B - C_A$ represent the cost difference. Further, assume that $x < 0$ denotes the choice of mode $A$, while $x > 0$ represents travel by mode $B$. The external parameters $a$ and $b$ are functions of the cost difference $AC$.

It is possible to construct functions $a(AC)$ and $b(AC)$ such that there exists a number $\lambda$ so that

If $AC$ is large and positive, then mode $A$ is the only choice and $x < 0$.
If $AC$ is large and negative, then mode $B$ is the only choice and $x > 0$.
If $0 < AC < \lambda$, then mode $A$ is the likely choice, but both are possible.
If $-\lambda < AC < 0$, then mode $B$ is the likely choice but both are possible.
If $AC = 0$, then both modes are equally likely.

The dashed path in Figure 1.2 shows what happens to the individual's choice if $AC$ is changed smoothly.

As will be noted in later sections, the foregoing setup can be well modeled by employing Thom's theory of catastrophes. The important point for the moment is that the basic model for the process is generated only by the disutility function $E(x, a, b)$. A more detailed description of the internal dynamics, which in most social situations are not available anyway, is not required. In fact, as we shall observe later, even the precise form of the disutility function $E$ need not be known *a priori*. All that is required is that we be willing to assume the *existence* of such a function. All else follows from the mathematics and the data (including the precise form of Figure 1.2 needed to model the situation quantitatively).

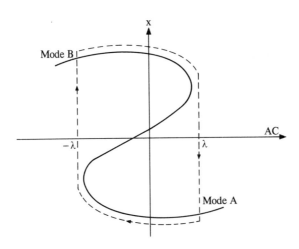

FIGURE 1.2 Binary choice of travel modes.

## MATHEMATICAL DESCRIPTIONS

The examples of the preceding section have underscored the point that many different types of mathematical description may be used to define a given situation abstractly. An important question to ask, however, is why we need any mathematical description at all. A partial answer was already given, when we cited the complex implications of existing knowledge and the need to abstract the essential features of descriptive models. However, a number of other equally important considerations compel us to make use of mathematical descriptions of one type or another:

*Compactness.* A verbal description of a process is likely to be cluttered up with an excess of ambiguous ideas that cloud the main issues. The compact symbolism of a mathematical model should eliminate fuzzy or ill-thought-out notions that may not be apparent in a lengthy verbal description. In short, a mathematical description provides us with the model-building analogue of the familiar picture that is worth a thousand words.

*Clarity.* By associating each symbol in the mathematical description with a known aspect of the process under study, we are able to see more clearly the interrelationships between the various process variables. Furthermore, it becomes far more apparent whether any essential variables have been omitted or, conversely, whether redundant variables have been inadvertently included in the process description.

*Computability.* Once the mathematical description has been agreed upon, it takes on a life of its own, more or less independent of the process itself. In other words, the mathematical description may be manipulated according to the conventional rules of logic in the expectation that nontrivial conclusions about the system may be arrived at. In addition, the mathematical model provides the basis for various computational studies, culminating, one hopes, in a *predictive*, rather than a descriptive, analysis of the system.

Let us now outline some of the principal types of mathematical description that will be used throughout this book.

### INTERNAL DESCRIPTIONS

Since the time of Newton, the standard mathematical description of a dynamical process has been in terms of differential (or difference) equations. Such equations describe the time evolution of a given system in terms of conveniently chosen variables, such as position, temperature, and velocity. The general form of such a description is

$$\dot{x} = f(x(t), u(t), t), \qquad x(0) = x_0$$
$$y(t) = h(x(t), u(t), t),$$

where $x(t)$ is an $n$-dimensional vector whose components represent the "state" of the process at time $t$, $y(t)$ is a $p$-dimensional vector of observed outputs, $u(t)$ is an $m$-dimensional vector of system inputs, and $x_0$ is the initial system state. In discrete time, these dynamics take the form of a difference equation

$$x(k+1) = F(x(k), u(k), k), \qquad x(0) = x_0,$$
$$y(k) = H(x(k), u(k), k).$$

The most important point to observe about such a description is that it is inherently local. The system equations describe the behavior of the process in a local neighborhood of the current state. Implicit in such a description is the assumption that precise local information may somehow be "pieced together" to obtain an understanding of the global (in time or space) behavior of the process. While this has proven to be a reasonably valid conjecture for numerous problems in physics and engineering, there is far less evidence for accepting this bold hypothesis in less well-understood systems, especially those in the realm of the social sciences.

In connection with the local versus global issue, it is interesting to note that up until the time of Newton and the invention of the calculus, local descriptions of the sort described above were totally unheard of. Rather, from antiquity, the description of physical processes was dominated by the Aristotelian view that, "in the order of Nature the State is prior to the household or individual. *For the whole must needs be prior to its parts.*" This viewpoint led to a physics in which the significance of set members is explained in terms of the significance of the set (the whole). Modern physical theories, of course, do exactly the opposite; the whole is "explained" in terms of the elementary (local) parts. The views of Aristotle dominated physical thought for many centuries until the experimentalist view pioneered by Galileo and legitimized by Newton took over the stage. The complexities of contemporary life as seen in problems of politics, economy, and sociology are stimulating a revival of interest in holistic theories, a turn of events that should call to mind that other Aristotelian notion of "moderation in all things."

Some simple examples of local descriptions are provided by familiar situations from elementary physics. For instance, the motion of a simple pendulum of unit mass swinging at the end of a cord of unit length is well known (via Newton's laws of motion) to be modeled by the dynamical equation

$$\ddot{x} + a\dot{x} + \sin x = u(t), \tag{1.1}$$

where $a$ is a frictional effect, $u(t)$ is an external force applied to the bob, and $x(t)$ represents the displacement of the pendulum from its rest position. Thus, Equation (1.1) describes the *instantaneous* rate of change of the

8

pendulum's position and velocity as a function of its current position and velocity—clearly a local description in the position–velocity state space. We emphasize that this feature is characteristic of *all* differential (difference) equation descriptions of dynamical systems.

EXTERNAL DESCRIPTIONS

The type of mathematical description of a system that is most familiar to the experimental scientist is an input–output relationship. In many ways, such a description is diametrically opposite to the specific local description previously discussed, as now all local detail is obliterated and the only information given is a rule (mapping) associating outputs with inputs. No explanatory information concerning the "internal" mechanism that transforms the inputs into outputs is given. For this reason, input–output relations are often referred to as *external* descriptions of a system, whereas the specific local description given earlier is called an *internal* description. Schematically, the situation is as shown in Figure 1.3.

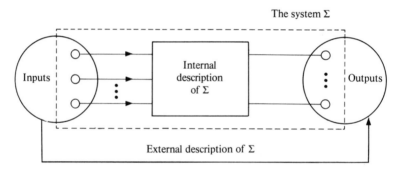

FIGURE 1.3    Internal–external description of Σ.

From a purely mechanistic point of view, the preceding internal–external descriptions suggest that we regard Σ as being a "machine" that transforms inputs into outputs according to a prescription laid down by the internal description: in other words, Σ is an information processor, in a generalized sense. It is evident that the internal description tells us substantially more about the workings of the system than the external since every internal description generates an external one. Model building, however, is concerned with the converse question: Can every external description be "explained" by an internal model? This question, the so-called *realization* problem, forms one of the cornerstones of mathematical system theory, about which more will be said later.

The crudest possible situation in which input–output descriptions arise is that in which we have only a table of elements (often, numbers) indicating the response of $\Sigma$ to various applied inputs (stimuli). If the set of possible input functions is denoted by $\Omega$, while the set of possible output functions is $\Gamma$, then the external description of $\Sigma$ is equivalent to a map

$$f: \Omega \to \Gamma.$$

As mentioned, in many problem areas $\Omega$ and $\Gamma$ are just finite sets of elements, with $f$ being a correspondence between them. Such situations often occur, for example, in psychology, economics, business, and the social sciences in general.

*Examples* Imagine a box that falls from a UFO. Assume that an experimenter has no knowledge of the nature of the box or its contents, but that he does possess certain resources for acting upon it (i.e., for applying inputs) and certain resources for observing its behavior. For the sake of definiteness, we assume that the sets $\Omega$ and $\Gamma$ consist of the readings that may be observed upon a set of dials on various measuring devices. A possible input–output description of the experiment might then be

| Time | Input | Output |
|------|-------|--------|
| 10:05 | Do nothing | Box emits a whistle at 240 Hz |
| 10:06 | Push the switch marked X | Pitch rises to 480 Hz and remains steady |
| 10:07 | Accidentally pushed the button marked "☠" | Box increases in temperature by 20°F and starts vibrating |

Note that this trivial example illustrates the fact that the inputs and outputs are functions of time—we can never conduct the same experiment twice! What may be done is to perform another experiment that differs from the first in some way that is agreed to be negligible.

A far less trivial example of an external system description is provided by the "behaviorist" school of psychology. A typical situation is one in which an experiment is performed and the experimental evidence is presented in a stimulus–response format. To a behaviorist, such an *external* description constitutes the sum total of all that one can ever learn about the structure of the workings of the organism under study. Of course, the "cognitive" school of thought would object to this in principle, their claim being that an *internal* model offers the only satisfactory explanation.

On the basis of rather general system-theoretic results, we shall later show that the behaviorist–cognitive dichotomy is actually an empty debate. Both schools are, in essence, making the same claim, and the debate, from a system-theoretic point of view, has about as much content as an argument over which side of a coin more accurately represents its value.

FINITE-STATE DESCRIPTIONS

Replacing the hypothesis of finite *dimensionality* of the state space with *finiteness*, we are led to a class of systems that may be analyzed by purely algebraic means. The importance of this change of finiteness condition cannot be overemphasized, since the set of finite-state systems includes all sequential digital computers.

The basic objects comprising a mathematical description of a finite-state system $\Sigma$ are

$U$, a set of admissible inputs
$Y$, a set of admissible outputs
$Q$, the set of states
$\lambda: Q \times U \to Q$, the next-state function
$\gamma: Q \times U \to Y$, the output function

Of course, it is assumed that the sets $U$, $Y$, and $Q$ are finite. We denote the system $\Sigma$ by the quintuple $\Sigma = (U, Y, Q, \lambda, \gamma)$. (Remark: In the literature, this is often called a *circuit*, with the machine characterized by the external input–output function $f: \Pi U \to Y$, where $\Pi U = \{(u_1, u_2, \ldots, u_n): n \geq 1$ and $u_j \in U\}$. In this situation, $f(u_1, u_2, \ldots, u_n) = Y_n$ is interpreted as the output at time $n$ if $u_j$ is the input at time $j$, $1 \leq j \leq n$.)

As noted, computational considerations ultimately force us to reduce every system problem to the above terms, explicitly or implicitly. Consequently, it is of considerable interest to thoroughly examine and understand the algebraic structure inherent in the finite-state description. This structure relies heavily upon the theory of finite semigroups, and much of it is beyond the modest aims of this introductory report. However, we shall develop a few of the elementary aspects in the chapter on complexity. For now, let us fix ideas with an example.

*Example*   Consider the situation in which the system $\Sigma$ consists of the rotational symmetries of an equilateral triangle. Some possible finite-state spaces might be

$$
\begin{array}{cccc}
& Q_1 & Q_2 & Q_3 \\
\triangle_{\,b\ \ c}^{\,a} & = [a, b, c], & 0, & 0 \\
\triangle_{\,a\ \ b}^{\,c} & = [c, a, b], & 2\pi/3, & 1 \\
\triangle_{\,c\ \ a}^{\,b} & = [b, c, a], & 4\pi/3, & 2.
\end{array}
$$

Any of the above state spaces, $Q_1$, $Q_2$, or $Q_3$, will suffice for describing $\Sigma$. However, some of them may be more convenient for calculating the actions of $\lambda$ upon the states. Here we have a good illustration of an important point: the state space of a system need not have an intrinsic connection to the physical process. It is purely a mathematical artifice introduced to ease the burden of determining the output response to given inputs.

Assume we have two possible state transition maps $\lambda_1$ and $\lambda_2$, corresponding to positive rotations of 120° and 240°, respectively, about the triangle's barycenter. We can then tabulate the result of these transformations in the different state spaces.

| | $q$ | $\lambda_1(q)$ | $\lambda_2(q)$ |
|---|---|---|---|
| $Q_1$: | $[a, b, c]$ | $[c, a, b]$ | $[b, c, a]$ |
| | $[c, a, b]$ | $[b, c, a]$ | $[a, b, c]$ |
| | $[b, c, a]$ | $[a, b, c]$ | $[c, a, b]$ |
| $Q_2$: | $0$ | $2\pi/3$ | $4\pi/3$ |
| | $2\pi/3$ | $4\pi/3$ | $0$ |
| | $4\pi/3$ | $0$ | $2\pi/3$ |
| $Q_3$: | $0$ | $1$ | $2$ |
| | $1$ | $2$ | $0$ |
| | $2$ | $0$ | $1$ |

More compactly, we have

$$
\lambda_1: \begin{array}{l} Q_1 \rightarrow Q_1; \\ Q_2 \rightarrow Q_2; \\ Q_3 \rightarrow Q_3; \end{array} \quad
\begin{array}{l} \lambda_1(\alpha, \beta, \gamma) = (\gamma, \alpha, \beta) \\ \lambda_1(q) = q + 2\pi/3 \,(\mathrm{mod}\ 2\pi) \\ \lambda_1(q) = q + 1 \,(\mathrm{mod}\ 3). \end{array}
$$

$$
\lambda_2: \begin{array}{l} Q_1 \rightarrow Q_1; \\ Q_2 \rightarrow Q_2; \\ Q_3 \rightarrow Q_3; \end{array} \quad
\begin{array}{l} \lambda_2(\alpha, \beta, \gamma) = (\beta, \gamma, \alpha) \\ \lambda_2(q) = q + 4\pi/3 \,(\mathrm{mod}\ 2\pi) \\ \lambda_2(q) = q + 2 \,(\mathrm{mod}\ 3). \end{array}
$$

The state space $Q_1$, which seems needlessly complex, comes into its own for more general systems $\Sigma$—for example, the general symmetries of the triangle where we might have transformations such as $\lambda_3$: reflection in the altitude. $Q_2$ and $Q_3$ do not have obvious extensions that also preserve simplicity of calculation with respect to more general actions.

Alternate ways of describing a system state space are called coordinatizations of $\Sigma$. It is of obvious interest to know if there are always coordinatizations that are "good" with respect to the actions of the system. We shall make the notion of "goodness" precise in a later chapter and show that an affirmative answer is possible for all systems that have a finite number of configurations with respect to the state-space actions. The key to this problem is the algebraic structure of the system state-space model. In fact, the famous Krohn-Rhodes decomposition theorem for finite semigroups establishes the relationship between arbitrary transformations on a finite state space and certain advantageous coordinatizations of their action.

POTENTIAL AND ENTROPY FUNCTIONS

As an alternative to the internal–external system descriptions given above, a number of investigators have studied systems more from a goal-directed or information-theoretic vantage point. The basis for such studies has been the mathematical description of a system in terms of a potential or an entropy function.

Arguing by analogy with classical mechanics and electromagnetic theory, a potential function description of a dynamical process would state that the response of the system to external inputs would be such that the state of the system moves to the minimum of a suitable potential function. Depending upon the particular system and assumptions of the investigator, such a dynamic may be *local* in the sense that movement is toward the relative minimum nearest the current state, or it may be *global*, in which case the system always moves to the absolute minimum of the assumed potential function. We illustrate the basic idea schematically in Figure 1.4, where we assume the system state is given by $x$ with $f(x; a)$ being the describing potential function depending upon an external parameter (input) $a$. Initially, the system is in the state $x(a)$. We then change $a$ to the value $a^*$, thereby changing the location of the minima of $f$. Under the *local* movement hypothesis, we have the picture $(A)$, while the *global* assumption yields the new system state as depicted in $(B)$.

In rough mathematical terms, the potential function description of a dynamical process consists of the following ingredients:

A system state (phase) space $X$
Possibly a collection of input functions $\Omega$
A smooth-mapping $f: X \times \Omega \to R$, the real numbers

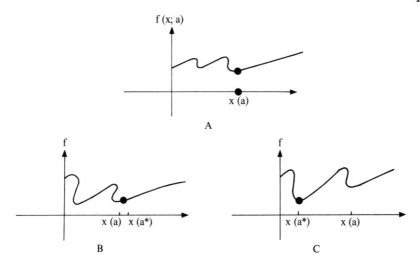

FIGURE 1.4 Potential function description. *A*, basic idea; *B*, local movement hypothesis; *C*, global movement.

The system dynamics are then assumed to operate according to the principle that for fixed input $\omega \in \Omega$, the observed state of the process will be a local minimum of $f$. To be perfectly precise, we must specify in more detail the sets $X$ and $\Omega$, and the properties of $f$. However, the foregoing setup will be sufficient for understanding the basic ideas. We shall fill in more details in Chapter 5.

In well-understood physical systems, potential-function descriptions have proven very useful alternatives to internal descriptions. In classical physics, the success of such descriptions is guaranteed by appeal to such well-established variational laws as Hamilton's principle, Fermat's principle, and d'Alembert's principle for generation of appropriate potential functions in any given situation. In most instances, internal description of physical processes may be obtained from the potential function description by means of the system Hamiltonian or the Euler–Lagrange equations.

In systems of the kind encountered in the social sciences, a potential function description is far less secure than in the physical sciences, due to the absence of reliable variational principles. However, in some cases arising in stability analyses and catastrophe theory, it is not necessary to know the precise form of the potential function, only to admit that one exists, in order to characterize important qualitative aspects of the system. Problems of this genre will form the basis for part of Chapter 5.

Closely related to the potential function description is the idea of describing a system's behavior by an *entropy* function. As is well known from traditional thermodynamics, entropy is a measure of the disorder present in a given physical setup. Intuitively, then, negative entropy, or *negentropy* for short, measures the orderliness, and the entropy-theoretic description of a dynamical process asserts that a system transforms negentropy in the input into information. Thus, we have the basic underlying principle: *all closed systems change so that the variation of entropy is minimized.* When stated in such a form, the connections between the potential function description and the entropy description become rather apparent.

To indicate the generality of the entropy description of a system $\Sigma$, we briefly summarize the main points of a relativistic information theory of such processses developed by G. Jumarie. The theory is founded upon the following set of axioms:

*Axiom 1.* The system $\Sigma$ is imbedded within a universe $\mathcal{U}$ and evolves only because it has an objective $v$ to perform.

*Axiom 2.* To achieve the objective $v$, $\Sigma$ takes information $I$ from its environment and uses this information to modify its organization (inner structure) $a$, to increase its negentropy state $n$, and to apply the action $A$ to its environment.

*Axiom 3 (Evolution Principle).* The *structural entropy* $E$ of $\Sigma$ is defined by the equation

$$dE = dI/n$$

and is a nondecreasing function of the evolution of $\Sigma$.

*Axiom 4.* The universe $\mathcal{U}$ is blind, in that it cannot observe its own evolution.

In the context of the above axioms, the system's state equation is given by

$$f(H_o, H_i, v) = 0,$$

where

$H_o =$ the external entropy of $\Sigma$ with respect to a fixed observer $R$
$H_i =$ the internal entropy of $\Sigma$ with respect to an observer $R$
$v =$ the objective of $\Sigma$ as seen by the observer $R$

Note the critical role played by the observer $R$ in the foregoing definitions. This approach emphasizes the role of the observer (or decision maker) when one defines a system and strongly suggests a kinematic approach based upon analogues of the Lorentz transformations between two observers $R$ and $R'$. We shall pursue this point in a moment.

Returning for a moment to the system state equation, we see that knowledge of the function $f$ would enable us to compute $E$ by virtue of the information exchange relation

$$dI = \alpha \, dH_o + \beta \, dH_i,$$

where $\alpha$ and $\beta$ are appropriate constants.

*Example A: Scalar Dynamics*  To consolidate these notions, consider the simple dynamical system

$$\dot{x} = u(t),$$

where $x$ and $u$ are scalar functions. It can be shown that the external entropy $H_o$ has the same properties as the time $t$; thus, we make the identification $t \rightarrow H_o$. Moreover, it is reasonable to identify $x$, the internal state, with the internal entropy $H_i$. Thus, the system dynamic is equivalent to the equation

$$dH_i - u(H_o)\, dH_o = 0.$$

Now we attempt to obtain the state function $f$ as given earlier. We should have

$$\frac{\partial f}{\partial H_o}\, dH_o + \frac{\partial f}{\partial H_i}\, dH_i + \frac{\partial f}{\partial v}\, dv = 0.$$

Lacking more information about the system, we shall assume that it has constant objective, hence $dv = 0$. We can now integrate the above equation to obtain the relation

$$f(H_i, H_o, v) = H_i - \int_{H_o^\circ}^{H_o} u(S)\, ds = 0,$$

where $H_o^\circ$ is the external entropy at the initial time $t_o$. The preceding analysis shows that the system $\dot{x} = u$ is not defined from the point of view of information exchange with its environment; more precisely, the information exchange with the environment is zero.

*Example B: Stationary Dynamics*  We now consider the dynamics

$$\dot{x} = \phi(x(t)),$$

which, utilizing the same identification as in Example A, gives

$$dH_i - \phi(H_i)\, dH_o = 0.$$

To obtain the state equation, we must have

$$\frac{\partial f}{\partial H_i} = 1 \Rightarrow f = H_i + \chi(H_o),$$

$$\frac{\partial f}{\partial H_o} = \phi(H_i) \Rightarrow \phi(H_i) = \chi(H_o),$$

an inconsistency. Thus, we cannot regard the system dynamics as being the state equation; rather, we must view it as the information exchange equation

$$dI = dH_i - \phi(H_i)\, dH_o$$
$$= 0.$$

Hence, this system exchanges no information with its environment and evolves with a constant structural entropy. This interpretation is in agreement with the autonomous character of the system.

Before leaving the entropy description of a dynamical process, we discuss the relativistic aspect. We noted earlier that the variables $H_o$, $H_i$, and $v$ depend upon the observer $R$. Such an interpretation generates the immediate question of what these quantities are, relative to another observer $R'$. Adopting the appropriate quantities relative to the observer $R$, standard relativity theory suggests a kinematic approach to the question in the Riemannian space defined by the geodesic

$$d\sigma^2(\Sigma \mid R) = c^2\, dH_o^2(\Sigma \mid R) - dH_i^2(\Sigma \mid R) - dv^2(\Sigma \mid R),$$

where the universal constant $c$ is defined by

$$H_i(\mathcal{U} \mid \mathcal{U}) = cH_o(\mathcal{U} \mid \mathcal{U}).$$

The Lorentz transformations relating $R$ and $R'$ are then

$$H_i(\Sigma \mid R') = \rho[H_i(\Sigma \mid R) + u(R \mid R')H_o(\Sigma \mid R)],$$
$$v(\Sigma \mid R') = v(\Sigma \mid R),$$
$$H_o(\Sigma \mid R') = \rho\left[H_o(\Sigma \mid R) + \frac{u(R \mid R')}{c^2} H_i(\Sigma \mid R)\right],$$
$$\rho \doteq [1 - u^2(R \mid R')/c^2]^{-1/2},$$

where

$$u(R \mid R') \doteq dH_i(R \mid R')/dH_o(R \mid R'),$$

that is, $u(R \mid R')$ is the organizability of $R$ from the viewpoint of $R'$.

In summary, the entropy approach to system analysis is based upon the view that the system under consideration is seen as an integral unit, as a whole. From this it follows that the system may be appreciated only in its contrast with the environment, that is, with the "universe" involved. The fact that the system is considered as a whole may be further specified in detail by the notion of "connection." The whole complex of connections and their characteristics leads to the ideas surrounding system "structure" and "complexity," which shall occupy us throughout this monograph. We now pass on to another type of system description that is particularly useful for such structural studies.

SETS AND RELATIONS

It is often stated that the abstract foundations of mathematics lie in set theory and relations among elements of sets. Taking this remark as our point of departure, it is certainly reasonable to think of defining a system in similar terms. Obviously, a useful definition will require that the elements of the defining sets and the relations linking the elements be tailored to the particular system. However, once such specification has been made, the sets–relations description of a system provides an extremely broad basis for analyzing not only the connective structure of a process, but also its dynamical behavior.

In general terms, we consider two finite sets $X$ and $Y$ whose elements are relevant to the system $\Sigma$. For instance, the sets of predators and prey in an ecosystem, the sets of vehicle types and roadways in a traffic study, or sets of urban facilities and required services. We define a binary relation $\lambda$ on the Cartesian product of $X$ and $Y$ to reflect the fact that, in the context of the given problem, the pair of elements $(x, y)$, $x \in X$, $y \in Y$ are related. Thus, $\lambda \subset X \times Y$.

To illustrate, consider a trivial example where $X$ is a set of consumer items and $Y$ is a set of service facilities. For definiteness,

$$X = \frac{\{\text{bread milk, stamps, shoes}\}}{\{x_1, x_2, x_3, x_4\}},$$

$$Y = \frac{\{\text{market, department store, bank, post office}\}}{\{y_1, y_2, y_3, y_4\}}$$

We define a relation $\lambda$ on $X \times Y$ by the rule

"$x_i$ is $\lambda$-related to $y_j$ if and only if good $x_i$ may be obtained at facility $y_j$."

Thus,

$$\lambda = \{(x_1, y_1), (x_2, y_1), (x_3, y_4), x_4, y_2)\}.$$

A convenient way to represent $\lambda$ is by the *incidence matrix*

$$\Lambda = \begin{array}{c|cccc} \lambda & y_1 & y_2 & y_3 & y_4 \\ \hline x_1 & 1 & 0 & 0 & 0 \\ x_2 & 1 & 0 & 0 & 0 \\ x_3 & 0 & 0 & 0 & 1 \\ x_4 & 0 & 1 & 0 & 0 \end{array}.$$

Here, we have

$$[\Lambda]_{ij} = \begin{cases} 1, & (x_i, y_j) \in \lambda \\ 0, & \text{otherwise} \end{cases}.$$

Geometrically, the relation $\lambda$ may be interpreted as defining a simplicial complex $K_X(Y; \lambda)$ in which the elements of $Y$ are regarded as *vertices*, while the elements of $X$ are the *simplices*. For instance, in the above example, the element $x_1$ (bread) is a 0-simplex consisting of the vertex $y_1$ (market). As long as $K$ contains no $r$-simplices with $r \geq 3$, we may also draw the picture of $K_X(Y; \lambda)$. The previous example has the form

$$\begin{array}{ccc} y_1 & y_2 & y_4 \\ \bullet & \bullet & \bullet \end{array},$$

not a very interesting geometrical structure. However, it does show that the complex has no connected components and that the vertex $y_3$ (bank) plays no role whatsoever in the analysis of $K_X(Y; \lambda)$.

Having defined appropriate sets $X$ and $Y$ and a relation $\lambda$, we can now speak of another relation induced by $\lambda$. This is the so-called "conjugate" relation $\lambda^*$ defined by reversing the roles of the sets $X$ and $Y$. Thus, $\lambda^* \subset Y \times X$, with the rule of association now being

"$y_i$ is $\lambda^*$-related to $x_j$ if and only if $x_j$ is $\lambda$-related to $y_i$."

Hence, we see that the incidence matrix for $\lambda^*$ is just the transpose of that for $\lambda$, i.e.,

$$\Lambda^* = \Lambda'.$$

The reversal of the roles of $X$ and $Y$ results in a geometrical complex $K_Y(X; \lambda^*)$ for which $X$ is the vertex set and $Y$ the set of simplices. In the above example, the reader may easily verify that the complex $K_Y(X; \lambda^*)$ has the geometrical form

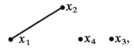

which is marginally more interesting than the totally disconnected structure of $K_X(Y; \lambda)$. Here we see that the vertices $x_1$ (bread) and $x_2$ (milk) are connected via the 1-simplex $y_1$ (market). We shall examine the implications of these connectivity notions, as well as the total topological structure contained in such incidence relations, in Chapter 3.

Before moving on to other matters, we give another example of system description by sets and binary relations to indicate the generality of the approach.

*Example: The Game of Chess*  The world chess champion Emmanuel Lasker once remarked, "There are 64 squares on the chess-board; if you control 33 of them you must have an advantage." Obviously, this over-simplifies the situation but does show that chessmasters have always been concerned with the "strategic" nature of the game. This feature can immediately be seen to be mathematically expressible as a relation between the set of pieces and the set of squares on the board. Thus, we consider two relations $\lambda_W$ and $\lambda_B$, where $\lambda_W$ gives the relation between the White pieces and the squares, while $\lambda_B$ does the same for the Black pieces.

Following the idea given above, we define the sets $X$ and $Y$ as

$$X = \frac{\{\text{pieces}\}}{\{QR, QN, QB, Q, K, KB, KN, KR, QRP, QNP, QBP, QP, KP, KBP, KNP, KRP\}}$$

$Y = \{\text{squares}\}$.

Here we have adopted the standard international notation for the pieces {King, Queen, Bishop, Knight, Rook, Pawns}, and we assume that the squares of the board are numbered in some consistent fashion. We define the relations $\lambda_W$, as follows:

"given $x_i$ and $y_j$, then $(x_i, y_j) \in \lambda_W$ if and only if piece $x_i$ *attacks* square $y_j$."

By "attacks" we mean that one of the following situations obtains:

If it is White's move, and if $x_i$ is not a Pawn or the King, then $x_i \to y_j$ is a legal move.
If $x_i$ is a Pawn, then $y_j$ is a capturing square for $x_i$.
If there is a White man on $y_j$, then $x_i$ is protecting this man.
If $x_i$ is the White King, then $y_j$ is adjacent to the square occupied by $x_i$.
If the square $y_j$ contains a Black man (other than the King) and if it is White's move, then $x_i$ capturing the Black man is a legal move.
The Black King is on $y_j$ and is in check to $x_i$.

A similar definition holds for the relation $\lambda_B$.

Note that $\lambda_W$ is a function of the mode of play—that is, it depends upon the state of play (whose move it is, and the current positioning of the men on the board). The relations $\lambda_W$ and $\lambda_B$ might be interpreted as giving the player's view of the board, while the conjugate relations $\lambda_W^*$ and $\lambda_B^*$ give the board's view of the player. We will return to a deeper analysis of this example in Chapter 3.

The astute reader will recognize some similarities between the sets–relation description of a system and the more common graph-theoretic description in terms of nodes and arcs (or vertices and links). Basically, the above definition coincides with the graph-theoretic version if we let $X = Y =$ the vertex set, with the links being defined by the relation $\lambda$. Obviously, a great deal of flexibility is lost in such an arrangement, as much of the multidimensional nature of the relation $\lambda$ is destroyed or, at best, obscured. However, the graph-theoretic setup is quite useful in many situations, but, as they have been extensively treated elsewhere, we shall not explore them in detail in this monograph. The references at the end of the chapter will provide an introduction for the curious reader.

Since the essence of system theory is dynamics, we must inquire about how the notion of dynamical change is incorporated into the sets/relation description of a process. This is accomplished by introducing the concept of a *pattern*. In general terms, a pattern $\Pi$ is a mapping that associates a number with each simplex in a complex: that is,

$$\Pi: \sigma^i \rightarrow k,$$

where $\sigma^i$ is a simplex from $K$, and $k$ is an appropriate number system (reals, integers, and so on). As each simplex in $K$ has a certain geometrical dimension associated with it determined by the number of its vertices, we see that the pattern $\Pi$ is actually a *graded* pattern

$$\Pi = \Pi_0 \oplus \Pi_1 \oplus \ldots \oplus \Pi_N,$$

where $N = \dim K =$ dimension of the largest simplex in $K$. Here each $\Pi_i$ is a mapping on only the $i$-dimensional simplices in $K$.

We give an example to clarify the pattern concept. Consider the predator–prey system given as Example 3 in the section on intuitive notions. There we had the sets

$$X = \text{set of prey},$$

$$Y = \text{set of predators},$$

with the incidence relation $\lambda$ being given by the matrix

| $\lambda$ | $x_1$ | $x_2$ | $x_3$ | $x_4$ | $x_5$ | $x_6$ | $x_7$ | $x_8$ |
|---|---|---|---|---|---|---|---|---|
| $y_1$ | 1 | 1 | 1 | 1 | 0 | 0 | 0 | 0 |
| $y_2$ | 1 | 0 | 1 | 0 | 0 | 0 | 0 | 0 |
| $\Lambda = y_3$ | 0 | 0 | 0 | 0 | 1 | 1 | 0 | 0 |
| $y_4$ | 0 | 1 | 0 | 0 | 1 | 0 | 1 | 1 |
| $y_5$ | 0 | 0 | 0 | 0 | 0 | 0 | 1 | 0 |
| $y_6$ | 0 | 1 | 0 | 0 | 1 | 0 | 0 | 0 |

Thus, $y_1$ (man) is a 3-simplex, $y_4$ (birds) is a 3-simplex, and so on. A pattern $\Pi$ would be a mapping that associates a number, say the population currently present, with each such simplex. Since the simplices are graded by their dimensions, so is $\Pi$. Thus,

$\Pi_0$: $\{y_5(\text{fish})\} \rightarrow$ current fish population

$\{y_2(\text{lions})\} \rightarrow$ current lion population

$\Pi_1$: $\{y_3(\text{elephants})\} \rightarrow$ current elephant population

$\{y_6(\text{horses})\} \rightarrow$ current horse population

$\Pi_2$: empty

$\Pi_3$: $\begin{array}{l}\{y_1(\text{man})\} \rightarrow \text{current human population}\\ \{y_4(\text{birds})\} \rightarrow \text{current bird population.}\end{array}$

The total pattern $\Pi$ for this ecosystem is

$$\Pi = \Pi_0 \oplus \Pi_1 \oplus \Pi_2 \oplus \Pi_3.$$

The notion of a system dynamic is now accounted for by *changes* in the pattern $\Pi$ at each moment of time. In Chapter 3 we shall take up a detailed study of the interpretation of such changes either as forces imposed upon the fixed geometry of the complex, or as "free" changes that are allowed by the geometry. The former correspond to classical Newtonian forces, while the latter are more in the spirit of Einsteinian or relativistic changes.


## NOTES AND REFERENCES

INTUITIVE NOTIONS

A far more extensive treatment of the Leontief-type economic models may be found in the following works:

Gale, D., The Theory of Linear Economic Models. McGraw-Hill, New York. 1960.

Baumol, W., Economic Theory and Operations Analysis. Prentice-Hall, Englewood Cliffs, New Jersey, 1965.

Leontief, W., "Mathematics in Economics," *Bull. Am. Math. Soc.* 60 (1954), 215–233.

Isard, W., and P. Kaniss, "The 1973 Nobel Prize for Economic Science," *Science*, 182 (1973), 568–569, 571.

The water reservoir example is taken from:

Szöllösi-Nagy, A., "State Space Approach to Hydrology," in *Symposium on Mathematical Modeling in Hydrology*, University College, Galway, Ireland, April 1974.

Similar examples of water resource models are given in:

Bazykin, A., "Elementary Model of Eutrophication," in *Analysis and Computation of Equilibria and Regions of Stability*, H. Grümm, ed., CP-75-8, International Institute for Applied Systems Analysis, Laxenburg, Austria, 1975.

Jorgensen, S., "A Eutrophication Model for a Lake," *Ecol. Mod.*, 2 (1976), 147–165.

22

MATHEMATICAL DESCRIPTIONS

Modern treatments of the state-variable (internal) descriptions of a process are given in the books listed below:

Casti, J., *Dynamical Systems and Their Applications: Linear Theory*, Academic, New York, 1977.
Brockett, R., *Finite-Dimensional Linear Systems*, Wiley, New York, 1970.

Kalman, R., P. Falb, and M. Arbib, *Topics in Mathematical System Theory*, McGraw-Hill, New York, 1969.

The input–output description of dynamical processes has, for the most part, been treated mathematically using the tools of functional analysis. A representative sampling of results in this area may be found in

Saeks, R., *Resolution Space, Operators and Systems*, Springer, Heidelberg, 1973.
Rosenbrock, H., *State-Space and Multivariable theory*, Nelson, London, 1970.
Luenberger, D., *Optimization by Vector Space Methods*, Wiley, New York, 1969.
Porter, W., *Modern Foundations of Systems Engineering*, Macmillan, New York, 1966.
Willems, J. C., *The Analysis of Feedback Systems*, MIT Press, Cambridge, Massachusetts, 1971.

The UFO example is adapted from the classic work of Ashby:

Ashby, W. R., *Introduction to Cybernetics*, Chapman and Hall, London, 1956.

For further material on finite-state descriptions, see the paper:

Krohn, K., R. Langer, and J. Rhodes, "Transformations, Semigroups and Metabolism," in *System Theory and Biology*, M. Mesarovic, ed., Springer, New York, 1968.

Variational formulations of problems not arising from a potential function are discussed in the paper:

Leitmann, G., "Some Remarks on Hamilton's Principle," *J. Applied Mechanics, Tran. ASME* December 1963, 623–625.

The entropy-theoretic description of a system, as well as the quoted axioms, may be found in

Jumarie, G., "A Relativistic Information Theory Model for General Systems: Lorentz Transformation of Organizability and Structural Entropy," *Int. J. Syst. Sci.*, 6 (1975), 865–886.

The references contained in this paper cite further work by the author in developing a most provocative "thermodynamic" theory of large-systems.
Description of a system using finite sets and binary relations was pioneered in the book:

Atkin, R. H., *Mathematical Structure in Human Affairs*, Heinemann, London, 1973.

Further developments and extensions are to be found in the forthcoming monograph:

Atkin, R. H., *Multidimensional Man*, Penguin, London (in press).

# 2 Basic Questions and Perspectives on System Theory

> What we need is imagination. We have to find a new view of the world.
> R. P. FEYNMAN

> Imagination is more important than knowledge.
> A. EINSTEIN

We have seen some of the principal means for describing dynamical processes and their interaction with man and the environment. Now we turn to the question of what to do with these descriptions. Philosophically, the mathematical descriptions enable us to abstract certain seemingly important features from a physical situation and to formalize the relationship between various system components. However, the way in which we manipulate these mathematical constructs in an attempt to gain insight into the process is determined by the type of questions we ask. Thus, in this chapter we shall examine several questions that are already considered in the systems literature; we re-examine them here for the sake of completeness. Such topics as stochastic effects, controlled dynamics, identification, and so forth, while not central to the theme of this book, continue to generate important system-theoretic results and form a partial backdrop for the development of our major themes: connectivity, complexity, and stability, including catastrophe theory.

Brief overviews of these areas will be given in this current chapter as a prelude to the detailed discussions of each topic given in the following chapters.

## CONTROLLED VERSUS FREE DYNAMICS

The celestial observers of antiquity took the first steps on the long evolutionary path to the systems analysis of today. However, their role was a purely passive one: to observe. The ancient astronomers had no means with which to influence the dynamical behavior of the systems they studied; they were forced to be content with a type of analysis consisting of observations,

23

classifications, and possible synthesis without the possibility of physical experiments to modify the observed phenomena. Such is the situation facing many workers in astrophysics, biology, linguistics, and sociology to the present day. Scholars in these areas are, for the time being, condemned to a life of observation without control.

Interesting and important as such observations are, it is unlikely that system theory as we know it today would have evolved to its current level of sophistication without the impetus of the desire to control events and the recognition of the possibility of doing so. In other words, the modern system analyst's principal role is that of an activist: to generate suitable external inputs to ensure that the system behaves in a satisfactory manner. There are clearly many unanswered questions involving psychological and moral considerations as well as physical constraints in such an interventionist philosophy. Nevertheless, the active–passive, controlled motion versus free dynamics dichotomy provides the simplest line of demarcation between the classical and modern viewpoints on systems analysis, and current evidence indicates no diminution of movement toward a more active role in any situation where it seems possible to influence the process.

As an illustration of the contrast between the classical and modern views of system study, we may think of the annual flooding taking place in the Nile delta. For thousands of years classical analysts observed the phenomenon, correlated it with celestial positions, predicted the time and duration of the next flood, and so on. In short, everything was done except control. History records the tragedies associated with the famines that occurred periodically because of this lack of control. Modern technology coupled with control engineering now makes such whimsical turns of nature a thing of the past. A series of dams and reservoirs on the Nile now provide a reasonably regular flow of water to the delta region. This flow of life-giving water is the result of an activist intervention into the natural dynamics of the hydrological process. However, we should also note that the type of regulation actually employed has been somewhat of a mixed blessing, in that poor planning has resulted in a reservoir network which has had *bad* effects on part of the region. For instance, salinity has now increased in the Mediterranean, since the flood control network prevents the escape of fresh water from the Nile, and the incidence of schistosomiasis along the lower Nile has risen, also as a result of the suppression of the seasonal cycle. There have been other important deleterious and unforeseen effects as well. Thus, the project represents a case of inadequately thought-out control. In short, the global consequences of the controlling actions were not thoroughly explored prior to construction of the project and the result has been a cure which is worse than the disease—a good object lesson for all large-scale system analysts to ponder!

The preceding "cybernetic," or regulatory, point of view implies a transformation of input by output in order to render an originally independent variable partially dependent in accordance with some rule of convergence to a certain standard or desired trajectory. The foregoing process may be made more complex if there is another "inverse" transformation that can change the standard itself. This situation represents a simulation of an evolutionary system.

The inverse transformation we have just discussed, consisting of input modification and change of behavior standard via measured output, is the essence of cybernetic control and regulation. That essence is more usably, precisely, and concretely given in the above explanation than by the usual terminology "feedback."

## IDENTIFICATION

The initial phase in formulating a mathematical model of a given situation is the process of identifying the relevant variables and their interrelationships. Depending upon the particular type of mathematical description that seems appropriate, the identification process may consist of such general issues as determining the dimension of the state space, the internal system dynamics, meaningful relations between sets of objects, and probability distributions for random influences. In fact, there is a circular chain here, since the identification process depends upon the type of mathematical description, which in turn depends upon the success of the identification process, and so on. The usual resolution of this dilemma is by means of iteration: a provisional mathematical description is chosen, then modified according to the degree of success of the identification leading to a new description, and so on.

Undoubtedly, the best-developed type of system identification problem is that of determining the internal description of a *linear*, constant-coefficient input–output map. For ease of exposition, assume that the given system operates in discrete time and that the initial time $t_0 = 0$, with the initial state $x_0 = 0$. It is then easily verified that the following relation holds between the system input function $u(t)$ and the output function $y(t)$:

$$y(t) = \sum_{t > \tau \geq 0} A_{t-\tau} u(\tau),$$

where the matrices $\{A_i\}$ are $p \times m$. Thus, the (possibly infinite) matrix sequence $\{A_1, A_2, \ldots\}$ *defines* the input–output description of $\Sigma$.

If an internal description of $\Sigma$ given by

$$x(t+1) = Fx(t) + Gu(t),$$

$$y(t) = Hx(t),$$

is to agree with the above external description, then the matrices $F$, $G$, and $H$ must be related to the sequence $\{A_i\}$ as

$$A_t = HF^{t-1}G, \qquad t = 1, 2, \ldots . \tag{2.1}$$

The *realization problem* for linear dynamical systems is to find $n \times n$, $n \times m$, and $p \times n$ matrices $F$, $G$, and $H$, respectively, such that the relations (2.1) hold, with the dimension of the internal state $n$ being as small as possible. In other words, we want the most compact model possible, consistent with the observed data.

Fortunately, good algorithms exist for carrying out the above realization under the crucial assumption: *the sequence $\{A_i\}$ possesses a finite-dimensional realization*. If the $\{A_i\}$ do possess a realization of dimension $n < \infty$, then the first $2n$ terms of $\{A_i\}$ uniquely determine all the remaining terms (Cayley–Hamilton theorem). The problem, of course, is to find this number $n$ from the data $\{A_i\}$.

As one might suspect, no such well-developed algorithms exist (yet) for general *nonlinear* input–output maps, although certain classes of problems possessing some type of linear or algebraic structure have been treated.

A situation that has been treated much more extensively than the very general external $\rightarrow$ internal type of identification problem is the so-called "parameter" identification problem. These problems generally arise when great confidence exists in the basic internal structure of a process, except that certain parameter values appearing within the structure are not known. Thus, we assume that the dynamics are given by a differential (or difference) equation

$$\dot{x} = f(x, u, a),$$

$$y(t) = h(x, a),$$

where $a$ is an unknown vector of parameters to be estimated on the basis of the observed system output $y(t)$. In some cases, the input function $u(t)$ is specially chosen to enhance the effect of the unknown parameters. What is important about the preceding situation is the assumption that the system structure functions $f$ and $h$ are known. We should also observe that no assumption of linearity is made on $f$ or $h$.

As a simple illustration of the above class of problems, consider the problem of logistical growth of a population described by the dynamics

$$\frac{dx}{dt} = rx\left(1 - \frac{x}{K}\right) - Ex, \qquad x(0) \doteq x_0.$$

Here $x(t)$ is the population at time $t$, $r$ is the net proportional growth rate of the population, $K$ is the environmental carrying capacity or saturation level, $E$ is the harvesting rate, and $x_0$ is the initial population. Assume that measurements can be made of the total population present at each instant, that is,

$$y(t) = x(t),$$

but that the carrying capacity $K$ is unknown. Thus, the parameter identification problem consists of estimating $K$ on the basis of observations of the total population. It is easy to see that, for this simple case, we have

$$K = \frac{-rx^2}{\dot{x} + (E - r)x}, \qquad \text{for each } t > 0.$$

Thus, observing $y(t)$ over any *interval* suffices to determine $K$. However, the more practical situation of a finite number of values of $y(t)$ introduces approximation procedures of various types.

More general versions of the preceding problem involving uncertainties in measuring $x(t)$, multiple species, and so on lead to mathematical problems of some complexity. We refer to the chapter references for details of many of the proposed solution methods.

The identification question for more general system descriptions of the potential function or sets–relation type is less well-structured and certainly less well-studied. Basically, these descriptions rely much more heavily upon the analyst's intuitive understanding of the process under study than do the external or internal differential equations type of description. Thus, the identification problem in such settings is much more of an art than a science, consisting primarily of isolating appropriate sets and relations (or energy functions) that lead to interpretable results. It is clearly of some interest to systematize the selection of meaningful sets and relations. We shall indicate some approaches to this task in Chapter 3.

## CONSTRAINTS

Good systems analysis, like good politics, is the art of the possible. When considering the mathematical formulation of a problem, the analyst must be aware of the external and internal constraints that may limit his freedom in choosing control strategies. Various considerations involving quantities of available resource, minimal demands that must be met, available technology, computing capability, manpower, time, and so on, all combine to severely reduce the options open to a decision maker.

We distinguish two fundamentally different types of constraints:

- *Internal*—constraints imposed by the system structure itself,
- *External*—constraints imposed upon the performance of the system by outside agencies.

Let us examine these constraints in a bit more detail.

Internal constraints arise as a result of restrictions involving the controlling or measuring process, that is, constraints upon how the system may interact with the outside world. Generally speaking, these types of constraints are most easily seen when we use an *internal* system description in terms of differential, or difference, equations. We illustrate the concept of an internal constraint with an example from the biomedical area.

*Example: Pharmacokinetics*   Consider a cardiac patient who receives the drug digitoxin and metabolizes it to digoxin. Since with digitoxin there is a rather fine edge between the lethal amount and the therapeutic amount, it is important to be able to determine the amount present in the body accurately when comtemplating additional doses.

The multicompartment model used to describe the kinetics and metabolism of digitoxin is shown in Figure 2.1. Here $X$ represents the digitoxin

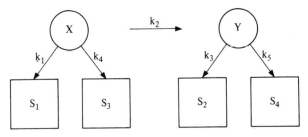

FIGURE 2.1   Multicompartment structure for digitoxin metabolism.

compartment of the body, $Y$ is the digoxin compartment, $S_1$ and $S_2$ are urinary excretion sinks, and $S_3$ and $S_4$ are nonurinary sinks, while the $k_i$ are diffusion rate constants, $i = 1, 2, \ldots, 5$.

It is more or less standard practice to assume that when a dose of digitoxin is given, approximately 92 percent of the dose is immediately taken up in compartment $X$ and that about 85 percent of the remaining 8 percent is instantly taken up in $Y$. The dynamics of the drug concentrations in the various compartments are assumed to be given by the equations

$$\dot{X} = -(k_1 + k_2 + k_4)X,$$
$$\dot{Y} = k_2 X - (k_3 + k_5)Y,$$
$$\dot{S}_1 = k_1 X,$$
$$\dot{S}_2 = k_3 Y,$$
$$\dot{S}_3 = k_4 X,$$
$$\dot{S}_4 = k_5 Y.$$

The initial conditions are

$$X(0) = 0.92D, \qquad Y(0) = (0.85)(0.08)D,$$

$$S_1(0) = S_2(0) = S_3(0) = S_4(0) = 0,$$

where $D$ represents the dose given.

We assume that only the urinary excretions of digitoxin and digoxin can be measured. Thus, the system outputs are

$$y_1(t) = S_1(t),$$

$$y_2(t) = S_2(t).$$

This assumption, which is very realistic in practice, constitutes what we have termed an internal constraint on the system. Because of this constraint, not all of the internal system variables are accessible to direct measurement.

In the context of the basic problem faced by the cardiologist, we would like to know whether measurements of the variables $y_1$ and $y_2$ suffice to determine the unknown initial dosage $D$. This is a problem of observability, whose treatment can be found in the references at the end of the chapter.

External constraints are of a qualitatively different character. As noted, such constraints arise not from physical or structural limitations in the process, but from the desires of the external decision maker. Generally, such considerations involve finite resource limitations, capacity considerations, minimal demand levels, and so on. The key point is that they are restrictions imposed from the outside and have nothing to do with mathematical restrictions induced by the model itself.

Typical examples of external constraints arise in management problems where a finite amount of money is available to achieve various objectives. For instance, consider a corporate advertising manager who has a budget of $M$ dollars, which he must allocate for ads in newspapers, magazines, TV, radio, and billboards, say. Assume that a sales amount $f_i(x_i)$ is generated as a result of allocating $x_i$ dollars to communications medium $i$, $i$ = newspapers, magazines, and so on. Here the $f_i(\cdot)$ are assumed to be known functions.

Clearly, since the corporation wishes to maximize sales, the advertising manager faces the problem of maximizing

$$\sum f_i(x_i)$$

over all allocations $\{x_{\text{news}}, x_{\text{mag}}, x_{\text{radio}}, x_{\text{TV}}, x_{\text{bill}}\}$, subject to the external constraint

$$\sum x_i \leq M.$$

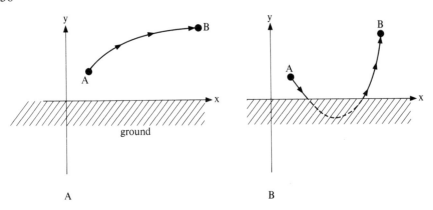

FIGURE 2.2   Aircraft trajectories.

Here we see the role of the external constraint. It arises from the finite advertising budget, not from the way in which the system is assumed to interact with the external world.

As another example of an external constraint, we cite the problem of a pilot who wishes to move from point $A$ to point $B$ in minimum time (see Figure 2.2). Depending upon the characteristics of the aircraft and other assumptions, a mathematical formulation of the situation may suggest the trajectory depicted in Figure 2.2b as being optimal. Such a situation clearly does not reflect the realistic constraints of the situation, which must be imposed from the outside to make the problem physically meaningful. The proper external constraint $(y > 0)$ will then yield an optimal trajectory more like that of Figure 2.2.a.

## STOCHASTIC EFFECTS

Although the main thrust of this monograph is such that we shall not treat uncertainties in any detail, it must be kept in mind in most realistic systems problems that virtually nothing is known (for sure)! Regardless of the particular mathematical description chosen, uncertainties will exist as to the dynamics, objectives, constraints, and other aspects. If we are fortunate, probability distributions will be known with confidence for the uncertain variables. In the majority of cases, even the probability distributions will be unknown, and we will be faced with an adaptive situation. In any case, we cannot consider an analysis complete without a thorough investigation of the uncertainties inherent in the model.

Throughout the remainder of this book, we shall adopt the bold hypothesis that all uncertain effects can be neglected. Thus, we are assuming perfect knowledge of input–output responses, state transitions, and so on. Clearly, such an assumption must be justified by results. We shall attempt to provide the appropriate rationalizations as we go along.

## OPTIMIZATION

One of the most vexing aspects of social and economic problems is the question of criterion. In other words, by what means should one course of action be compared with another? Fortunately, dynamical processes arising in physics and biology often have reasonably well-understood objectives, generally arising from various minimum principles or conservation laws. However, the transference of these principles to a social setting is forced, at best, and is usually impossible.

Since our objective in this volume is to study system structure independent of optimization aspects, we shall have the luxury of avoiding the "choice of criterion" quandary. But, to indicate the magnitude of the problem, let us consider a simple example illustrating how selection of different criteria can lock the decision maker into qualitatively distinct control policies.

Consider a situation in which the system dynamics are given by the scalar linear differential equation

$$\frac{dx}{dt} = u(t), \qquad x(0) = c,$$

where $u$ is the input or control function. Furthermore, assume that the control resource that may be expended is subject to the restriction

$$|u(t)| \leq 1, \qquad \text{for all} \quad t \geq 0.$$

Such a situation might arise, for example, in controlling an automobile, where $u$ would represent the speed.

One criterion that might be imposed upon the above process is to demand that the initial state $c$ be transferred to a prescribed state, say $x = 0$, in minimum time. It is well known that the solution to this problem is given by

$$u^*(t) = \begin{cases} +1, & c < 0 \\ -1, & c > 0, \end{cases}$$

that is, a "bang-bang" control law is optimal. On the other hand, assume that one wants to minimize the deviation of the state and the total control energy used, with the cost given by the quadratic form

$$J = \int_0^T (x^2 + u^2) \, dt.$$

In this case, it is easy to show that the optimal control law has the form

$$u^*(t) = \tanh{(T-t)}x(t),$$

a feedback solution.

The preceding results show that even the qualitative character of the optimal control law is critically shaped by the choice of criterion. In the first case, we have a law that swings from one extreme to the other, depending upon the initial state. In the second case, the optimal law is generated by the system action itself and exhibits no discontinuities whatsoever. The important point is that the dynamics themselves remain the same. Only the choice of criterion brings about the fundamental difference in the optimal laws.

## GLOBAL PERSPECTIVES

As we have repeatedly emphasized, the development of global, as opposed to local, system properties is the goal of our study. In many ways, this is a reaffirmation of the "holist" philosophy of structures that, as noted earlier, reigned supreme in scientific studies from the time of Aristotle until the seventeenth century. At that time, the "reductionist" view, later exemplified by Newton's equations of motion, took over the stage and has dominated scientific philosophy and practice until quite recently. However, pressures of problems that do not yield to the reductionist approaches are now generating renewed interest and study of the holist, or global, approaches. Our goal is to catalogue a few of the more promising directions, involving questions of connective structure, complexity, and stability.

To illustrate the conceptual difference between local and global descriptions in simple fashion, consider the familiar situation of the simple pendulum depicted in Figure 2.3. If we let $x(t)$ denote the position of the pendulum as measured from the vertical, then in the *local* neighborhood of *any* such position, we have the dynamical equation of motion

$$\ddot{x} + \sin x = 0, \qquad x(0) = x_0, \qquad \dot{x}(0) = 0,$$

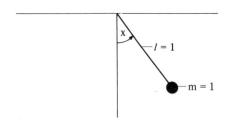

FIGURE 2.3   The simple pendulum.

where we have normalized units. This equation is a description of the local behavior of the pendulum in the (infinitesimal) neighborhood of any position $x(t)$. Using this description, a reductionist would attempt to "piece together" the local description at many points, thereby arriving (hopefully) at an understanding of the global behavior. Sometimes such an approach is successful, but unanticipated obstacles often complicate the reductionist's life.

A holist might analyze the pendulum from the following viewpoint. He would notice that certain global properties of the system must hold and, as a result, any local behavior must be such as to adhere to the constraints imposed by the global situation. If these constraints are sufficiently restrictive, the globalist would argue that all local motion is rigidly determined by the global restrictions.

For the pendulum, such a global constraint is provided by Hamilton's principle, which holds that the global system motion must be such that the total energy of the system is minimized. Introducing the Hamiltonian

$$H = \text{kinetic energy} + \text{potential energy},$$

we see that the system motion must be such that

$$H(x, \dot{x}) = (1/2)\dot{x}^2 + 1 - \cos x$$

is minimized. Hamilton's equations of motion then lead to the dynamics given earlier. The critical point here is that the local equations of motion are now deduced as a consequence of a global principle and not on the basis of local arguments and an appeal to Newton's second law. Conceptually, this is a fundamental difference.

As we might suspect, in the types of systems encountered in the social, economic, and management sphere, the search for global understanding will have to do without such well-established and unambiguous concepts as Hamilton's principle. In fact, there exists no such general laws for such systems, at least not yet. Thus, we shall have to be content with presenting a number of different global system properties and various techniques for operating with them in the hope that illumination of different facets of the picture will give insight into the structures involved.

As a more contemporary example of the use of global approaches to system problems, we consider the following road congestion situation. In view of the many parameters involved in road traffic interactions, the analyst tries to "piece together" the local descriptions provided by queuing theory, Monte Carlo simulations, and other methods. Using this approach, many details can be revealed, but in most cases it is not clear how the results obtained can be transferred to other traffic situations. A holist in this case may remember an analogy from the mechanics of particles and may try to describe the type of traffic situations by a simple time equation, neglecting

34

distances between vehicles, reasons for jams, and so on. His characteristic parameter in this case will be $q$, the vehicle density in vehicles per hour on a road interval of 1 kilometer length. The time $T_A$ in minutes, which is needed by a vehicle to travel 1 kilometer of the road under consideration, can be expressed as the sum of two quantities:

$$T_A = T_{A0} + k \cdot n_A,$$

with

$T_{A0}$ = time needed to travel a road interval of $A = 1$ km, if not delayed by other vehicles ($q \approx 0$) ($T_{A0} = 0.5$ min/km, for instance, corresponds to a free traffic speed of 120 km/h).

$k \cdot n_A$ = additional time needed for the interval $A = 1$ km, which is proportional to the number $n_A$ of vehicles, which are present in $A$ during the time interval $T_A$ (i.e., the delay under congestion conditions is a linear function of the number of deceleration and acceleration events or of the number $n_A$ of participating vehicles).

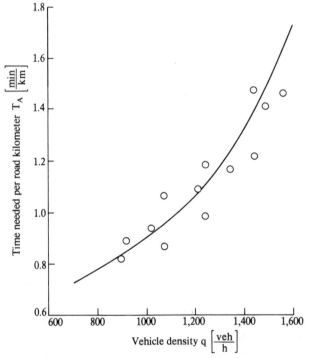

FIGURE 2.4 Delay caused by traffic jam. Time equation: $T_A = T_{A0} + k\dfrac{q}{60} \cdot T_A$. Curve for $T_{A0} = 0.50$ and $k = 0.0266$.

The number $n_A$ is a product of traffic density $q$ and time duration $T_A$:

$$n_A = \frac{q \cdot T_A}{60}.$$

Resolving the whole expression for $T_A$, we get

$$T_A = \frac{T_{A0}}{1 - k\frac{q}{60}}.$$

As illustrated in Figure 2.4, $T_A = f(q)$ is a convex curve: each additional vehicle, which causes an increment of $q$, is not only delayed in the interval A, but is itself the reason for a further delay of the following vehicles. For $T_{A0} = 0.5$ and $k = 0.0266$, Figure 2.4 shows a fair agreement between experimental data, and this simple equation for $q$ gives values well below the theoretical "total jam" density $q_\infty = 2,255$ vehicles/hour.

The traffic congestion problem shows how the holist's approach rather than a "local" description can provide a meaningful model of the time delay in a traffic jam.

## CONNECTIVITY AND GRAPHS

We now turn to the major topics of the book: connectivity, complexity, and stability. Each of these focal points will be briefly examined in the remaining sections of this chapter as a prelude to the detailed treatment of each presented in the remainder of the book.

Perhaps the most basic of all qualitative systems properties is the connective structure of the system. On intuitive grounds it seems evident that without a connective structure, there would be no system at all, since the very essence of the systems concept relates to notions of "something" being related, that is, connected to "something" else. Various strategies have been proposed for capturing the connective structure in mathematical terms, with the most successful being ideas stemming from graph theory and algebraic (combinatorial) topology. Of course, it should come as no surprise that the appropriate mathematical tools are basically algebraic in nature, since, more than any other branch of mathematics, algebra is concerned with the question of determining how "simple pieces" are put together. We shall go into the algebraic issues surrounding system connectivity in the next chapter, but for purposes of orientation we present some of the main issues now as a preliminary roadmap.

The essence of the connectivity issue is to understand the mathematical structures describing how the components of a system $\Sigma$ are related to each

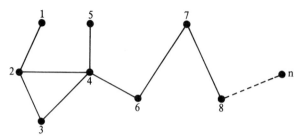

FIGURE 2.5   Graph-theoretic representation of $\Sigma$.

other. If we imagine a system in which it is possible to distinguish $n$ different components (subsystems), then we might try to represent the connective structure of $\Sigma$ by a graph (Figure 2.5).

Here the $n$ nodes represent the $n$ subsystems of $\Sigma$, and an arc connecting subsystems $i$ and $j$ denotes that these two subsystems are related, or connected, in some fashion. For example, $i$ receives inputs from $j$, $i$ regulates $j$, and so on. Many refinements of the basic setup are clearly possible. For instance, we could introduce an orientation upon the arcs to form a *directed* graph (digraph). Such a representation of $\Sigma$ would enable us to study more detailed situations in which $i$ affects $j$, but not conversely. We could also study various strengths of connectivity by associating a numerical value with each directed arc, and so forth. All of these considerations are directed toward the basic goal of determining which components of $\Sigma$ affect other components and by how much. Basically, graph-theoretic models give us some insight into how it might be possible to decompose $\Sigma$ into small pieces without destroying the main features which make $\Sigma$ a system.

Let us examine the following simple system to indicate the main ideas.

*Example: Food Webs and Ecological Niches*   We consider an ecological system consisting of a set of animals or plants. The *food web* of the community is a digraph whose vertex set is the set of all species in the community. An arc is drawn from species $i$ to species $j$ if $i$ is a prey of $j$. We have already seen examples of this setup in connection with the sets–relation description of a system. Here we examine a different system

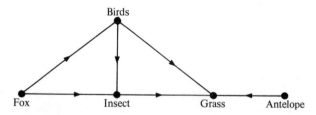

FIGURE 2.6   Digraph of a simple ecosystem.

consisting of five species: birds, insects, grass, antelope, and fox. A plausible digraph representing this system given as Figure 2.6.

From the food web graph we can generate the *adjacency* matrix, which corresponds to the incidence matrix for the sets–relation description, as well as several other interesting quantities characterizing important aspects of the system. For instance, the adjacency matrix of the above system is

|  |  | $j$ | | | | |
|---|---|---|---|---|---|---|
| $i$ |  | 1 | 2 | 3 | 4 | 5 |
| Birds | 1 | 0 | 0 | 1 | 1 | 0 |
| Fox | 2 | 1 | 0 | 1 | 0 | 0 |
| Insect | 3 | 0 | 0 | 0 | 1 | 0 |
| Grass | 4 | 0 | 0 | 0 | 0 | 0 |
| Antelope | 5 | 0 | 0 | 0 | 1 | 0 |

We shall return to this example in the next chapter, where we examine its connective structure using algebro-topological tools. For now, it is sufficient to note that some of the components (grass, for instance) seem to be more central to the system than others (e.g., birds). These observations, which are self-evident from Figure 2.6, are related to such ecological notions as trophic level and competition and will be formalized in later sections. The main point to note is that the graph-theoretical description enables us to visualize some of the inherent *geometry* present in the adjacency matrix.

Important as the graph-theoretic analyses are for visualizing connectivity patterns, they face inherent geometric, as well as analytical, obstacles, when it comes to accounting for the dimensionality of the systems components. On general principles, one would expect that attempting to account for multidimensional structure by planar graphs or, more generally, graphs drawn in the plane (they are not the same), would destroy or, at best, obscure much of the geometric structure of the system. Thus, we turn to an alternative characterization of system connectivity inspired by topological considerations.

## CONNECTIVITY AND SIMPLICIAL COMPLEXES

Roughly speaking, a simplicial complex consists of a set of vertices $X$ and set of simplices $Y$ formed from the vertices according to a given binary relation $\lambda$. The simplicial complex $K_Y(X; \lambda)$ then consists of the set of simplices $Y$ linked together through shared faces, i.e., through common vertices. For example, in the food web example given above, we might take

$$Y = X = \{\text{birds, fox, insects, grass, antelope}\},$$

with the relation $\lambda$ being that simplex $y_i$ consists of all those vertices $x_j$ such that $x_j$ is a prey of $y_i$. Thus, we would have

$$y_1 = \text{Birds} = 1-\text{simplex consisting of the vertices}$$
$$\text{Insects and Grass}$$

$$y_2 = \text{Fox} = 1-\text{simplex consisting of the vertices}$$
$$\text{Birds and Insects}$$

and so on. (Note that an $n$-simplex consists of $n+1$ vertices and that the dimension of a simplex is equal to the number of its vertices minus 1).

Generally, we represent a $p$-simplex $\sigma_P$ by a convex polyhedron with $(p+1)$-vertices in the euclidean space $E^p$ and the complex $K_Y(X; \lambda)$ by a collection of such polyhedra in some suitable space $E^\alpha$. Although it would be safe to choose $\alpha = $ sum of all the simplex dimensions in $K_Y(X; \lambda)$, the fact that many simplices share a common face suggests that a smaller value of $\alpha$ might suffice. In fact, it can be shown that if dim $K_Y(X; \lambda) = n$, then a sufficient value for $\alpha$ is $\alpha = 2n + 1$. For instance, if dim $K_Y(X; \lambda) = 1$, the highest order $\sigma_p$ is $p = 1$, and we expect to need a three-dimensional space $E^3$ to represent an arbitrary complex of dimension one geometrically. This is illustrated by the old game of trying to draw in a plane (in $E^2$) the lines that join three houses $H1$, $H2$, and $H3$ with the three utilities gas, electricity, and water and to do so without any of the lines crossing. The fact that this cannot be done without such a crossing illustrates the theorem. In Figure 2.7 we show the dilemma in $E^2$, and in Figure 2.8 we show its solution in $E^3$.

Utilizing geometric intuition, we may study the multidimensional connectivity structure of the complex $K_Y(X; \lambda)$ in many different ways by algebraic

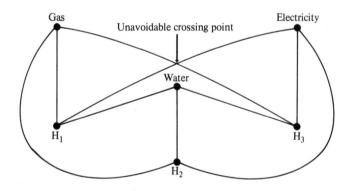

FIGURE 2.7   Crossing problem in $E^2$.

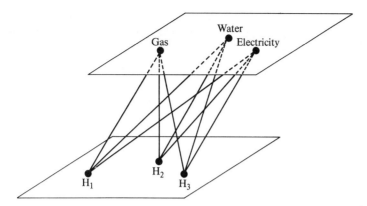

FIGURE 2.8  Solution of the crossing problem in $E^3$.

means. Since we shall thoroughly study these matters in the next chapter, let us now indicate only a few of the high points:

- *q-connectivity.*  It is of concern to examine those chains of connection in $K_Y(X; \lambda)$ such that each simplex in the chain shares $q + 1$ vertices with its adjacent neighbors, $q = 0, 1, 2, \ldots \dim K - 1$. Geometrically, these chains provide much of the local multidimensional information concerning how the simplices are connected to each to form the complex. We might envision a situation in which we could only "see" in dimensions $\geq q$ (with special glasses, say); then viewing $K_Y(X; \lambda)$ would show the complex being split into $Q_q$ disjoint pieces. Such a geometrical idea can be formulated into the notion of an algebraic theory of *q-connection*, providing much insight into the transfer of information within the complex.

- *Eccentricity.*  To understand how individual simplices "fit" into the complex, we can introduce the concept of *eccentricity*. Here we measure both the relative importance of the simplex to the complex as a whole (by its dimension) and its relative importance as an agent of connection (by the maximum number of vertices it shares with any other simplex). Eccentricity then enables us to visualize and measure how well integrated each simplex is into the entire complex.

- *Patterns.*  As already noted in Chapter 1, the notion of a system dynamic may be superimposed on the complex by introducing a mapping from each simplex of $K_Y(X; \lambda)$ into an appropriate number field:

$$\Pi: \sigma_i^r \to k, \qquad i = 0, 1, \ldots, \dim K,$$

$$r = 1, 2, \ldots, \text{card } K.$$

The pattern $\Pi$ embodies the dynamical changes taking place in the complex as time unfolds. Since each simplex $\sigma_i$ has a characteristic geometric

40

dimension, so do the numerical quantities associated with $\sigma_i$, and these features are intertwined with the geometric structure of $K$ through the chains of connection. As we shall point out later, the geometric structure then imposes various constraints upon the change of pattern, that is, upon the system dynamics.

• *Homotopy.* It is of theoretical and applied interest to ask "how close" a given simplex or chain is to another simplex or chain in the complex. This question can be precisely formulated and studied by introducing the notion of homotopy into the situation. Basically, homotopy is concerned with the question of whether a given chain may be deformed into another chain without meeting any geometrical obstacles during the deformation process. For instance, the curves $A$ and $A'$ on the torus of Figure 2.9 are homotopic,

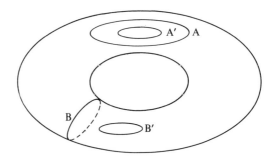

FIGURE 2.9   Homotopy on a torus.

while the curves $B$ and $B'$ are not, since the geometric obstacle of the "hole" in the center prevents $B$ from being continuously deformed into $B'$. Notions analogous to this simple geometrical situation can be defined for the complex $K_Y(X; \lambda)$ and prove useful in analyzing its structure.

Although the preceding geometrical concepts are elementary from a purely mathematical viewpoint, they represent a great deal of the information needed to understand the static geometry of a given relation and the dynamical implications of its associated connectivity structure. Such sweeping claims will be validated by numerous examples in the next chapter.

COMPLEXITY

Of all the adjectives in common use in the systems analysis literature, there can be little doubt that the most overworked and least precise is the descriptor "complex." In a vague intuitive sense, a complex system refers to one whose static structure or dynamical behavior is "unpredictable," "counterintuitive," "complicated," or the like. In short, a complex system is something quite complex—one of the principal tautologies of systems analysis!

Fortunately, stimulated by problems arising in computer science, a number of investigators have begun to make a methodological assault on the concept of complexity and to devise various means to quantify the notion. We shall discuss a number of these results in a later chapter. For now, let us discuss only some of the main ideas and the basic philosophical points surrounding this important qualitative concept.

Basically, complexity refers to two major aspects of a system: (a) the mathematical *structure of the irreducible component subsystems* of the process and (b) *the manner in which the components are connected* to form the system. These points imply, of course, that complexity is an attribute of the system itself, obscuring the fact that it is actually a relationship between an observer and the thing observed. However, this relativistic aspect will be suppressed throughout our introductory treatment in this book.

The first point noted above implies that the apparent complexity of a system can be lowered by grouping its variables into subsystems, as for example, in a schematic diagram of a radio, where the various system pieces (resistors, transistors, and so on) are grouped into components, such as tuning circuits and power supply. The goal of such a decomposition, of course, is to enable the analyst to see the system as less complex by being able to interpret it as a nearly decomposable collection of interrelated subsystems. We should note, however, that although the interactions between subsystems may (hopefully) be weak, this does not imply that they are negligible.

The second main point interfaces strongly with the connectivity concepts discussed previously. Such issues as dimensionality, hierarchy, length of connective chains, and data paths all fall into this broad category. Questions involving dynamical behavior are clearly intimately involved with both the structure of the "pieces," as well as with how the pieces are put together.

Fundamentally, then, the analyst must concern himself with two aspects of the complexity question—the structural or *static* complexity involving the connectivity and structure of the subsystems and the *dynamical* complexity surrounding the time behavior of the system. That these measures may be relatively independent is illustrated by simple cases. For instance, a wristwatch certainly possesses a high degree of static complexity but its dynamical complexity is essentially zero, assuming it is operating as designed. On the other hand, consider the nonlinear oscillator described by the Van der Pol equation

$$\ddot{x} + \lambda(x^2 - 1) + x = 0.$$

As is well known, this system can have complicated "flip-flop" behavior depending upon the parameter λ, and, in fact, it is precisely this "complicated" behavior that makes the circuit of theoretical and applied interest. However, from a structural view, the Van der Pol oscillator is certainly not a complex circuit.

To illustrate some other aspects of the type of counterintuitive behavior that seems to characterize complex systems, consider the idealized *linear* social process depicted in Figure 2.10. As is evident from the structural setup, this example is for illustration only, and the social assumptions should not necessarily be taken seriously.

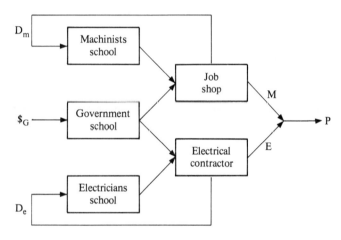

FIGURE 2.10   Simplified industrial economy of a developing country.

In Figure 2.10, we have a developing country whose nonagricultural economy has two kinds of workers and two factories: Machinists work in the job shop and electricians work for the electrical contractor. Both the job shop and the electrical contractor have a capacity for a fixed number of workers, and they try to operate at full capacity. Workers leave the work force sufficiently often that the number of workers is equal to the yearly output of the schools. There are three schools: two small schools, specializing in training machinists and electricians, and one large government school, which trains an equal number of both kinds of workers. The government trains two workers per dollar. The private schools train one worker per unit of demand, but, because these schools can be more selective in their students, they train their students to twice the productive capacity of the government-trained worker. The government subsidizes the factories so that they will take all workers trained in the government school. The following equations describe the situation:

$$M = D_m - {}^\$G,$$
$$P = D_m + {}^\$G + D_e,$$
$$E = {}^\$G + D_e,$$

where

> $M$ = number of machinists
> $E$ = number of electricians
> $P$ = total productive capacity (in terms of privately trained students)
> $D_m$ = demand for machinists
> $D_e$ = demand for electricians
> ${}^\$G$ = yearly output of the government school

Note that the scaling in the equations is unimportant, as the phenomena we shall present are invariant under scaling.

Assume that the control problem is such that it is desired to control the number of machinists and electricians and the total productive capacity. The controllers are the two factories and the government. The government controls $P$ with ${}^\$G$, while the job shop controls $M$ with $D_m$ and the electrical contractor controls $E$ with $D_e$.

The above situation generates the following paradoxical behavior: Suppose that the two factories have been operating at full worker capacity. The government then increases ${}^\$G$ by one unit. In turn, the two factories decrease $D_e$ and $D_m$ each by a unit amount to avoid overflowing. The net effect on $P$ of the changes in $D_m$ and $D_e$ is minus two units. Thus, the overall effect on $P$ of a single-unit *increase* in ${}^\$G$ is a unit *decrease* in P. This conclusion is independent of the detailed control strategies and depends *only* upon the structure of control and the objectives as seen by each controller.

The paradox could be removed if the government could manipulate $D_m$ or $D_e$ instead of ${}^\$G$. However, the basic problem arises because of the effect of other control actions on the apparent relationship between a controlled variable ($M$, $P$, or $E$) and the corresponding decision variable ($D_m$, ${}^\$G$, and $D_e$). The moral of the example is that seemingly elementary systems can give rise to very unexpected (and unpleasant) outcomes if the complexity of interactions is not thoroughly understood. Another important point to note is that, contrary to conventional wisdom, the nonintuitive aspects are *not* due to nonlinearities, stochastic effects, or the like. They are attributable solely to the system structure and the interactive connections and constraints of the composite subsystems.

The preceding example serves to illustrate still another important complexity concept—namely, the distinction between *design complexity* and *control complexity.* Roughly speaking, design complexity corresponds to a combination of the static and dynamic complexity when no controlling action is present or, more generally, to the transformation process in which full use of system potential is made. However, this transformation process may not result in stable configurations. For instance, unstable configurations may result from a gap between computability requirements of the entire system and the computational capacities of the connected subsystems attempting to realize the entire system.

By control complexity, we understand the complexity level that results from computations that keep the entire system under complete control. Unstable configurations may occur if some subsystems are unable to compute (adjust) fast enough in order to adapt to changes of input (external stimuli).

The relation between design and control complexity is called *evolution complexity,* and a system is said to be in *perfect balance* whenever the utilization of its potentialities is complete, that is, when design and control complexity coincide.

*Example: Jacob–Monod Gene Model* We assume the cell is divided into two parts: metabolism $M$ and genetic control $G$. One way to consider the interaction within the cell is as follows. $G$ is attempting to control $M$, where $G$ samples the output of $M$ and then applies a correction input into $M$ (the usual feedback setup of control theory). If $G$ accomplishes its action according to the design complexity and does not compute more or less than is required, then stable configurations will result and design and control complexity will coincide. Otherwise, a breakdown may occur.

Other models of a more realistic nature are explored in Chapter 4, where we consider applications of complexity concepts to the following types of dynamic systems:

• Competitive economic models of resource allocation and models of the "tragedy of the commons" type;
• Specific models of resource depletion and environmental pollution
• Structural models of spatiotemporal development

In summary, we can say that complexity is a multivalued concept involving static, dynamic, and control aspects. Static complexity represents essentially the complexity of the subsystems that realize the system, dynamic complexity involves the computational length required by the subsystem interconnection to realize the process, and control complexity represents a measure of computational requirements needed to keep the system behaving in a prescribed fashion. Ideally, a mathematical theory of complexity should reach a level similar to a theory of probability. Whereas probability can be conceived as a measure of uncertainty in particular situations, complexity may be considered as a measure of understanding of the system's behavior.


## STABILITY

Following connectivity and complexity, the third leg of our system-theoretic triangle in this book is stability. In rough terms, we have seen the relevance of connectivity and complexity to the understanding of system structure, but, for the most part, the dynamical behavior of the process has been underplayed. The variety of stability concepts will rectify this situation.

Unfortunately for the analyst, the term "stability" has been vastly overworked in the systems literature, having been used to denote everything from classical Lyapunov stability to organizational rigidity. The only common ground among all these uses of the stability concept has been that stability means the capability of something (the system, perhaps) to react to changes in its environment (e.g. perturbations, random disturbances) and still maintain approximately the same dynamical behavior over a certain time period (possibly infinite). Clearly, there is no hope for a mathematical study of stability with such a vague, shadowy "definition". But, it does provide the intuitive basis for more precise definitions and results.

For the sake of exposition, it is convenient to divide stability studies into two broad categories. The first we shall term *"classical,"* using the word to denote concepts and results centering upon external perturbations acting upon a fixed system: that is, the system, itself, does not change, only its external environment. A simple example of such a situation is again the classical pendulum, depicted in Figure 2.11.

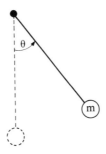

FIGURE 2.11  Simple pendulum.

If the equilibrium position ($\theta = 0$) is perturbed to the position $\theta^*$, we can ask whether the position $\theta = 0$ will again be reached after a sufficiently long, possibly infinite, time interval. It is evident both from the physics and from the mathematics that this will indeed be the case for all perturbations $\theta \neq 180°$. Thus, the position $\theta = 0$ is a *stable* equilibrium (in the sense of Lyapunov). The position $\theta = 180°$ is an unstable equilibrium, as an arbitrarily small perturbation from it will ultimately send the system to the stable position $\theta = 0$. The main point here is that the system dynamics are not affected by the initial displacement. Thus, we have a classical situation in which only the external environment (the displacing agent) is changing, not the system structure.

For the most part, classical stability analyses are concerned with the equilibrium points of the system and the dynamical behavior of the process in the neighborhood of these points. Various techniques for analyzing such situations have been perfected to a high degree; they will be discussed in Chapter 5.

Important as such classical equilibrium-centered concepts are in physics and engineering, their utility in systems arising in biology, economics, and the social sciences must be viewed with some reservation. The basic problem is that systems of this kind almost always operate far from equilibrium and are constantly being subjected to modifications that change the equilibrium positions. In short, the time constants of these problems are much too great for equilibrium analyses to be of more than marginal value in many cases. Of course, the systems of physics and engineering generally have much shorter transient times, and so the classical notions have proven very useful for studying electronic circuits, vibrations of plates, and so forth. However, what's good for the goose may not necessarily be good for the gander, too, and a careful analysis of the situation must be made before attempting to apply such ideas in other areas. (Workers in areas such as equilibrium economics, equilibrium ecology, and steady-state urban growth, please take note!)

The modern stability counterpart to the equilibrium-oriented classical view is the concept of *structural stability*. Here we are concerned with how the qualitative behavior of the system trajectories change when the system itself undergoes perturbation. Thus, we are studying the behavior of a given system with respect to the behavior of all "nearby" systems. If the target system behaves "about the same" as its neighbors, then we say it is structurally stable. Otherwise, it is structurally unstable. To make these notions precise, we must be very specific about what constitutes a nearby system, the class of perturbations allowed, and the meaning of similar behavior. However, the general idea is clear: a sufficiently small perturbation to the dynamics of a structurally stable system will result in a correspondingly small change in its dynamical behavior.

Let us consider the classic example of a structurally *unstable* system—the undamped simple harmonic oscillator. The system dynamics are

$$\ddot{x} + c_1 \dot{x} + c_2 x = 0$$

$$x(0) = a, \qquad \dot{x}(0) = 0.$$

We are interested in studying the effects of the parameters $c_1$ and $c_2$ upon the system trajectories. On physical grounds, we consider only the systems for which $c_1 \geq 0$, $c_2 > 0$.

Considering the motion in the $(x, \dot{x})$-plane, we see easily that if $c_1 = 0$, the trajectories are concentric circles centered at the origin with radii $a\sqrt{c_2}$ (see Figure 2.12). Assume now that we introduce some damping into the system.

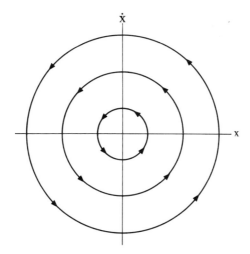

FIGURE 2.12   Trajectories of the undamped oscillator.

Mathematically, this means that $c_1 > 0$. If $c_1^2 > 4c_2$, the equilibrium point $x = \dot{x} = 0$ in the $(x, \dot{x})$-plane will be a *node* (Figure 2.13a); otherwise, it is a *focus* (Figure 2.13b).

In either case the origin is stable with respect to perturbation in $c_1$ or $c_2$. This situation is in stark contrast to the undamped case $c_1 = 0$ in which the origin is a *center* and its qualitative character may be changed by an arbitrarily small change of $c_1$. Thus, the systems with $c_1 \neq 0$ are structurally stable, in that the qualitative character of the equilibrium point (node, focus) is preserved under small changes of the system structure.

Since the structural stability ideas are closely related to the behavior of system trajectories as they move toward an equilibrium point, we must be concerned with those regions of the state space that correspond to *domains*

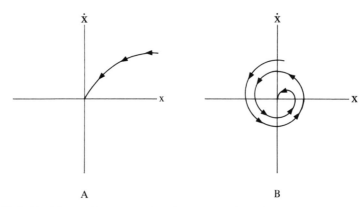

FIGURE 2.13   Phase plane portraits of system trajectories.

*of attraction or repulsion* for a given equilibrium. That is, given a particular equilibrium $x^*$, assumed for simplicity to be a fixed point, what initial points of the system will ultimately (as $t \to \infty$) end up at $x^*$? Graphically, we have the situation shown in Figure 2.14. Even in two dimensions, the situation can become quite complicated when we allow limit cycles and periodic

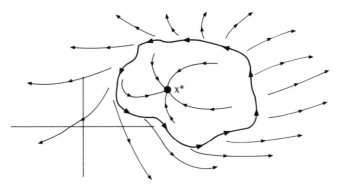

FIGURE 2.14   The domain of attraction of a fixed point in $R^2$.

trajectories as equilibria, and the picture in more than two dimensions is still very unclear. However, much is known about characterizng the domain of attraction and the associated structural stability questions, which we shall explore in the last chapter of this volume.

A slightly more complicated example of a structurally unstable situation is seen in the following ecological problem.

*Example: Antisymmetric Predator–Prey System*   Here we assume that $m$ species interact with the population of the $i$th species, denoted by $N_i(t)$. If $a_i$ represents the birth rate of species $i$, while $\alpha_{ij}$ is the rate of predation of species $i$ by species $j$, then the Lotka–Volterra system dynamics are

$$\frac{dN_i(t)}{dt} = N_i(t)\left[a_i - \sum_{j=1}^{m} \alpha_{ij}N_j(t)\right].$$

The nontrivial equilibrium populations $N_i^*$ must satisfy the linear algebraic system

$$\sum_{j=1}^{m} \alpha_{ij}N_j^* = a_i.$$

Under the questionable assumption that the interaction matrix $A = [\alpha_{ij}]$ is *antisymmetric*, i.e., $\alpha_{ij} = -\alpha_{ji}$, it can be shown that the system exhibits purely oscillatory behavior when it is displaced from any equilibrium, since the characteristic values of any antisymmetric matrix are purely imaginary. (It should be noted that the antisymmetry assumption is biologically equivalent to saying that the biochemical conversion of 1 gram of prey species $j$ is a constant for all members of the $i$th predator type; that is, the constant is independent of the type of prey being eaten.) In addition, it can be shown that the quantity

$$Q = \sum_{i=1}^{m} [N_i(t) - N_i^* \log N_i(t)]$$

is constant along trajectories of the system.

The above conservation law is a consequence of the oscillatory character of the system and is analogous to the conservation of mechanical energy associated with the ideal frictionless pendulum studied earlier. However, as soon as we lose the precise antisymmetric character of $A$, then the system equilibria become either nodes or foci (stable or unstable). Hence, again the introduction of an arbitrarily small change in the system destroys the qualitative behavior of the trajectories. Hence, the system is structurally unstable. Furthermore, the antisymmetric models apply only to a system with an *even* number of species, since antisymmetry implies that the characteristic values of $A$ occur in imaginary pairs. If $m$ is odd, then the unpaired characteristic value must be zero, giving rise to a singularity in the interaction matrix. Thus, the foregoing system might also be said to be structurally unstable with respect to perturbations in dimension, although we shall not pursue this type of instability in subsequent chapters.

## CATASTROPHES AND RESILIENCE

Since the location of system equilibria and their associated domain of attraction depends upon the precise dynamics of the system under study, it is

50

of great interest to know how these objects change as the system is perturbed to a nearby system. It is of the greatest practical concern to know if such a perturbation will result in a given state of the system shifting from one domain of attraction to another, since such a shift has dramatic implications for long-term behavior. Catastrophe theory has been developed as one tool for analyzing such situations.

In the standard catastrophe theory setup, we assume that we are interested in a process whose dynamics are governed by some potential function and that the stable equilibria of the process correspond to local minima of this potential. It is imperative to note that precise knowledge of the potential function itself is not needed to apply the theory, only the assumption that such a function exists. We then assume that a certain number of output variables are measured, being generated by the system as a result of input parameters. In the "elementary" catastrophe theory, the equilibrium outputs are all assumed to be simple fixed points. Roughly speaking, we fix a level of the input parameters, wait (infinitely long!) for the steady-state output to appear, then reset the input variables to new values and repeat the process. In this way, we obtain a surface of equilibria in the output space, graphed as a function of the input parameters. In loose terms, a "catastrophe" occurs when there is a discontinuous change in the output space behavior as a result of a smooth change of inputs.

We illustrate the situation in a system with two inputs and one output (the "cusp" catastrophe).

*Example: Central Place Theory*   In geographic analysis, one measure of the diversity of goods and services available in a given region is its "central place" level. Of course, there are many factors that influence the central place level, but two of the most important are population and expendable income per capita. Thus, suppose we wish to analyze the changes in equilibrium central place levels as a function of changes in population and expendable income in a given region. Since no one really knows how the central place dynamics operate anyway, there seems to be no reason to hesitate to assume that some unknown potential function governs the situation and that the equilibrium central place levels (for fixed population and income levels) correspond to local minima of this function.

Letting population and expendable income be the input parameters, with the central place level (dimensionless) being the output, the catastrophe-theoretic results in Chapter 5 lead to the picture in Figure 2.15. The manifold *M* represents the various equilibrium central place levels as a function of the two inputs. The most interesting features of the surface *M* are the two *fold* lines I and II, which meet at the *cusp* point 0. In the figure, these lines have also been projected onto the population–income plane.

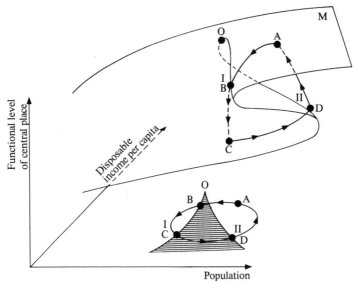

FIGURE 2.15   Catastrophe manifold for central place theory.

The cusp manifold *M* makes it clear how discontinuities in central place level may occur through seemingly minor population or income shifts. One such cycle *ABCD* is depicted in the figure. Here a decrease in population leads (with no change in per capita income) to the point *B*, whereupon a further population change discontinuously drops the central place level to *C*. Increasing population (again with constant per capita income) then moves the system to *D*, where the central place level then jumps back to *A*. It is important for the reader to understand that the cycle *ABCD* is *not* the dynamical motion of the system! It is only a sequence of *equilibrium* central place levels, parametrized by population and income. In Figure 2.15, we have also projected the cycle *ABCD* onto the input space, so that we can follow changes there. Note that as the inputs first enter the shaded cusp region, nothing unusual happens to the central place level. The level drops precipitously only at *B*, when the system *leaves* the critical region. The system then reenters the cusp region, again with no interesting central place changes until it leaves the region at *D*. The point to note is that discontinuous central place changes (up or down) occur only when the system crosses out of the cusp region by traversing the fold line opposite to that which it passed to enter into the critical region. We shall explore much more of the geometry of this situation in the last chapter.

In order to connect the catastrophe theory picture with our earlier remarks on the importance of the domain of attraction, we note that the

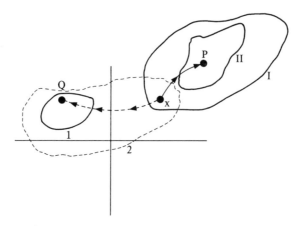

FIGURE 2.16    Shifting domains of attraction.

passage from the domain of attraction of one attractor to another corresponds to the situation shown in Figure 2.16. The point $x$ initially lies in the
domain of the attractor $P$. Because of changes in the system dynamics, the
domain of attraction of $P$ shrinks from I to II, while that of $Q$ expands from
1 to 2. The point $x$ is now drawn toward $Q$ rather than $P$. Of course, the
locations of $P$ and $Q$ themselves depend upon the system structure, so the
points in the figure are actually regions containing $P$ and $Q$. What is
important is that the regions $P$ and $Q$ are disconnected. Thus, perturbations
in the system structure that lead to the picture shown in Figure 2.16
generate a discontinuity in the output, if the output observed happens to be
the location of the equilibrium.

Returning to the catastrophe theory discussion, we see that the fold lines
correspond to exactly that combination of input parameters that leads to
discontinuous changes in the equilibria. Hence, the catastrophe theory
picture allows us to characterize changes in the domain of attraction
geometrically *without* having to go through the intermediate state space.
We should note that catastrophe theory tells us little about where a given
domain of attraction lies in state space; it tells us only about what regions of
input (or parameter) space may lead to a given state being transferred from
one domain to another. Often this is sufficient for applied work.

We close this chapter with a few words on the concept of *resilience*. It has
been recognized, especially by ecologists, that one of the most desirable
qualitative features that a system can possess is the ability to absorb
impulses (expected or not) without entering into a fatal type of behavior. In
other words, resilience should measure, in some sense, the ability of the
system to persist. Naturally, to make mathematical sense of this concept,
precise definitions are needed of the type of impulses allowed and the
meaning of "persist." We shall attempt some of this in Chapter 5.

Even this intuitive description of resilience shows that the notion is intimately tied up with the question of system domains of attraction and the change of these regions by artificial or natural causes. If such changes cause the current system state to be shifted into the domain of a "fatal attractor," then clearly we would say the system is not resilient to that class of impulses or inputs. Otherwise, it is resilient to a greater or lesser degree. One of our objectives in Chapter 5 will be to provide plausible measures of resilience and examples of resilient and nonresilient (rigid?) systems.

## NOTES AND REFERENCES

### CONTROLLED VERSUS FREE DYNAMICS

A most informative and entertaining treatment of the passive-observer/activist-controller dichotomy may be found in:

Bellman, R., *Some Vistas of Modern Mathematics*, University of Kentucky Press, Lexington, Kentucky, 1968.

The importance of this dichotomy, or paradigm, cannot be overemphasized since it provides the primary point of departure between modern system theory and classical ordinary differential equations.

### IDENTIFICATION

The general problem of system identification encompasses not only the limited parametric modeling ideas sketched in the text but the more general problems of determination of hierarchical levels, dimension, relationship among subsystems, and so forth. Excellent nontechnical introductions to much of the philosophy behind system modeling and identification are the books:

Weinberg, G., *Introduction to General Systems Thinking*, Wiley, New York, 1975.
Vemuri, V., *Modeling of Complex Systems: An Introduction*, Academic Press, New York, 1978.

A more technical presentation of the current state of the art in parametric identifications may be found in:

Mehra, R. K., and D. Lainiotis, eds., *System Identification: Advances and Case Studies*, Academic, New York, 1976.
Rajbman, N. S., "The Application of Identification Methods in the USSR: A Survey," *Automatica*, 12 (1976), 73–95.
Astrom, K., and P. Eyekhoff, "System Identification—A Survey," *Automatica*, 7 (1971), 123–162.

### CONSTRAINTS

Adaptation of external system constraints in a multiparticipant, multigoal environment is discussed in:

Lewin, A. Y., and M. Shakun, *Policy Sciences: Methodologies and Cases*, Pergamon, New York, 1976.

54

The pharmacokinetics example is adapted from:

Jeliffe, R., *et al.*, "A Mathematical Study of the Metabolic Conversion of Digitoxin to Digoxin in Man," USC Report EE-347, University of Southern California, Los Angeles, 1967.

The problem is treated from the viewpoint of observability in the book:

Casti, J., *Dynamical Systems and their Applications: Linear Theory*, Academic, New York, 1977.

OPTIMIZATION

Many outstanding books have been written in recent years dealing with the question of optimal control for systems described by differential (or difference) equations. As a representative list, we suggest:

Kirk, D., *Optimal Control Theory: An Introduction*, Prentice-Hall, Englewood Cliffs, New Jersey, 1971.
Bellman, R., *Introduction to the Mathematical Theory of Control Processes*, Vols. 1 and 2, Academic, New York, 1967, 1971.
Barnett, S., *Introduction to Mathematical Control Theory*, Clarendon Press, Oxford, 1975.
Bryson, A., and Y. C. Ho, *Applied Optimal Control*, Blaisdell, Waltham, Massachusetts, 1969.

For systems described in external form, or by graphs, sets/relations, and so on, there is no literature at all concerning optimal control. No doubt this is due to the relative newness of these approaches to system characterization, and it is to be expected that optimization results will follow in due course.

GLOBAL PERSPECTIVES

The issue of global system structure is at the heart of the current "general" system theory movement and its emphasis on the *holistic* structure of large systems, in contrast to the Aristotelian reductionist philosophy. A brilliant elucidation of the main points in the holist/reductionist debate is found in the works:

Koestler, A., *Janus*, Random House, New York, 1978.
Koestler, A., and J. Smythies, eds., *Beyond Reductionism*, Macmillan, New York, 1969.

See also:

Weinberg, G., *Introduction to General Systems Thinking*, Wiley, New York, 1975.
Bertalanffy, L. von, *General System Theory*, Braziller, New York, 1963.
Klir, G., *Trends in General System Theory*, Wiley, New York, 1972.

We are indebted to Dr. J. Dathe for the road traffic example of this section. Good sources for further material on this type of traffic problem are:

Ashton, W. D., *The Theory of Road Traffic Flow*, Methuen, London, 1966.
Dathe, J. "Time-Delay Equations for Traffic Jams," in *Proc. Oper. Res. 1978*, C. Schneeweiss, ed., Physica Verlag, Würzburg, 1979.

CONNECTIVITY AND GRAPHS

Most of the published connectivity studies for systems have utilized various graph-theoretic concepts to identify the system components and connectivities. Some sources for much of this work are:

Roberts, F., *Discrete Mathematical Models*, Prentice-Hall, Englewood Cliffs, New Jersey, 1976.
Harary, F., R. Norman, and D. Cartwright, *Structural Models: An Introduction to the Theory of Directed Graphs*, Wiley, New York, 1965.
Berge, C., *The Theory of Graphs and Its Applications*, Methuen, London, 1962.

CONNECTIVITY AND SIMPLICIAL COMPLEXES

The concepts of $q$-connection, eccentricity, and pattern are thoroughly explored in:

Atkin, R. H., *Mathematical Structure in Human Affairs*, Heinemann, London, 1973.

Classical notions of algebraic topology, such as homology, homotopy, and Betti number, are presented in:

Giblin, P. *Graphs, Surfaces and Homology*, Chapman and Hall, London, 1977.
Wallace, A. D., *Introduction to Algebraic Topology*, Pergamon, London, 1957.

COMPLEXITY

The industrial economy example is taken from:

Bristol, E., "The Counterintuitive Behavior of Complex Systems," *IEEE Systems, Man & Cybernetics Newsletter*, March 1975.

For a more detailed discussion of design and control complexity, see:

Gottinger, H., "Complexity and Information Technology in Dynamic Systems," *Kybernetes*, 4 (1975), 129–141.

STABILITY

Among the many outstanding books on all aspects of stability theory, we recommend:

Bellman, R., *Stability Theory of Differential Equations*, McGraw-Hill, New York, 1953.
Hahn, W., *Stability of Motion*, Springer, Berlin, 1967.
Hirsch, M., and S. Smale, *Differential Equations, Dynamical Systems, and Linear Algebra*, Academic, New York, 1974.

A collection of reprints of classical papers on the stability of nonlinear systems is:

Aggarwal, J. K., and M. Vidyasagar, eds., *Nonlinear Systems: Stability Analysis*, Dowden, Hutchinson and Ross, Stroudsburg, Pennsylvania, 1977.

CATASTROPHE AND RESILIENCE

The current fashionable (and controversial) subject of catastrophe theory is well summarized in the books:

Zeeman, E., *Catastrophe Theory: Selected Papers, 1972–77*, Addison-Wesley, Reading, Massachusetts, 1977.

Poston, T., and I. Stewart, *Catastrophe Theory and Its Applications*, Pitman, London, 1978.

The central place example is taken from:

Casti, J., and H. Swain, "Catastrophe Theory and Urban Systems," *IFIP Conference on Optimization*, Nice, France, September 1975.

The concept of resilience appears to have originated in the ecological community. For a general discussion see:

Holling, C. S., "Resilience and Stability of Ecosystems," *Annual Rev. Ecol. Syst.*, 4 (1973), 1–23.

Watters, C., "Foreclosure of Options in Sequential Resource Development Decisions," RR-75-12, International Institute for Applied Systems Analysis, Laxenburg, Austria, 1975.

# 3 Connectivity

In elementary books on systems analysis, one often sees a statement such as "a system is a collection of interrelated elements." While this hardly suffices as a definition, the intuitive notion that a system constitutes a *connected* set of objects is made explicit. One might even say that connectivity is the very essence of the "large-scale" system concept, since, *a fortiori*, a system whose components do not interact is unlikely to pose much of an analytical problem (or to represent a very interesting physical process).

The question to be addressed in this chapter is how to describe the connective structure of a system in mathematical terms. In view of the many different mathematical formulations of a system given in the preceding chapters, it will be necessary to consider the connectivity question from several points of view; however, all the viewpoints will have the objective of making explicit the essential connections between system components and the manner in which these connections influence the behavior of the process.

To illustrate, consider an input–output description given by the set of linear algebraic equations

$$Ax = b.$$

If we identify each component of $x$ with a subsystems and regard $b$ as the system input, it is clear that the off-diagonal terms in $A$ determine the interaction between component subsystems and any analysis of the connective structure of the process must be centered upon the zero/nonzero pattern and the magnitude of these elements. We shall present a substantial generalization of this basic concept below within the framework of a linear dynamical process. On the other hand, if our system is described qualitatively by a planar graph, where an arc between two nodes indicates that the subsystems represented by the nodes are connected in some fashion, the relevant object for studying the connective structure is the system interconnection matrix $E$, whose $(i, j)$ element is 1 if and only if subsystems $i$ and $j$ are connected, 0 otherwise. As will be shown later, the off-diagonal elements of $E$, while important, do not tell the whole story of the system's connective structure, and a more topological, rather than algebraic, approach is required.

The picture that will emerge from our analysis is that connective structure is a multifaceted, multidimensional notion that requires tools from both algebra and topology to characterize adequately the way in which a system is composed from its components. Depending upon the manner in which the system is described, different aspects of the connectivity question will present themselves and different questions will be appropriate. Our goal will be to survey the most interesting of these questions and to attempt to supply an array of mathematical tools for their resolution.

Since connectivity is essentially an *algebraic* notion, this chapter is heavily flavored by mathematical constructs and ideas from abstract algebra and topology. In particular, the first half of the chapter is devoted to a semi-intuitive discussion of simplicial complexes and algebraic topology in order to provide a suitable framework for analyzing connectivity when a set–relation model of a system is employed. The second half of the chapter shifts to the algebraic theory of semigroups as a suitable mathematical basis for studying connectivity in a dynamical context. In addition, the semigroup material will be extensively employed in the complexity studies of the following chapter.

## COMPLEXES AND CONNECTIONS

As observed in Chapter 1, the simplicial complex forms the natural mathematical generalization of a planar graph, an extension that is critical to examination of the multidimensional nature of a given binary relation. For geometrical, as well as expository, reasons, we begin our study of connective structure by examining complexes.

As simplicial complexes are nothing more than collections of simplices joined through a sharing of vertices, the most natural connective concept here is the dimensional one, that is, the dimension of the face shared by two simplices. Since we are interested in the complex, it is most appropriate to consider the idea of a *chain of connection*, reflecting the fact that two simplices may share no common face, yet be connected to each other by an intermediate sequence of simplices. Taking account of the dimensional aspects of the situation, we are led to the concept of *q-connectivity*.

*Definition 3.1.* Given two simplices $\sigma_i$ and $\sigma_j$ in a complex $K$, we say they are joined by a *chain of q-connection* if there exists a sequence of simplices

$\{\sigma_{\alpha_i}\}_{i=1}^{n}$ in $K$ such that

1. $\sigma_i$ is a face of $\sigma_{\alpha_1}$
2. $\sigma_{\alpha_n}$ is a face of $\sigma_j$
3. $\sigma_{\alpha_i}$ and $\sigma_{\alpha_{i+1}}$ share a common face of dimension, say, $\beta_i$
4. $q = \min\{i, \beta_1, \beta_2, \ldots, \beta_n, j\}$

(Here we employ the standard convention that a subscript on a simplex indicates its geometrical dimension, e.g., $\dim \sigma_s = s$.)

It is easily verified that the concept of $q$-connection defines an equivalence relation upon the simplices of $K$. Thus, a natural way to examine the global connective structure of the complex $K$ is provided by studying the $q$-equivalence classes. For each dimensional level $q = 0, 1, \ldots, \dim K$, we shall determine the number of distinct equivalence classes $Q_q$ and shall call this the operation of performing a "$q$-analysis" of $K$. The vector

$$Q = (Q_{\dim K}, \ldots, Q_1, Q_0)$$

will be called the *first structure vector* of the complex.

The information contained in $Q$ captures some of the global structure of the complex $K$ in the following sense. In order for two simplices $A$ and $B$ to belong to the same $q$-connected component of $K$, there must exist a chain of intermediate simplices connecting $A$ and $B$ such that the "weakest link," dimensionally speaking, in this chain has dimension greater than or equal to $q$. It is evident from Definition 3.1 that if two simplices are $q$-connected, then they are also $q-1, q-2, \ldots, 0$ connected as well. Hence, we may regard $K$ as being constructed out of multidimensional tubes of simplices, and the vector $Q$ tells how many tubes of each dimension there are in $K$.

Alternatively, we may conceive of $q$-connection in the following manner. Imagine being able to view the complex through a pair of spectacles that enable one to see only in dimension $q$ and higher. Looking at a geometrical representation of $K$ through such spectacles, we would see the complex split up into $Q_q$ disjoint (disconnected) pieces. Hence, we note in passing that the number $Q_0$ is identical with the topologist's zeroth Betti number, although the other $Q_q, q \geq 1$, do not coincide with the higher Betti numbers. $Q_0$, of course, represents the number of disconnected components of $K$, when $K$ is viewed at all dimensional levels.

In order to fix the preceding ideas firmly, consider the elementary example of a system characterizing the goods–service facilities of a primitive town as presented in Chapter 1. Imagine that the set

$$X = \{\text{bread, milk, stamps, shoes}\}$$

represents the goods of interest, while the set

$$Y = \{\text{market, department store, bank, post office}\}$$

represents the service facilities. A natural relation $\lambda \subset Y \times X$ linking these two sets is

$(y_i, x_j) \in \lambda$    if and only if good $y_i$ is obtainable at facility $x_j$.

Then clearly

$$\lambda = \{(y_1, x_1), (y_1, x_2), (y_2, x_4), (y_4, x_3)\}.$$

The incidence matrix $\Lambda$ for this relation is

|  | $x_1$ | $x_2$ | $x_3$ | $x_4$ |
|---|---|---|---|---|
| $\lambda$ | | | | |
| $y_1$ | 1 | 1 | 0 | 0 |
| $\Lambda = y_2$ | 0 | 0 | 0 | 1 |
| $y_3$ | 0 | 0 | 0 | 0 |
| $y_4$ | 0 | 0 | 1 | 0 |

while the geometrical view of the complex is given as

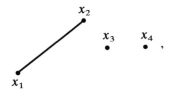

where we use $X$ as the vertex set, $Y$ as the simplex set. Note that the "empty" simplex $y_3$ does not belong to the complex $K_Y(X; \lambda)$ unless we agree to augment $K$ by adding the empty vertex $\varnothing$ to $X$, representing a $(-1)$-dimensional simplex.

As is evident from the geometry, the above complex consists of the 1-simplex $y_1$, and the two 0-simplices $y_2$ and $y_4$. Clearly, this "system" displays a very low level of connectivity. By inspection, we can see that $Q_1 = 1$, the simplex $y_1$, while $Q_0 = 3$, the disjoint 0-components being the simplices $y_1$, $y_2$, and $y_4$. Hence, the first structure vector for this complex is

$$Q = (1 \quad 3).$$

## ECCENTRICITY

While the preceding type of analysis can be quite revealing as far as the global connective structure is concerned, it provides little information about the way in which any individual simplex fits into the total complex. Since the simplices themselves represent meaningful entities within the problem context, it is important to determine how well "integrated" each individual simplex is into the whole structure. In an attempt to capture this concept, we introduce the idea of "eccentricity."

*Definition 3.2.* The *eccentricity* of a simplex $\sigma$ is given by the formula

$$\text{ecc}\,(\sigma) = \frac{\hat{q} - \check{q}}{\check{q} + 1},$$

where $\hat{q}$ is the dimension of $\sigma$ as a simplex, and $\check{q}$ is the largest $q$ value at which $\sigma$ is connected to some other simplex in $K$.

The difference $\hat{q} - \check{q}$ is a measure of the unusual, "nonconforming" nature of $\sigma$; however, $\hat{q} - \check{q} = 2$ is presumably more revealing if $\check{q} = 1$ than if $\check{q} = 10$. Thus, we use the ratio above rather than the absolute difference $\hat{q} - \check{q}$ as a measure of eccentricity. Note also that $\text{ecc}\,(\sigma) = \infty$ if $\check{q} = -1$, that is, if $\sigma$ is not connected to any other simplex in $K$. This agrees with our intuition that a simplex is maximally eccentric if it is totally disconnected from the remainder of the complex.

With regard to the simple complex of the previous section, it is easily computed that

$$\text{ecc}\,(y_1) = \infty, \qquad \text{ecc}\,(y_2) = \infty, \qquad \text{ecc}\,(y_4) = \infty,$$

indicating that each simplex is totally disconnected from the others. We shall present a more interesting example of the eccentricity notion in the next chapter.


## HOLES AND OBSTRUCTIONS

As noted above, the $q$-analysis of a simplicial complex provides information about the multidimensional chains of connection of the simplices comprising $K$. A question of interest centers on the structure *between* these chains. We might regard $K$ as being a type of multidimensional Swiss cheese with the chains of $q$-connection forming the substance of the cheese. We now wish to study the structure of the holes in the cheese. First, we must turn to a bit of advanced mathematics, but we shall return to "reality" again in the section on predator–prey relations (p. 70).

In the language of algebraic topology, the study of the multidimensional holes in a complex is called *homology theory* and involves the concepts of chains and boundaries. We restrict the discussion to the case of a relation $\lambda$ between two finite sets $X$ and $Y$; in particular, $\lambda \subset Y \times X$ and $\lambda^* \subset X \times Y$.

Either of the two simplicial complexes $K_Y(X; \lambda)$, $K_X(Y; \lambda^*)$ possesses a finite dimension and a finite number of simplices.

We therefore take the case of such a complex, say, $K_Y(X; \lambda)$, in which $\dim K = n$; we assume that we have an orientation on $K$, induced by an ordering of the vertex set $X$, and that this is displayed by labeling the vertices $x_1, x_2, \ldots, x_k$, with $k \geq n+1$. We select an integer $p$ such that $0 \leq p \leq n$ and we label all the simplices of dimension $p$ as $\sigma_p^i$, $i = 1, 2, \ldots, h_p$, where we suppose that there are $h_p$ $p$-simplices in $K$.

We now form the formal linear sum of these $p$-simplices and call any such combination a *p-chain*, allowing multiples of any one $\sigma_p$. We denote the totality of these $p$-chains by $C_p$ and one member of $C_p$ by $c_p$. Thus a typical $p$-chain is

$$c_p = m_1 \sigma_p^1 + m_2 \sigma_p^2 + \ldots + m_{h_p} \sigma_p^{h_p},$$

with each $m_i \in J$ where $J$ is an arbitrary Abelian group. We can then regard this set $C_p$ as a group (an additive Abelian group) under the operation $+$, by demanding

$$c_p + c_p' - (m_1 + m_1') \sigma_p^1 + \ldots + (m_{h_p} + m_{h_p}') \sigma_p^{h_p}$$

together with the identity (zero) $0_p$ for which each $m_i = 0$. Combining every group $C_p$, for $p = 0, 1, \ldots, n$, we obtain by the direct sum the chain group $C.$, written

$$C. = C_0 \oplus C_1 \oplus \ldots \oplus C_n.$$

Any element in $C.$ is of the form

$$c. = c_0 + c_1 + \ldots + c_n.$$

With every $p$-chain $c_p$ we now associate a certain $(p-1)$-chain, called its *boundary*, and denoted by $\partial c_p$. We define $\partial c_p$ precisely in terms of the boundary of a simplex $\partial \sigma_p$, and if $c_p = \sum_i m_i \sigma_p^i$, we take

$$\partial c_p = \sum_i m_i \, \partial \sigma_p^i.$$

In other words, we require that $\partial$ be a homomorphism from $C_p$ into $C_{p-1}$.

If a typical $\sigma_p$ is $\sigma_p = \langle x_1 x_2 \ldots x_{p+1} \rangle$, we define $\partial \sigma_p$ by

$$\partial \sigma_p = \partial \langle x_1 x_2 \ldots x_{p+1} \rangle = \sum_i (-1)^{i+1} \langle x_1 x_2 \ldots \hat{x}_i \ldots x_{p+1} \rangle$$

where $\hat{x}_i$ means that the vertex $x_i$ is omitted.

Figure 3.1 shows a geometric representation of a $\sigma_2 = \langle x_1 x_2 x_3 \rangle$, together with the orientation and the induced orientations on the edges. In this case

$$\partial \sigma_2 = \partial \langle x_1 x_2 x_3 \rangle$$
$$= (-1)^2 \langle x_2 x_3 \rangle + (-1)^3 \langle x_1 x_3 \rangle + (-1)^4 \langle x_1 x_2 \rangle;$$

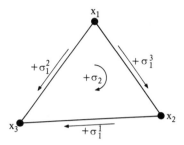

FIGURE 3.1   A 2-simplex with its faces oriented.

this means that

$$\partial\sigma_2 = \sigma_1^1 - \sigma_1^2 + \sigma_1^3,$$

which is a 1-chain, a member of $C_1$.

The boundary of a chain can be seen as its image under the operator $\partial$, which is a map

$$\partial: C_p \to C_{p-1} \qquad \text{for} \qquad p = 1, \ldots n.$$

Not only is $\partial$ a homomorphism (it preserves the additive structure), but it is easily seen to be nilpotent—that is to say, $\partial(\partial c_p) = 0$ in $C_{p-2}$, or

$$\partial^2 = 0 \quad \text{(the zero map).}$$

In the case shown in Figure 3.1, we have

$$\begin{aligned}
\partial^2\sigma_2 &= \partial(\partial\sigma_2) = \partial(\sigma_1^1 - \sigma_1^2 + \sigma_1^3) \\
&= \partial\langle x_2 x_3\rangle - \partial\langle x_1 x_3\rangle + \partial\langle x_1 x_2\rangle \\
&= \langle x_3\rangle - \langle x_2\rangle - (\langle x_3\rangle - \langle x_1\rangle) + \langle x_2\rangle - \langle x_1\rangle \\
&= 0.
\end{aligned}$$

Since $\partial: C_p \to C_{p-1}$ is a homomorphism, the image of $C_p$ under $\partial$ must be a subgroup of $C_{p-1}$; we denote this image $\partial C_p$ variously by im $\partial$ or by $B_{p-1}$, and, because $\partial$ is nilpotent, we see that

$$\partial B_{p-1} = 0 \quad \text{in } C_{p-2}, \text{or} \quad \partial(\text{im } \partial) = 0.$$

Those $p$-chains $c_p \in C_p$ that are such that their boundaries vanish (that is, $\partial c_p = 0$) are called $p$-cycles. They form a subgroup of $C_p$, being the kernel of the homomorphism $\partial$, and are usually denoted by the symbols $z_p$, the whole subgroup being $Z_p$. The members of $B_p$ (which is $\partial C_{p+1}$) are clearly cycles too, by the above, and so $B_p \subset Z_p$. In fact $B_p$ is a subgroup of $Z_p$.

The members of $B_p$ are called *bounding cycles* (they are cycles in an identical or trivial sense), and those members of $Z_p$ that are not members of $B_p$ can be identified as representatives of the elements of the factor group (or quotient group) $Z_p/B_p$. The members of this factor group are of the form

$$z_p + B_p,$$

and, if we select one member, say $z_p$, out of this equivalence class, we can also denote it by $[z_p]$. When two $p$-cycles $z_p^1$ and $z_p^2$ differ by a $p$-boundary, then $z_p^1 - z_p^2 \in B_p$ and we say that $z_p^1$ and $z_p^2$ are homologous (often written as $z_p^1 \sim z_p^2$). This is a relation on the set of cycles, and it is easy to see that it is an equivalence relation. The quotient set $Z_p/\sim$, under the relation of "being homologous to," is the quotient group $Z_p/B_p$, the group structure being determined by the operation $+$ on the members $z_p + B_p$. In this group structure, the set $B_p$ acts as the additive identity (the "zero"), since

$$(z_p + B_p) + B_p = z_p + B_p$$

for all $z_p$.

This $p$th factor group $Z_p/B_p$ is what is called the $p$th *homology group* and is denoted by $H_p$:

$$H_p = Z_p/B_p, \qquad p = 0, 1, \ldots, n.$$

The group of cycles $Z_p$ being mapped to zero by the homomorphism $\partial$ is what is known as the kernel of $\partial$ (written ker $\partial$) and so we find the alternative form

$$H_p = \ker \partial / \operatorname{im} \partial.$$

The operation of $\partial$ on the graded group $C.$ can be indicated by the sequence:

$$C. = C_0 \oplus C_1 \oplus C_2 \oplus \ldots C_p \overset{\partial}{\oplus} C_{p+1} \ldots \oplus C_n,$$

together with the symbolic diagram of Figure 3.2, where $B_p$ is represented by the shaded bull's-eye in $C_p$; $Z_p$ is the inner ring surrounding this shaded portion.

When $H_p = 0$, there is only one equivalence class in the factor group and this is $B_p$; every $z_p \in B_p$; every cycle is a bounding cycle. When $H_p \neq 0$, there is more than one element in the factor group and so there must be at least

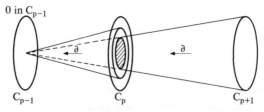

FIGURE 3.2    A nilpotent $\partial$ operating on a graded group C.

one cycle that is not a bounding cycle at this level. In Figure 3.1 we have $H_1 = 0$ because the only 1-cycle is the combination $\sigma_1^1 - \sigma_1^2 + \sigma_1^3$ (and multiples thereof), and this is $\partial \sigma_2$. Because there is no $C_3$, there cannot be a $B_2$ (the $\sigma_2$ is not the boundary of anything) and since $\partial \sigma_2 \neq 0$, $Z_2$ is also empty. Under these conditions we also write $H_2 = 0$. When $H_p = 0$ we speak of the homology being trivial at the $p$-level; when we say that "the homology is trivial," without specifying the values of $p$, we mean that $H_p = 0$ for all values of $p$ other than $p = 0$. This latter group $H_0$ is never zero, except possibly when the complex $K$ is augmented by inclusion of the simplex whose vertex set is empty.

We can see in Figure 3.1 that the homology is trivial, and also that $H_0 \neq 0$, for any $c_0$ is of the form

$$c_0 = m \langle x_1 \rangle + m_2 \langle x_2 \rangle + m_3 \langle x_3 \rangle,$$

and, taking the boundary of a point to be zero, it follows that $c_0$ must be a 0-cycle, $c_0 \in Z_0$. But the vertices $x_1, x_2, x_3$ form part of an arcwise-connected structure in the sense that 1-chains $c_1, c_1'$ exist such that

$$\langle x_2 \rangle = \langle x_1 \rangle + \partial c_1$$
$$\langle x_3 \rangle = \langle x_1 \rangle + \partial c_1'$$

(in fact, we need only take $c_1 = \sigma_1^3$ and $c_1' = \sigma_1^2$). Hence we have

$$c_0 = z_0 = (m_1 + m_2 + m_3) \langle x_1 \rangle + \partial(\text{some 1-chain}).$$

Hence the vertex $x_1$ acts like a specially chosen 0-cycle $\hat{z}_0$; all the possible 0-cycles in the structure can be generated by writing

$$z_0 = m \hat{z}_0 + \partial(\text{some 1-chain}),$$

and $\hat{z}_0$, consisting of a single point, cannot be the boundary of any 1-chain. Hence $\hat{z}_0 \notin B_0$ and so $H_0 \neq 0$; in fact $H_0$ contains a single generator, and, being an additive group, it is isomorphic therefore to the additive group $J$ (which is generated by a single symbol, namely, 1). Thus we see that for the complex represented in Figure 3.1,

$$H_0 = J,$$

or, preferably, we should use the symbol for isomorphism and write $H_0 \cong J$.

The above argument shows that this structure is characteristic of the complex's being arcwise connected, and we can therefore generalize it to give the result:

if $K$ possesses $k$ connected components, then

$$H_0(K) = J \oplus J \oplus \ldots \oplus J$$

with $k$ summands. This number $k$ is also known as the zero-order Betti number of $K$; it then is written as $\beta_0$.

## BETTI NUMBERS AND TORSION

The groups $C_p$, $Z_p$, $B_p$ already discussed are examples of finitely generated free groups, there being no linear dependencies between the generators of any of them. But this property of being "free" is not necessarily true of the factor group $H_p$. Indeed, in general, we find that $H_p$ can be written as the direct sum of two parts, of which one is a free group and the other is not. To explain this idea, and to illustrate it by a practical example, we write our general $H_p$ in the form

$$H_p = G_p^0 \oplus \operatorname{Tor} H_p,$$

where $G_p^0$ is to be a free group and $\operatorname{Tor} H_p$ is to be called the torsion subgroup of $H_p$. Any element of $\operatorname{Tor} H_p$, say $h$, is such that $nh = 0$ for some finite integer $n$ (with 0 being the additive identity of the group $H_p$). In the context of boundaries and cycles, this means that $h$ can be written in the form $h = z_p + B_p$, because $h \in H_p$, and that there is an $n$ such that

$$nh = nz_p + nB_p;$$

this element must be in $B_p$ (the zero of the factor group). But this means that, although $z_p \notin B_p$, it must be that $nz_p \in B_p$ for this particular value of $n$. This rather strange behavior of certain torsion cycles is the property that the subgroup $\operatorname{Tor} H_p$ characterizes.

Members of the free group $G_p^0$ cannot behave in this way; if $z_p \in G_p^0$ and $z_p \notin B_p$, then $nz_p \notin B_p$ for any nonzero value of $n$. For this reason a free group is often called an infinite cyclic group, in contrast to the finite cyclic groups that go to make up $\operatorname{Tor} H_p$. Thus $G_p^0$ will consist of summands of type $J$ (the number of summands will equal the number of distinct generators of $G_p^0$), while $\operatorname{Tor} H_p$ will consist of summands of type $J_m$ (the additive integers modulo $m$ if $J =$ integers) for some choices of $m$. This must be so because a group like $J_m$ is an additive Abelian group with the property that if $h \in J_m$ then $mh = 0$. If $\operatorname{Tor} H_p$ contains a number of subgroups then each one will be isomorphic to some $J_m$, for a suitable $m$.

The number of generators of $G_p^0$ (the number of free generators of $H_p$) is called the $p$th Betti number of the complex $K$, sometimes written as $\beta_p$.

## $p$-HOLES

We have seen (Figure 3.1) the case of a complex $K$ possessing a trivial homological structure; in that example, $H_1 = 0$ because the triangle $\sigma_2$ is filled in. If we cut out the inside of this $\sigma_2$, leaving only the edges, then we find that $H_1 = J$, because there is now a single generator in the shape of

$$\sigma_1^1 - \sigma_1^2 + \sigma_1^3,$$

which is not the boundary of a $\sigma_2$, the $\sigma_2$ having been removed. Thus the single generator of $H_1$ represents the presence in $K$ of a hole, bounded by 1-simplices (edges), which we shall call a 1-dimensional hole. If the complex $K$ contained two hollowed-out triangles, then $H_1$ would be isomorphic to the direct sum of $J$ and $J$, written $H_1 = J \oplus J$. Similarly if a geometrical representation of the complex $K$ possessed a spherical hole (bounded by the surface of a sphere), we would find that $H_2$ would contain a single generator $\hat{z}_2 \in B_2$; and if we found that $H_2 = J \oplus J$, we could interpret it as meaning that $K$ possessed two 2-dimensional holes.

In general, then, we wish to stress the interpretation of the free group $G_p^0$ as an algebraic representation of the occurrence of $p$-dimensional holes in the complex $K$; the precise number of these holes is given by the $p$th Betti number $\beta_p$. A geometrical representation of the complex—as far as $G_p^0$ is concerned—therefore looks like a sort of multidimensional Swiss cheese.

The $q$-connectivity analysis discussed above is dedicated to showing us the structure of the "cheese" in between the holes. The possible interpretation of the torsion subgroup Tor $H_p$ is more elusive in this cheeselike context, but the following example shows that it can have a very practical significance in another.

*Example* Denote the faces of a gambler's die by the symbols $v^1, v^2, v^3, v^4, v^5, v^6$. Let these be the vertices of a 5-simplex and let $K$ be this simplex together with all its faces; for example, a typical 1-simplex is the pair $\langle v^i v^j \rangle$ with $i \neq j$. Impose the induced orientation on $K$, induced by the natural ordering of the vertices. Now conduct a series of experiments in which the die is successively thrown until there is a repetition of a die-face; in this, interpret the sequence $\{v^i, v^j\}$ as the negative of the sequence $\{v^j, v^i\}$. The result of a series of successive throws is to observe an element in the graded chain group

$$C_. = C_0 \oplus C_1 \oplus C_2 \oplus C_3 \oplus C_4 \oplus C_5.$$

Notice that the boundary of the run $\langle 123 \rangle$ is the 1-chain $\langle 12 \rangle$, $\langle 23 \rangle$, $\langle 31 \rangle$.

In the first place, we expect the experimenter to be able to observe every possible distinct run and series of runs. It would then follow that in the graded chain group every cycle is a boundary and so

$$H_p = 0 \qquad \text{for} \qquad p = 1, 2, 3, 4;$$

thus the homology is trivial.

But now let us alter the arrangement so that the experimenter suffers the handicap of working with a laboratory assistant who sees to it (by doctoring the records) that, let us say, the run $\langle 123 \rangle$ never occurs—either by itself or as a face of any other run. This results in a drastic alteration of the complex $K$ and its associated chain group. For example, the sequence

$\langle 123456 \rangle$ never occurs, since it contains $\langle 123 \rangle$. Furthermore, in the new complex $K'$, there exists a cycle

$$z_1 = \langle 12 \rangle + \langle 23 \rangle + \langle 31 \rangle$$

that is not a boundary. Hence the intervention of the assistant is reflected in an increase in the first Betti number $\beta_1$ from the value 0 to the value 1. The assistant is responsible for punching a hole in the complex; the homology group $H_1$ is now isomorphic to $J$.

Let us go further and alter the arrangements yet again. Suppose that the experiment is conducted by two fair-minded gamblers. They begin by noticing that the probabilities of distinct runs corresponding to typical simplices $\sigma_1, \sigma_2, \sigma_3, \sigma_4, \sigma_5$ are 5/6, 5/9, 5/18, 5/54, and 5/324. Since they intend to bet on the experiment, our two gamblers agree to weight the simplices so as to even up the chances. They do this by introducing new (weighted) simplices as generators for the new chain group $C'$. These generators $\sigma_i'$ are related to the old generators $\sigma_i$ by the formulae

$$\sigma_1' = 54\sigma_1; \qquad \sigma_2' = 36\sigma_2; \qquad \sigma_3' = 18\sigma_3; \qquad \sigma_4' = 6\sigma_4; \qquad \sigma_5' = \sigma_5.$$

Now the homology has been altered once more; for example,

$$54\{\langle 12 \rangle + \langle 23 \rangle + \langle 31 \rangle\}$$

is in $Z_1'$ but not in $B_1'$, because the latter consists of multiples of $108 \sum_i \sigma_1^i$, 108 being the lowest common multiple of 36 and 54. Hence there exists a cycle $z_1$ such that $2z_1 \in B_1'$. This makes a contribution to $H_1$ of the summand $J_2$; $H_1$ now contains a torsion subgroup Tor $H_1$. In fact,

$$H_1 = J_2 \oplus J_2 \oplus \ldots \oplus J_2,$$

there being 10 summands in all. The other $H_p$ are not affected, and $H_p = 0$ for $p = 2, 3, 4$.

The gambler's complex therefore possesses torsion that is expressed in $H_1$. It is thereby clear that the torsion can be introduced into $H(K)$ in different ways, which give different summands $J_m$, by altering the odds on the outcome of the experiments. Thus $\sigma_1' = 48\sigma_1$ leads to 10 summands $J_3$, with

$$H_1 = J_3 \oplus J_3 \oplus \ldots \oplus J_3.$$

## COCHAINS AND COBOUNDARIES

We can associate with a chain group $C$. (with coefficients in $J$) a dual concept, namely that of mappings from $C$. into $J$. In doing this we introduce the concept of a cochain, dual to that of a chain; every such cochain is a mapping from $C$, into $J$:

$$c^p: C_p \to J.$$

Precisely, we denote a $p$-cochain by $c^p$, and we also demand additivity

$$c^p(c_p + c'_p) = c^p(c_p) + c^p(c'_p).$$

We can build up any particular $p$-cochain $c^p$ in terms of a set of mappings from the $p$-simplices $\sigma_p$ into $J$. Hence, prior to the notion of a cochain, we can have the notion of a cosimplex $\sigma^p$, which is simply a mapping

$$\sigma^p: \{\sigma^i_p\} \to J,$$

without any additive structure assumed. If there are $h_p$ $p$-simplices in $K$ we can define a basis for the cosimplices as the set of $h_p$ mappings $\{\sigma^p_i, i = 1, 2, \ldots, h_p\}$ where

$$\sigma^p_i(\sigma^j_p) = 0 \quad \text{if} \quad i \neq j$$
$$= 1 \quad \text{if} \quad i = j.$$

Then every cosimplex $\sigma^p$ is the sum of the $\sigma^p_i$; that is,

$$\sigma^p = \sum_i \sigma^p_i,$$

and every $p$-cochain is a linear combination

$$c^p = \sum_i m_i \sigma^p_i,$$

together with the linearity condition. The zero cochain map (for any $p$) is the one defined by $m_i = 0$, for all values of $i$, and the whole set of $p$-cochains form an additive group $C^p$. Hence the graded cochain group is the direct sum

$$C^{\cdot} = C^0 \oplus C^1 \oplus \ldots \oplus C^n,$$

where $n = \dim K$. To complete the duality, we can define a coboundary operator $\delta$ which is the adjoint of $\partial$. Adopting the inner product notation $(c_p, c^p)$ for the value (in $J$) of $c^p(c_p)$, we define $\delta$ by

$$(\partial c_{p+1}, c^p) = (c_{p+1}, \delta c^p),$$

which shows that $\delta: C^p \to C^{p+1}$. It is also clear that $\delta$ is nilpotent, $\delta^2 = 0$, since

$$0 = (0, c^p) = (\partial^2 c_{p+2}, c^p)$$
$$= (\partial c_{p+2}, \delta c^p)$$
$$= (c_{p+2}, \delta^2 c^p) \quad \text{for all choices of } c_{p+2},$$

and so $\delta^2 c^p$ must be the zero map. We now have the dual cohomology groups, $H^p(K;J)$ defined by

$$H^p = Z^p/B^p = \ker \delta/\text{im }\delta.$$

## PREDATOR–PREY RELATIONS: A HOMOLOGICAL EXAMPLE

The preceding homological considerations can be well illustrated by examination of a classical ecological situation, the predator–prey ecosystem. Graphically, we have the system shown in Figure 3.3, consisting of the fifteen species indicated. An arrow from species $i$ to species $j$ denotes that $i$ preys on $j$.

Since the only objects present in the food web are the species themselves, it is natural to define the sets $X$ and $Y$ to be the same, namely, $X = Y = $ the collection of all species in the web. We shall use the notation $x_i$ $(=y_i)$ to denote the $i$th species numbered according to the key in Figure 3.3.

Each species in the web may be either a predator or prey (or both). Thus, to obtain a complete picture of the interconnections in the food web we define *two* relations on the set $X \times X$: the predator relation $\lambda_{PRD}$ and the prey relation $\lambda_{PRY}$. These relations are defined in the obvious way. For instance, $(x_i, x_j) \in \lambda_{PRD}$ if and only if $x_i$ is a predator of $x_j$, $i, j = 1, 2, \ldots, 15$. The incidence matrix for $\lambda_{PRD}$ is easily obtained from Figure 3.3 as

$$\Lambda_{PRD} =$$

| $\lambda_{PRD}$ | $X_1$ | $X_2$ | $X_3$ | $X_4$ | $X_5$ | $X_6$ | $X_7$ | $X_8$ | $X_9$ | $X_{10}$ | $X_{11}$ | $X_{12}$ | $X_{13}$ | $X_{14}$ | $X_{15}$ |
|---|---|---|---|---|---|---|---|---|---|---|---|---|---|---|---|
| $X_1$ | 0 | 0 | 1 | 0 | 0 | 0 | 1 | 0 | 0 | 1 | 0 | 0 | 0 | 0 | 0 |
| $X_2$ | 0 | 0 | 0 | 0 | 0 | 0 | 1 | 0 | 0 | 0 | 0 | 0 | 0 | 0 | 0 |
| $X_3$ | 0 | 0 | 0 | 0 | 0 | 0 | 1 | 0 | 0 | 0 | 0 | 0 | 0 | 0 | 0 |
| $X_4$ | 0 | 1 | 0 | 0 | 1 | 1 | 0 | 1 | 0 | 1 | 1 | 0 | 0 | 0 | 0 |
| $X_5$ | 0 | 0 | 0 | 0 | 0 | 1 | 0 | 0 | 0 | 0 | 0 | 0 | 1 | 0 | 0 |
| $X_6$ | 0 | 0 | 0 | 0 | 0 | 0 | 1 | 0 | 0 | 0 | 0 | 0 | 0 | 0 | 0 |
| $X_7$ | 0 | 0 | 0 | 0 | 0 | 0 | 0 | 0 | 0 | 0 | 0 | 0 | 0 | 0 | 0 |
| $X_8$ | 0 | 0 | 0 | 0 | 0 | 0 | 1 | 0 | 0 | 0 | 0 | 0 | 0 | 0 | 0 |
| $X_9$ | 0 | 1 | 0 | 0 | 0 | 1 | 0 | 0 | 0 | 0 | 0 | 0 | 0 | 0 | 0 |
| $X_{10}$ | 0 | 0 | 0 | 0 | 0 | 0 | 0 | 0 | 0 | 0 | 0 | 0 | 0 | 0 | 0 |
| $X_{11}$ | 0 | 0 | 0 | 0 | 0 | 1 | 0 | 0 | 0 | 0 | 0 | 0 | 0 | 0 | 0 |
| $X_{12}$ | 0 | 0 | 0 | 0 | 0 | 1 | 0 | 0 | 0 | 1 | 0 | 0 | 0 | 0 | 0 |
| $X_{13}$ | 0 | 0 | 0 | 0 | 0 | 1 | 0 | 0 | 0 | 0 | 0 | 0 | 0 | 0 | 0 |
| $X_{14}$ | 0 | 1 | 0 | 0 | 0 | 0 | 0 | 0 | 0 | 1 | 0 | 0 | 0 | 0 | 0 |
| $X_{15}$ | 0 | 0 | 1 | 0 | 0 | 0 | 0 | 1 | 0 | 1 | 0 | 1 | 0 | 0 | 0 |

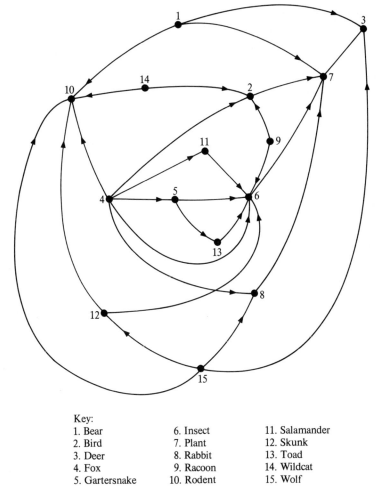

Key:
1. Bear
2. Bird
3. Deer
4. Fox
5. Gartersnake
6. Insect
7. Plant
8. Rabbit
9. Racoon
10. Rodent
11. Salamander
12. Skunk
13. Toad
14. Wildcat
15. Wolf

FIGURE 3.3  Predator–prey ecosystem.

Performing the $q$-analysis, we obtain the predator connectivity pattern:

$$
\begin{aligned}
\text{at} \quad q &= 5, & Q_5 &= 1, & \{x_4\} \\
q &= 4, & Q_4 &= 1, & \{x_4\} \\
q &= 3, & Q_3 &= 2, & \{x_4\}, \{x_{15}\} \\
q &= 2, & Q_2 &= 3, & \{x_4\}, \{x_1\}, \{x_{15}\} \\
q &= 1, & Q_1 &= 2, & \{x_1, x_4, x_9, x_{12}, x_{14}, x_{15}\}, \{x_5\} \\
q &= 0, & Q_0 &= 1, & \{\text{all except } x_7, x_{10}\}
\end{aligned}
$$

The structure vector is

$$Q = \begin{pmatrix} 5 & & & & & & 0 \\ 1 & 1 & 2 & 3 & 2 & 1 \end{pmatrix}.$$

The analysis shows that from the predator viewpoint, the complex is well-connected at the high and low $q$ values, but splits into several disconnected components at the intermediate $q$ levels.

Since more than a single component at a level $p$ comes about because there exist two $p$-dimensional species that are not $p$-connected, the notion of a *geometrical obstruction* is suggested. Hence, we define the obstruction vector $\hat{Q} = Q - U$, where $U$ is the vector all of whose components are 1. The components of $\hat{Q}$ measure the obstruction of a "free flow of information" in the complex at each dimensional level. In the preceding example, the obstruction at the $q = 3$ level means that the simplices $x_4$ (fox) and $x_{15}$ (wolf), while they each feed on at least four species, are not connected (directly or indirectly) by any four species, and, consequently, an unimpeded exchange of prey between fox and wolf is impossible at the 3-level. In other words, the obstruction vector is a rough indicator of alternatives available to predators at each $q$-level.

We remarked earlier that the integration of individual simplices into the complex may be studied by computing their eccentricities. Following Definition 3.2, we obtain the predator eccentricities shown in Table 3.1.

TABLE 3.1   Predator Eccentricities

| Species | Eccentricity | Species | Eccentricity | Species | Eccentricity |
|---------|--------------|---------|--------------|---------|--------------|
| 1 | 1/2 | 6 | 0 | 11 | 0 |
| 2 | 0 | 7 | $\infty$ | 12 | 0 |
| 3 | 0 | 8 | 0 | 13 | 0 |
| 4 | 2 | 9 | 0 | 14 | 0 |
| 5 | 1 | 10 | $\infty$ | 15 | 1 |

Thus, aside from species 7 (plant) and 10 (rodent), which are not even in the predator complex, we see that the least homogeneous member is species 4 (fox). This comes about principally because the fox has so many prey that he does not share with any other high-dimensional animal.

These results indicate that eccentricity is a measure of flexibility of species in their feeding—i.e., a measure of their ability to absorb changes in the web without starving. Again, this interpretation calls to mind the resilience concept, but now at the individual species level.

A totally analogous discussion and analysis can also be carried out for the prey relation $\lambda_{PRY}$. To conserve space, we present the final results of the

$q$-analysis and eccentricity calculations as checks for any reader who feels sufficiently motivated to carry out the details for himself. The $q$-analysis gives

$$
\begin{aligned}
\text{at} \quad q = 5, \quad & Q_5 = 1, \quad \{x_6\} \\
q = 4, \quad & Q_4 = 3, \quad \{x_6\}, \{x_7\}, \{x_{10}\}, \\
q = 3, \quad & Q_3 = 3, \quad \{x_6\}, \{x_7\}, \{x_{10}\}, \\
q = 2, \quad & Q_2 = 4, \quad \{x_6\}, \{x_7\}, \{x_{10}\}, \{x_2\} \\
q = 1, \quad & Q_1 = 2, \quad \{x_2, x_3, x_6, x_8, x_{10}\}, \{x_7\}, \\
q = 0, \quad & Q_0 = 1, \quad \{\text{all except } x_1, x_4, x_9, x_{14}, x_{15}\}.
\end{aligned}
$$

The structure vector is $Q = (\overset{5}{1} \ 3 \ 3 \ 4 \ 2 \ \overset{0}{1})$.

The eccentricities are shown in Table 3.2. Again, as in the predator complex, we see that the high-dimensional simplices $x_6$ (insects), $x_7$ (plants), and $x_{10}$ (rodent) have the highest eccentricities (except for those species that

TABLE 3.2  Prey Eccentricities

| Species | Eccentricity | Species | Eccentricity | Species | Eccentricity |
|---------|-------------|---------|-------------|---------|-------------|
| 1 | $\infty$ | 6 | 2 | 11 | 0 |
| 2 | 1/2 | 7 | 4 | 12 | 0 |
| 3 | 0 | 8 | 0 | 13 | 0 |
| 4 | $\infty$ | 9 | $\infty$ | 14 | $\infty$ |
| 5 | 0 | 10 | 3/2 | 15 | $\infty$ |

are absent from the complex), indicating that they are relatively unaffected by minor changes in the food web. Of course, since the prey relation reflects the web from the viewpoint of the prey, this means that addition or deletion of *predators* would likely have little effect on the high-dimensional prey species—they will continue to provide meals for much of the complex.

From a homological point of view, we examine the relation $\lambda_{\text{PRD}}$ for nontrivial bounding cycles. At dimension level $q = 1$, we have the four simplices $\sigma^5, \sigma^9, \sigma^{12}, \sigma^{14}$. It is easily verified that

$$
\partial(\sigma^9 + \sigma^{12} - \sigma^{14}) = 0,
$$

which means that the chain $\sigma^9 + \sigma^{12} - \sigma^{14}$ is a candidate for a bounding cycle. The question is whether there is a 2-cycle in $K$ whose boundary equals $\sigma^9 + \sigma^{12} - \sigma^{14}$. Since the only 2-simplex in $K$ is $\sigma_2 = \langle x_3 x_7 x_{10} \rangle$, whose boundary is $\langle x_7 x_{10} \rangle - \langle x_3 x_{10} \rangle + \langle x_3 x_7 \rangle \neq \sigma^9 + \sigma^{12} - \sigma^{14}$, we see that $\sigma^9 + \sigma^{12} - \sigma^{14}$ is a 1-cycle, which is not a bounding cycle. Thus, we see that

$$
Z_1 = \{\sigma^9 + \sigma^{12} - \sigma^{14}\},
$$

which implies trivially that $Z_1$ is generated by the cycle $\sigma^9 + \sigma^{12} - \sigma^{14}$. Similarly, since $\sigma_2 = \langle x_3 x_7 x_{10} \rangle$ is the only 2-simplex,

$$B_1 = \{\langle x_7 x_{10} \rangle - \langle x_3 x_{10} \rangle + \langle x_3 x_7 \rangle\}$$

is the only bounding 1-cycle and we have the homology groups

$$H_1 = Z_1 / B_1, \qquad H_0 \cong J.$$

Since there exists no integer $n$ such that $n(\sigma^9 + \sigma^{12} - \sigma^{14}) \in B_1$, the complex has no torsion, and, finally,

$$H_1 \cong J.$$

The Betti numbers are $\beta_1 = \beta_0 = 1$, with all other $\beta_i = 0$, $i = 2, \ldots, 5$.

The conclusion of the preceding analysis is that the predator complex contains a "hole" at the 1-level, which is bounded by 1-simplices. The physical interpretation of this hole is not entirely obvious, but it intuitively means that there exists a type of cyclic, or periodic, circulation of prey between the predators raccoon, skunk, and wildcat at the 1-dimensional level. A deeper interpretation would require a more detailed analysis of the dynamics of the system.

A similar analysis for the prey complex shows that the homology is trivial at all levels, so that no nontrivial bounding cycles exist.


## HIERARCHICAL SYSTEMS AND COVERS

In recent years, a theme running through much of mathematical system theory research has been the idea of hierarchical decision making. The basic idea is to recognize that problems of communication and uncertainty in large systems makes centralized decision making inefficient, if not totally ineffective. Consequently, for reasonable system behavior and organization, it is necessary to decompose the system into subsystems under the command of local controllers, whose decisions are coordinated with those of controllers at other hierarchical levels. A quick glance at the organization chart of any large firm or institution will confirm the universality of such decision making structures.

Since hierarchical organization is clearly dependent upon the manner in which the system pieces (subsystems) are connected, the question naturally arises of how the preceding topological connectivity concepts may be extended to include the hierarchical considerations. Our approach to this question shall be through the use of the set-theoretic concept of a *cover*.

*Definition 3.3.* A (finite) collection of sets $A = \{A_i\}_{i=1}^n$ forms a *cover* of the (finite) set $X$ if and only if

$$A_i \in \mathcal{P}(X), \quad \text{the power set of} \quad X$$

and

$$X = \bigcup_{i=1}^{n} A_i.$$

If, in addition, we know that $A_i \cap A_j = \varnothing$ (the empty set), then $A$ is called a *partition* of $X$.

By the foregoing definition, we see that the elements of $A$ are *subsets* of $X$ (see Figure 3.4). Consequently, we can regard the $A_i$ as being at the $(N+1)$-level if the elements of $X$ are assumed to be at the $N$-level. (Here we use $N$ to indicate a nominal, or normal level with no quantitative significance attached to the symbol $N$.)

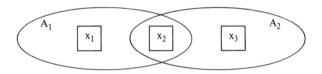

FIGURE 3.4   A cover of $X$.

We may now define a hierarchy $H$ by relations of the type $(A_i, X_j) \in \mu$ if and only if $X_j \in A_i$. Such a relation $\mu$ will also be represented by an incidence matrix of zeros and ones, just as for the $N$-level relation $\lambda$. The idea can also be extended in an obvious way to additional hierarchical levels and diagonally across levels, as is depicted in Figure 3.5.

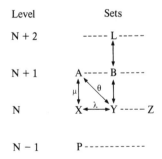

FIGURE 3.5   Hierarchical levels of sets and relations.

The hierarchical notions just considered are also intimately connected with Bertrand Russell's famous "theory of types," in which he insisted that we must not confuse the elements of a set with "sets of elements" with "sets of sets of elements," and so on. Such profound logical distinctions immediately enable us to sort out many logical paradoxes, among them the barber paradox:

In a certain town, every man either shaves himself or is shaved by the (male) barber. Does the barber shave himself?

The problem here is that if $X =$ set of men in the town, then the barber as a barber and not a man is not really a member of $X$, but rather a member of the *power set* of $X$, namely the subset of $X$ consisting of those men who shave themselves. Thus, we cannot ask questions of members of $\mathcal{P}(X)$ as if they were members only of $X$.

## APPLICATIONS OF $q$-CONNECTIVITY TO CHESS AND SHAKESPEAREAN DRAMA

As an entertaining way of illustrating some aspects of $q$-analysis, we consider the game of chess and Shakespeare's play *A Midsummer Night's Dream*. In addition to being fields of study that are, by and large, outside the realm of traditional systems analysis methodology, these examples provide ample ammunition to support the proposition that almost every aspect of human affairs contains some nontrivial mathematical aspects, provided we are clever enough to employ the right kind of mathematics.

### CHESS

It is almost a tautology to state that the game of chess is a relationship (of some type) between the playing pieces and the squares of the chessboard. Thus, to employ the $q$-analysis approach to analyzing connective structure, the sets $X$ and $Y$ are relatively clear, viz,

$$X = \{\text{playing pieces}\}, \qquad Y = \{\text{squares of the board}\}.$$

For reasons that will become apparent in a moment, it is convenient to partition $X$ into the two subsets $X_W$, consisting of the pieces of White, and $X_B$, the Black pieces.

One relation between $X$ and $Y$, which at first sight seems promising, is to say that $(x_i, y_j) \in \lambda$ if and only if piece $x_i$ occupies square $y_j$. However, following up the consequences of this relation does not lead to any interesting insights into the structural aspects of a given board situation. The problem is that this relation does not incorporate any of the rules of the game. Hence, a more elaborate relation between $X$ and $Y$ is needed.

As it turns out, a very useful relationship between the pieces and the squares is provided by the notion of a piece "attacking" a square, as noted earlier, in Chapter 1. Since we have made the separation of $X$ into White and Black pieces, there are two relationships $\lambda_W$ and $\lambda_B$ induced by the above rules for White and Black, respectively.

While the rules given in Chapter 1 defining the relations $\lambda_W$ and $\lambda_B$ characterize the player's view of the board (since we regard the squares as the vertices in the complex, while the pieces are the simplices), the conjugate relations $\lambda_W^*$ and $\lambda_B^*$, obtained by interchanging the roles of $X$ and $Y$, provide the board's view of the players. Presumably, all four relations are needed to characterize a given situation at any mode of play.

The implications of the preceding ideas for positional analysis and automated chess-playing have been extensively pursued elsewhere and the interested reader should consult the chapter references for details. We only note here that if one compares the *maximum* dimension of the pieces as simplices generated by the relations $\lambda_W$ and $\lambda_B$ with the classical piece values, we obtain Table 3.3.

TABLE 3.3 Comparison of Chess Piece Values

| Piece | Max. Dimension | Classical Value |
|-------|------|------|
| Pawn | 1 | 1 |
| Knight | 7 | 3 |
| Bishop | 12 | 3 |
| Rook | 13 | 5 |
| Queen | 26 | 9 |

We see in the table that the relative differences between the simplicial values correspond rather closely to the relative strengths obtained on empirical grounds. The only real discrepancy is the Knight vs Bishop, where the simplicial values would suggest the Bishop as being somewhat more valuable. However, this conclusion is conditioned by the assumption that the values are calculated on the basis of an open board with no obstacles, i.e. they are the maximal possible values. In general, the strength depends upon the particular situation, as any chess player knows.

The hierarchical considerations introduced above are particularly relevant for the chess-playing setup, since such well-known chess concepts as strong squares and weak squares, control of the center, and strong or open files may all be mathematically interpreted in the language of sets, covers, and dimensions. Thus, $q$-analysis certainly seems to provide a totally new approach to the analysis of chess situations, one that may surely be coupled with efficient computers and searching algorithms to yield an effective computational approach to the game.

78

A MIDSUMMER NIGHT'S DREAM

We close our discussion of topological connectivity by examining Shakespeare's *A Midsummer Night's Dream* from a $q$-analysis point of view. Our objective, of course, is not to provide an in-depth literary critique, but rather to give some insight into the use of $q$-analysis as a language of structure in an area ordinarily far removed from traditional systems methodology.

As always, our starting point is the identification of relevant sets and relations.

We somewhat arbitrarily divide the play into three main sets:

$A$ = the play, the acts, the scenes, the subscenes
$B$ = the characters
$C$ = the commentary, the play, the subplots, the speeches

The elements of these sets and their various hierarchical levels are as follows:

*Set A*

| | |
|---|---|
| $(N+2)$-level | The play |
| $(N+1)$-level | The acts $\{a_1, a_2, a_3, a_4, a_5\}$ |
| $N$-level | The scenes $\{s_1, s_2, \ldots, s_9\}$ |
| $(N-1)$-level | The subscenes $\{SB_1, \ldots, SB_{26}\}$ |

(Based upon major changes in the physical composition of the play, i.e., upon the entrance and exit of characters.)

*Set B*

All levels of $N$  The characters $\{c_1, c_2, \ldots, c_{21}\}$ {Theseus, Hippolyta, Egeus, *et al.*}

*Set C*

$(N+3)$-level  The commentary

(This is the speech made by Puck at the end of the play. This speech is addressed directly to the audience and, therefore, lies outside the action of the play; it is an apologia for the preceding events.)

$(N+2)$-level  The play
$(N+1)$-level  The plots $\{P_1, P_2, P_3\}$

$P_1$: The court of Theseus, comprising mainly the preparations for his wedding with Hippolyta and the rehearsal and performance of the play by Bottom and his friends, and the consideration of and resolution by Theseus of the problems surrounding Hermia and her two suitors.

$P_2$:  The world of the fairies, comprising the quarrel between Oberon and Titania and the trick played by him on her with its consequences for both Titania and Bottom.

$P_3$:  The world of the lovers, comprising the basic predicament of Hermia, Demetrius, and Lysander and the interference by Oberon and Puck and its consequences.

|  |  |
|---|---|
| $N$-level | The subplots $\{PS_1, \ldots, PS_8\}$ |

$PS_1$:  Theseus' role in the life of the four lovers

$PS_2$  The relationship between Theseus and Hippolyta and their wedding celebrations

$PS_3$:  The rehearsal and performance of the play by Bottom and his friends

$PS_4$:  The general world of the fairies: their songs and powers

$PS_5$:  The relationship between Oberon and Titania

$PS_6$:  Oberon's trick on Titania and its consequences for her and Bottom

$PS_7$:  The basic predicament of the four lovers

$PS_8$:  The interference by Oberon and Puck in the lives of the four lovers and its consequences

|  |  |
|---|---|
| $(N-1)$-level | The speeches $\{SP_1, \ldots, SP_{104}\}$ |

(There are 104 speeches, defined as any words uttered by any character that import to the audience a development of the plot of which the audience was previously unaware.)

The binary relations linking the above sets at the various hierarchical levels are fairly evident by inspection of the sets themselves. For example, if

$$Y = \text{plots}, \qquad X = \text{characters},$$

then it is natural to define $\lambda \subset Y \times X$ as

$$(y_i, x_j) \in \lambda \Leftrightarrow \text{character } x_j \text{ enters into plot } y_i.$$

The general hierarchical structure of the play is depicted in Figure 3.6.

80

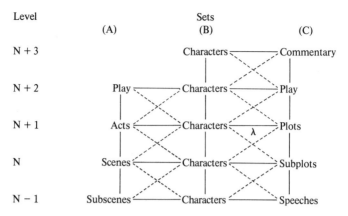

FIGURE 3.6   Connective structure of *A Midsummer Night's Dream.*

Utilizing obvious relations such as λ, incidence matrices may be generated linking sets at the various levels, $q$-analysis performed, and a number of interesting results obtained. Some typical examples are examined in the following sections.

$Y$ = PLOTS $(N+1)$-LEVEL, $X$ = CHARACTERS $(N+1)$-LEVEL

In $K_Y(X)$ all three plots come in as separate components only at connectivity level $q = 8$. This means that the plots can only be distinguished as separate entities by an audience following nine characters. Likewise, at $q = 6$, there are only two components, $\{P_1, P_2\}$ and $\{P_3\}$. Thus, if the audience can follow only seven characters, then they see the play as consisting essentially of only two plots, with $P_1$ and $P_2$ (the court of Theseus and the world of the lovers) confused.

In the conjugate complex $K_X(Y)$, the characters Hermia, Lysander, Demetrius, and Helena dominate the structure at $q = 2$. Therefore, an audience following all three plots as separate entities sees the play as being about the lovers.

$Y$ = PLOTS $(N+1)$-LEVEL, $X$ = SCENES $N$-LEVEL

In $K_Y(X)$ there are three components at $q = 5$. Thus, an audience following six scenes can see all three plots as separate entities. Plots $P_2$ and $P_3$ become combined at $q = 4$, giving two components, and consequently the audience will see these two plots as one when following five scenes. All three plots are combined at $q = 2$, i.e., when the audience follow three scenes. This is different from the analysis of plots and characters above, where plots $P_1$ and $P_3$ became confused.

In $K_X(Y)$ the structure is dominated at $q = 2$ by the scene dealing with Oberon's trick on Titania and their reconciliation and resolution of the lovers' dilemma and the scene concerning the culmination of the wedding celebrations of Theseus and Hippolyta in the performance of the play by Bottom and his friends.

$Y = $ SUBPLOTS $(N-1)$-LEVEL, $X = $ SPEECHES $N$-LEVEL

In $K_Y(X)$ the structure is dominated by the subplot $PS_8$ at $q = 35$, followed by subplots $PS_3$ at $q = 26$ and $PS_6$ at $q = 10$. Thus, $PS_8$ will be fully understood by an audience only when they have heard 36 speeches, while $PS_3$ requires 27 speeches and $PS_6$ only 11 speeches for this understanding. The $q$-analysis gives an indication of the complexity of the subplots. The critical $q$-value is $q = 5$, implying that all subplots require a minimum of six speeches to be fully understood by the audience.

In $K_X(Y)$ have a trivial structure at the critical level $q = 0$. This means that each speech is concerned with only one subplot, which, by our earlier definition of a speech, is so.

## ALGEBRAIC CONNECTIVITY

Despite the seemingly quantitative description of system connectivity provided by the $q$-analysis structure vector, it must still be admitted that the topological analysis presented above is primarily qualitative in spirit. Local system details are "fuzzed over" to obtain a global description without very specific information concerning the nature or structure of the subsystems (simplices). Such an outcome is due mainly to the manner in which we chose to describe the system by sets and binary relations. In those situations where much more is known about local system structure, the connectivity issue may often be more fruitfully examined using tools from algebra rather than from geometry. An introduction to these ideas will be our goal in the sections to follow.

Just as in the topological situation, a key ingredient in our algebraic connectivity development will be a *finiteness* condition. In the topological case, the relevant condition was that the two sets $X$ and $Y$ be finite; in the algebraic case, the conditions will enter through the system state space, since we shall be concerned now with systems described in *internal form* by differential or difference equations. For systems whose dynamics are linear, it turns out that the relevant finiteness condition is that the state space be *finite-dimensional*, while for nonlinear processes we demand a *finite* state space since, in general, the state space of a nonlinear system may not even be a vector space and the notion of dimensionality may be meaningless.

The principal thrust of the algebraic connectivity results is to provide a systematic procedure for decomposing a given system into its mathematically irreducible subsystems and to show how these systems are put together to form the composite process. It should be noted that these mathematical subsystems, or elementary "building blocks," do not in general correspond to any natural decomposition that the system may possess as a result of its physical structure. This is an unfortunate and unavoidable part of the process of translating reality into computationally efficient mathematical models. Once we have formulated a satisfactory model of a given situation, the model should take on a mathematical life of its own, with contact being made with the physical process again only after the mathematical machinery has (we hope) done its job. Basically, it's a question of choosing one set of coordinates convenient for modeling the physics while doing the mathematics and computation in another set, more convenient for mathematicians and machines. If things are set up properly, we should be able to shift back and forth between the two coordinate sets at will.

## LINEAR SYSTEMS

To simplify our exposition, let us begin by considering the linear dynamical system described in internal form by the differential equation

$$\frac{dx}{dt} = Fx(t) + Gu(t), \tag{$\kappa$}$$

with the system output given by

$$y(t) = Hx(t).$$

Here $x$, $u$, and $y$ are $n$-, $m$-, and $p$-dimensional vector functions, respectively, with $F$, $G$, $H$ being constant matrices of appropriate sizes.

Perhaps the most convenient way to illustrate the algebraic aspects of linear systems is to form the "transfer function" matrix associated with the system $\Sigma$. Denoting the Laplace transform of the vectors $x$, $u$, and $y$ by $\bar{x}$, $\bar{u}$, and $\bar{y}$, respectively, it is a simple exercise to verify that the relationship between the transformed input and output is

$$\bar{y}(z) = H(zI - F)^{-1} G\bar{u}(z)$$
$$= W(z)\bar{u}(z),$$

where $z$ is the transform variable. The matrix $W(z)$ is called the transfer matrix and is clearly an external description of the dynamical behavior of $\Sigma$. Without further comment, we shall assume that $W(z)$ is a proper rational matrix, i.e., all components of $W(z)$ are irreducible. Study of the internal connections linking the input and output channels of $\Sigma$ is equivalent to study of the cyclic structure of $W(z)$, as the following result shows.

*Realization Theorem.  Every proper rational transfer function matrix W may be realized as the direct sum of the systems*

$$\sum_i = (F_i, G_i, H_i),$$

*where $G_i$, $H_i$ are computed as below and $F_i$ is a cyclic matrix with characteristic polynomial $\psi_i$, the ith invariant factor of the matrix W.*

The proof of this result requires more preliminary background than is appropriate here; the interested reader may consult the chapter references for details. The important point of the theorem is to show that the basic building blocks of the system $\Sigma$ are formed by computing the invariant factors of $W$. From polynomial algebra, we know that if $\psi$ is the least common denominator of the matrix $W$, then $\psi W$ is a polynomial matrix, and the invariant factor algorithm enables us to calculate a representation

$$\psi W = PLQ \bmod \psi,$$

where det $P$, det $Q$ are units in the ring $K[z]/K[z]\psi$, while $L$ is a diagonal matrix unique up to units in the same ring (here $K =$ arbitrary number field). As it turns out, the elements $\psi_i$ of the theorem are related to the elements of $L$ as

$$\psi_i = l_{n-i+1}, \qquad i = 1, 2, \ldots, q$$

with $n =$ degree of least common denominator of $W$.

To form the entries of $\Sigma_i$, we proceed as follows:

1. For each invariant factor $\psi_i$ of $W$, choose a cyclic matrix $F_i$ such that the characteristic polynomial $\chi_{F_i} = \psi_i$ (e.g., let $F_i =$ companion matrix of $\psi_i$), $i = 1, 2, \ldots, q$.

2. Let $L = (l_1, l_2, \ldots)$, $p_i = i$th column of $P$, $q_i' = i$th row of $Q$ in the above representation of $\psi W$. Let $v_i$, $w_i$ be polynomial vectors such that

$$\chi_{F_i}(zI - F_i)^{-1} = v_i(z)w_i'(z) \bmod \chi_{F_i}.$$

(Such vectors are unique up to units in $K[z]/K[z]\chi_{F_i}$.)

3. The equations

$$H_i v_i = (l_i/\mu_i)p_i \bmod \psi_i,$$
$$w_i' G_i = q_i' \bmod \psi_i,$$

have a unique solutions $H_i$, $G_i$ where $\mu_i =$ greatest common factor of $l_i$ and $\psi$.

*Conclusion* The size (dimension) of the blocks (subsystems) that comprise the total external description of $\Sigma$ equals the degrees of the invariant factors of the matrix $W$.

Diagrammatically, the situation is as depicted in Figure 3.7.

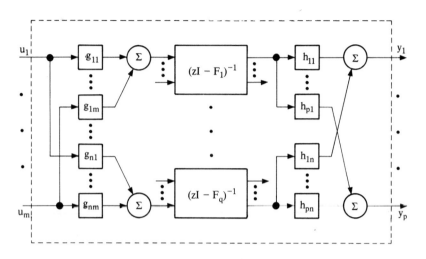

FIGURE 3.7   General structure of a linear system.

The above *canonical* (minimal dimension) structure of a linear system is characterized by the high degree of connectivity between its component parts. Figure 3.7 should be contrasted with the usual picture of a linear system given in elementary textbooks (Figure 3.8). Figure 3.8, while appealing from a visual viewpoint, is the result of an arbitrary choice of connections and will seldom be canonical; it may bear no relation at all to the actual system $\Sigma$ giving rise to $W$. Thus, the "right" way to visualize the system is Figure 3.7, not Figure 3.8.

To fix the preceding ideas, let us consider a simple numerical example. Let

$$W(z) = \begin{bmatrix} \dfrac{1}{z+1} & 0 & 0 \\ 0 & \dfrac{1}{z+2} & 0 \\ 0 & 0 & \dfrac{1}{z+3} \end{bmatrix}$$

We have $\psi(z) = (z+1)(z+2)(z+3)$, and the invariant factors of $\psi W$ are

$$\Lambda = \begin{bmatrix} 1 & 0 & 0 \\ 0 & 1 & 0 \\ 0 & 0 & \psi \end{bmatrix}.$$

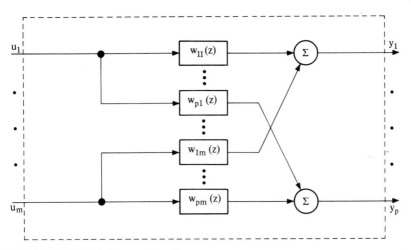

FIGURE 3.8 Usual picture of a linear system.

Hence,

$$L = \begin{bmatrix} 1 & 0 & 0 \\ 0 & 0 & 0 \\ 0 & 0 & 0 \end{bmatrix},$$

$$P = \begin{bmatrix} (z+2)(z+3) & 1 & 0 \\ 2(z+1)(z+3) & 2 & 2 \\ (z+1)(z+2) & 1 & 2 \end{bmatrix},$$

$$Q = \begin{bmatrix} 1/2(z+2)(z+3) & -1/2(z+1)(z+3) & 1/2(z+1)(z+2) \\ -1 & 1 & -1 \\ 0 & -1/2 & 1 \end{bmatrix}.$$

We can take the vectors $v(z)$, $w(z)$ as

$$v(z) = \begin{bmatrix} 1 \\ z \\ z^2 \end{bmatrix}, \qquad w(z) = \begin{bmatrix} z^2 + 6z + 11 \\ z + 6 \\ 1 \end{bmatrix}.$$

The reader can check that a canonical internal model of the transfer matrix $W(z)$ is given by

$$F = \begin{bmatrix} 0 & 1 & 0 \\ 0 & 0 & 1 \\ -6 & -11 & -6 \end{bmatrix}$$

$$G = \begin{bmatrix} 1/2 & -1/2 & 1/2 \\ -1/2 & 1 & 3/2 \\ 1/2 & -5/2 & 9/2 \end{bmatrix}, \qquad H = \begin{bmatrix} 6 & 5 & 1 \\ 6 & 8 & 2 \\ 2 & 3 & 1 \end{bmatrix}.$$

86

An easy consequence of the realization theorem is that *all* canonical models are equivalent up to a change of coordinates $x \to Tx$ in the state space. This fact illustrates a point made earlier that behaviorist/cognitive debates are vacuous at the system-theoretic level.

*Example: Societal Dynamics*  As a more concrete illustration of the use of transfer matrices, we consider a highly simplified model of the evolution of societies according to the basic ideas of A. Toynbee. The model we present is very elementary chiefly because

• It assumes that an entire society may be divided into only two "strata": a majority, belonging to the lower stratum and a ruling minority.
• It refers explicitly only to the production of goods.

It will become clear that the basic principles involved in construction of the model may be employed to produce much more realistic versions by addition of suitable "blocks" and "connections."

The starting point of the model is Figure 3.9, where the block $B$

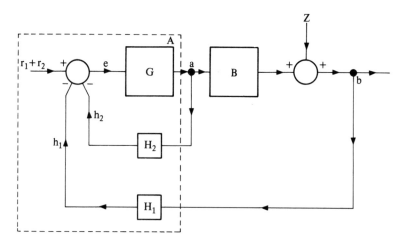

FIGURE 3.9  Block diagram of societal structure.

corresponds to the subsystem that supplies a quantity $b$ of goods (e.g., agricultural output) under the action $a$ supplied by the workers of the society. The mechanism relating $a$ to $b$ is repressnted by the block $A$. The disturbance input $Z$ allows us to take into account the variation of produced goods that do not depend upon the work level $a$.

The decomposition of block $A$ has been done on the assumption that the majority, belonging to the lower stratum of society, accomplish the work *a* for two different reasons:

1. Because this activity enables it to satisfy its needs
2. Because of moral obligation or physical coercion by the ruling minority

Aspect (1) is accounted for by the feedback loop $G$–$B$–$H_1$, where $H_1$ corresponds to the criteria adopted by the given society for resource distribution. The output $n_1$ is compared with a reference level $1^-$, which denotes the needs of this stratum. The value $r_1$, in fact, differs from society to society and from epoch to epoch. For instance, in some societies based upon slavery, $r_1$ approaches the limits of pure survival; in present-day consumer-oriented Western society, $r_1$ is much higher than in any earlier epochs. The difference between "needs" $r_1$ and "availability" $h_1$ forms a component $e_1$ of the global "stimulus" to work $e$.

Aspect (2) is taken into account by feedback loop $G$–$H_2$. In this case, it is work $a$ and not production $b$ that is "fed back" and compared with the reference level $r_2$ in order to generate $e_2$. The output $h_2$ of block $H_2$ measures the labor employed for $a$. As noted, $r_2$ may be fixed by the moral norms of the society or by physical compulsion, as for instance in slavery-based societies.

For quantitative analysis of the dynamic behavior of the model, we must associate to each block a functional relationship connecting the input with the output. As a first attempt, we shall characterize each block by a suitable transfer function.

In simple cases, block $B$ may be characterized by means of a pure delay. Since a first-order transfer function cannot take the initial delay into account, we shall adopt a second-order transfer function with two real poles:

$$B(Z) = \frac{k_B}{(1 + T_1 Z)(1 + T_2 Z)}.$$

For the other blocks, we can adopt the first-order transfer functions.

$$G(Z) = \frac{k_g}{1 + T_3 Z},$$

$$H_1(Z) = \frac{k_{H_1}}{1 + T_4 Z},$$

$$H_2(Z) = \frac{k_{H_2}}{1 + T_5 Z}.$$

The overall transfer function of the societal model is

$$W(Z) = \frac{G(Z)B(Z)}{1 + G(Z)H_2(Z) + G(Z)B(Z)H_1(Z)}.$$

Carrying out the algebraic operations to find the numerator and denominator of $W(Z)$, it is a simple task to write down a suitable *internal* model of the society. However, identification of the model parameters is a very hard task. A trial-and-error procedure could be adopted, for example, if we referred to a given, well-defined production sector and to a given historical period. Alternately, if sufficient data were available, the parameter of the linear model could be inferred using modern system identification techniques. However the analysis is carried out, the above model would allow us to determine the influence of the various parameters on societal behavior and to forecast the effects of parameter variation.

## NONLINEAR PROBLEMS

While the algebra of the preceding section proves exceedingly helpful in studying the fundamental structure of linear dynamical processes, an analogous development for general nonlinear systems seems beyond the scope of such techniques. This is not surprising, since, for example, a nonlinear system may have a state space that is not even a vector space, implying that the previous essentially linear algebraic ideas will be of no particular use.

In order to treat a broad class of nonlinear problems, we return to our metaprinciple of finiteness and argue that since finite dimensionality of the state space is, in general, meaningless, perhaps assuming a *finite* state space would lead to a meaningful approach. Recalling our discussion in Chapter 1 of finite-state descriptions of dynamical systems, we shall use the notion of a *finite semigroup of transformations* to replace the finite-dimensional linear operators (matrices) $F$, $G$, and $H$ of the linear theory. The shift to the finite-state/semigroup setting will enable us to give a decomposition result (the Krohn–Rhodes theorem) that will accomplish much the same thing for nonlinear problems that the invariant factor theorem does for linear processes. Unfortunately, a small amount of elementary algebraic material will first be required.

## SEMIGROUPS AND WREATH PRODUCTS

As discussed in Chapter 1, we assume the state space of the process under study is denoted by $Q$ and that $Q$ contains only a *finite* number of elements. Assume that $\mathcal{F}$ is a set of transformations defined on $Q$, i.e.,

$$\mathcal{F}: Q \to Q,$$

and let the product of two elements $f_1$ and $f_2$ from $\mathcal{F}$ be defined in the usual way as

$$(f_1 f_2): Q \to Q,$$

$$(f_1 f_2)q = f_2(f_1(q)).$$

This definition corresponds to the usual composition of two transformations and is well known to be associative, i.e.,

$$[f_1(f_2 f_3)]q = [(f_1 f_2)f_3]q \quad \text{for all} \quad f_1, f_2, f_3 \in \mathscr{F}, \qquad q \in Q.$$

Since any system of operations which is both closed and associative forms a *semigroup*, we can generate a semigroup from $\mathscr{F}$ by taking all products of elements in $\mathscr{F}$. We call this the semigroup of $\mathscr{F}$ and is denoted as $\mathscr{F}^*$.

The pair of objects $(Q, \mathscr{F}^*)$ forms what is called a *transformation semigroup*, and, since we are concerned with finite $Q$, it is a *finite transformation semigroup*. (Note: The order of $(Q, \mathscr{F}^*)$ equals the number of distinct transformations in $\mathscr{F}^*$, which is clearly finite if $Q$ is.)

Our goal is to make a connection between arbitrary transformations on a finite state space and certain advantageous coordinatizations of the action of these transformations. To accomplish this objective, we introduce the idea of *wreath product coordinates*.

Suppose that $Q$ is coordinatized by the Cartesian product

$$Q = X_1 \times X_2 \times \ldots \times X_n,$$

i.e., each $q \in Q$ has a representation $q = (x_1, x_2, \ldots, x_n)$, $x_i \in X_i$, $i = 1, 2, \ldots, n$. Then we say that the action of $\mathscr{F}^*$ on $Q$ is *triangularized* if each $f \in \mathscr{F}^*$ may be represented as an $n$-tuple $f = (f_1, f_2, \ldots, f_n) \in F_1 \times F_2 \times \ldots \times F_n$, where

$$f(q) = f(x_1, x_2, \ldots, x_n) = (f_1(x_1), f_2(x_1, x_2), \ldots, f_n(x_1, x_2, \ldots, x_n)) = q',$$

i.e., $f_k : X_1 \times X_2 \times \ldots X_k \to X_k$. Thus, triangularization means that each coordinate of $q'$ is dependent only upon that coordinate and its predecessors.

The second key concept that we need is the idea of $k$th *coordinate action*. The $k$th coordinate action of $(Q, \mathscr{F}^*) = (X_1 \times X_2 \times \ldots \times X_n; F_1 \times F_2 \times \ldots \times F_n)$ is the transformation semigroup $(X_k, G_k^*)$, where $G_k$ is the set of all transformations $g$ on $X_k$ such that

$$g: X_k \to X_k, \qquad g(z) = f_k(a_1, a_2, \ldots, a_{k-1}, z),$$

where $(a_1, a_2, \ldots, a_{k-1})$ is an arbitrary but fixed element of $X_1 \times X_2 \times \ldots \times X_{k-1}$ and $f_k \in F_k$. In other words, the elements of $G_k$ not only map $X_k$ to itself but also must form part of a triangularization of $\mathscr{F}^*$.

If the action of $\mathscr{F}^*$ on $Q$ may be triangularized by the coordination $Q = X_1 \times X_2 \times \ldots \times X_n$, then $Q$ is said to be a wreath product of its coordinate action, i.e.,

$$(Q, \mathscr{F}^*) = (X_1, G_1^*)w(X_2, G_2^*)w \ldots w(X_n, G_n^*).$$

The set $X_1 \times X_2 \times \ldots \times X_n$ then forms wreath product coordinates for $Q$, while the set $G_1 \times G_2 \times \ldots \times G_n$ forms wreath product coordinates for $\mathscr{F}^*$.

*Example*   Let $Q = R^2$ and take $X_1 = X_2 = R^1$. Further, let $f: R^2 \to R^2$ be an upper triangular matrix

$$f = \begin{bmatrix} f_{11} & f_{12} \\ 0 & f_{22} \end{bmatrix}.$$

We take the component transformation $f_i$ to be the operator determined by the leading $i \times i$ block of $f$, followed by projection onto the $i$th coordinate.

## THE KROHN–RHODES DECOMPOSITION THEOREM

The preceding development has been directed toward describing the underlying structure of finite semigroups. In finite group theory, such a structural theorem has been known for many years, the so-called Jordan–Hölder theorem, which asserts that any finite group may be built from a fixed set of simple groups (the Jordan–Hölder factors) and that the building set is unique (up to isomorphism). The Krohn–Rhodes result provides an analogue for finite transformation semigroups. A rough statement of the Krohn–Rhodes theorem is as follows (a more precise statement will be given in a moment).

*Theorem (Krohn-Rhodes).   Any finite state space $Q$ may be coordinatized so that any set of phenomena observed on it is triangularized. Furthermore, the coordinate actions will be either (a) simple permutation groups closely associated with $(Q, \mathscr{F}^*)$ or (b) one of three possible transformation semigroups, the largest of which has order three.*

As a consequence of this remarkable result, we see that *any* system with finite state space may be conveniently coordinatized and that the coordinate actions will be decomposable into particularly simple form: the permutation groups mentioned in (a) will be such that they *divide* the orginal semigroup $(X, \mathscr{F}^*)$ (definitions later), while the semigroups of (b) will be elementary "flip-flops." Thus, regardless of the complexity of system behavior, it will be possible to analyze the process by studying simpler objects put together in a manner specified by the wreath product construction.

In order to give a precise statement of the Krohn–Rhodes result, it is necessary to introduce the notion of one semigroup *dividing* another.

*Definition 3.4.*   We say the transformation semigroup $(X, S)$ *divides* $(Y, T)$

and write $(X, S) \mid (Y, T)$ if and only if

1. There exists a subset $Y'$ of $Y$ and a subsemigroup $T'$ of $T$ such that $Y'$ is invariant under the action of $T'$.
2. There exists a map $\theta \colon Y' \twoheadrightarrow X (\twoheadrightarrow$ denotes *onto*) and an epimorphism $\phi \colon T' \to S$ such that $\theta(yt) = \theta(y)\phi(t)$ for all $y \in Y'$, $t \in T'$.

Realization of a given system (machine) by component subsystems (machines) hooked together corresponds to semigroup division. We can now state the basic problem addressed by the Krohn–Rhodes theorem.

*Problem:* Let $X$ be the state space on which a finite semigroup $\mathscr{F}^*$ of transformations acts. Is it possible to find decompositions of $(X, \mathscr{F}^*)$ into transformation subsemigroups $(X_k, G_k^*)$, $k = 1, \ldots, n$, such that one obtains the minimal solution of $(X, \mathscr{F}) \mid (X_n, G_n^*)w(X_{n-1}, G_{n-1}^*)w \ldots w(X_1, G_1^*)$? If so, what is the structure of the component pieces $(X_i, G_i^*)$, and what is the maximal value of $n$ that will satisfy the division condition?

In machine-theoretic language, the corresponding problem is to factor a finite-state machine into the largest possible number of component machines, obtaining a so-called *prime* decomposition of the original machine. We shall return to this point in some detail in the next chapter, on system complexity.

The last notions we need before stating the Krohn–Rhodes result are the ideas of a *flip-flop* semigroup and a *prime* group.

*Definition 3.5.* Let $a \neq b$ and consider the semigroup $(\{a, b\}, \{C_a, C_b, Id\})$, where $xC_a = a$, $xC_b = b$, $xId = x$ for $x = a$ or $b$. We also write this semigroup as $(\{a, b\}, U_3)$. The semigroup $(\{a, b\}, U_3)$ is called the *order-three flip-flop*.

*Definition 3.6.* We say a finite group $G$ is *prime* if $G$ is simple and $G \neq \{Id\}$. (Recall that a group is simple if it has no nontrivial normal subgroups, where $N$ is normal in $G$ if and only if $Ng = gN$ for all $g \in G$.)

If $S$ is a semigroup, then Primes $(S) = \{G \colon G \text{ is prime and } G \mid S\}$.

Finally, we can state the Krohn–Rhodes theorem.

*Prime Decomposition Theorem for Finite Semigroups.* *Let the finite semigroup* $(X, \mathscr{F}^*)$ *be given. Then there exists a wreath product decomposition* $(X_1, G_1^*), \ldots, (X_n, G_n^*)$ *such that*

$$(X, \mathscr{F}^*) \mid (X_n, G_n^*)w \ldots w(X_1, G_1^*),$$

*and for each factor* $(X_j, G_j^*)$ *either*

$G_j^* \in Primes\ (\mathscr{F}^*)$ *and* $(X_j, G_j^*)$ *is a faithful transitive permutation group, or*

$$(X_j, G_j^*) = (\{a, b\}, U_3).$$

The proof of this result is much too complicated to be given here. We note, however, that by comparison with the Jordan–Hölder theorem, the Krohn–Rhodes result implies that finite semigroup theory is equivalent to finite group theory plus the "flip-flop" operation.

## DECOMPOSITION OF ANALYTIC SYSTEMS

If the state space of a given process is not finite, but finite-dimensional, a decomposition result like the Krohn–Rhodes theorem can still be given, although the mathematical details are considerably more complex.

To suggest the basic flavor, consider an internal description of a system $\Sigma$ given by the differential equation

$$\dot{x} = f(x, u),$$

where the state space $M$ is an analytic manifold, $u \in \Omega \subset R^m$, and $f$ is a real analytic function of $x$, continuous in $u$ and satisfying a Lipschitz condition in $x$ uniformly in $u$.

For each $u \in \Omega$, we obtain a vector field $f(\cdot, u)$ on $M$ and define the Lie algebra of $\Sigma$ to be the smallest subalgebra of $V(M)$ (the set of analytic vector fields on $M$) that contains all such vector fields, using the Lie bracket operation $[\cdot, \cdot]$ to form a new vector field from two given fields, i.e., $[v, w] = (\partial w/\partial x)(w) - (\partial w/\partial x)(v)$.

Using the preceding terminology, a finite-dimensional analogue of the Krohn–Rhodes result is

*Krener's Theorem.* *If the Lie algebra of $\Sigma$ is finite-dimensional, then $\Sigma$ admits a decomposition into the parallel cascade of systems with simple Lie algebras followed by a cascade of one-dimensional systems.*

Several comments about the above result are appropriate:

1. A Lie algebra is simple if it is not abelian (commutative) and if it contains no nontrivial ideals. Thus, in Krener's theorem, the simple Lie algebras are the analogues of the simple groups in the Krohn–Rhodes result. The analogy breaks down, however, between the one-dimensional systems and the flip-flops (combinatorial semigroups), since flip-flops correspond to the nongroup part of the finite-state machine: However, we do note that, up to isomorphism, there are only two one-dimensional systems, those on the

circle and those on the line. Thus, the "simple" elements of the decomposition are still two in number, corresponding to the combinatorial semigroups $U_3$ and $D_1$ (see Chapter 4, pp. 109).

2. In a certain sense, the above theorem is the best that one can hope for in the way of a decomposition result for finite-dimensional systems. The reason is that a finite-dimensional system $\Sigma$ is *indecomposable* if and only if the Lie algebra of $\Sigma$ is one-dimensional or simple. Notice that this theorem gives necessary and sufficient conditions for the decomposition of any finite-dimensional analytic system.

As an example of the foregoing results, consider the bilinear system $\Sigma$ described by the matrix equation

$$\dot{X} = \sum_{i=1}^{3} u_i B_i x, \qquad X(0) = I, \qquad (\Sigma)$$

where

$$B_1 = \begin{bmatrix} 1 & 0 \\ 0 & -1 \end{bmatrix}, \qquad B_2 = \begin{bmatrix} 0 & 1 \\ 0 & 0 \end{bmatrix}, \qquad B_3 = \begin{bmatrix} 0 & 0 \\ 1 & 0 \end{bmatrix}.$$

We take the state space to be $M = SL(2, R)$, the group of real $2 \times 2$ matrices of determinant 1 and the input space $\Omega = R^3$.

After some algebra, the devoted reader will find that $\Sigma$ admits the nontrivial parallel cascade decomposition

$$\dot{X}_1 = u_1 B_1 X_1,$$
$$\dot{X}_2 = (X_1)^{-1}(u_2 B_2 + u_3 B_3) X_1 X_2,$$

where

$$X = X_1 X_2.$$

Among other things, this example illustrates the point that for nonlinear systems the "right" state space is usually not $R^n$. Much current work in algebraic system theory is devoted to various aspects of this question.

## NOTES AND REFERENCES

An interesting exploitation of the off-diagonal elements in the interconnection matrix for system decomposition is given in the paper:

Steward, D. V., "Partitioning and Tearing System of Equations," *SIAM J. Num. Anal.*, 2 (1965), 345–365.

This paper is a readable version of the "tearing" method developed by G. Kron to study electrical networks. A summary of this work is the book:

Happ, H., *The Theory of Network Diakoptics*, Academic, New York, 1970.

An exposition of Kron's approach that touches upon the topological considerations studied in this book is:

Roth, J. P., "An Application of Algebraic Topology: Kron's Method of Tearing," *Quart. Appl. Math.*, 17 (1959), 1–14.

COMPLEXES AND CONNECTIONS; ECCENTRICITY

The material on $q$-connectivity and eccentricity is taken from the pioneering work of Atkin. A complete exposition, with numerous examples, is found in the works:

Atkin, R. H., *Mathematical Structure in Human Affairs*, Heinemann, London, 1974.
Atkin, R. H., *Combinatorial Connectivities in Social Systems*, Birkhauser, Basel, 1976.
Atkin, R. H., *Multidimensional Man*, Penguin, London (in press).

See also:

Atkin, R. H., and J. Casti, "Polyhedral Dynamics and the Geometry of Systems," *RR*-77-6, International Institute for Applied Systems Analysis, Laxenburg, Austria, March 1977.

HOLES AND OBSTRUCTIONS; BETTI NUMBERS AND TORSION; $p$-HOLES; COCHAINS AND BOUNDARIES

The homology material follows that given in the appendix of:

Atkin, R., *Mathematical Structure in Human Affairs*, Heinemann, London, 1973.

Elementary concepts of algebraic topology are covered in the texts:

Alexandrov, P., *Basic Concepts of Topology*, Dover, New York, 1961.
Giblin, P., *Graphs, Surfaces and Homology*, Chapman and Hall, London, 1977.
Franz, W., *Algebraic Topology*, Ungar, New York, 1968.

More extensive and advanced texts are:

Hilton, P., and S. Wylie, *Homology Theory*, Cambridge University Press, Cambridge, 1960.
Spanier, E., *Algebraic Topology*, McGraw-Hill, New York, 1966.

PREDATOR–PREY RELATIONS: A HOMOLOGICAL EXAMPLE

The predator–prey example is taken from:

Casti, J., "Connectivity, Complexity and Resilience in Complex Ecosystems," in *IFAC Symposium on Bio- and Ecosystems*, Leipzig, Germany, 1977.

APPLICATIONS OF $q$-CONNECTIVITY TO CHESS AND SHAKESPEAREAN COMEDY

The Shakespearean example is taken from the forthcoming work:

Atkin, R., *Multidimensional Man*, Penguin, London (in press).

ALGEBRAIC CONNECTIVITY

The general applicability of the "finiteness principle" in mathematical system theory is well illustrated in:

Eilenberg, S., *Automata, Languages and Machines*, Vols. A and B, Academic, New York, 1974, 1976.

See also:

Kalman, R., P. Falb, and M. Arbib, *Topics in Mathematical System Theory*, McGraw-Hill, New York, 1969.


LINEAR SYSTEMS

The results on linear system realization follow Chapter 10 of the Kalman *et al.*, book just cited. See also:

Kalman, R., "Irreducible Realizations and the Degree of a Rational Matrix," *SIAM J. Appl. Math.*, 13 (1965), 520–544.

The societal dynamics model follows the work:

Cobelli, C., A. Lepschy, and S. Milo, "A Tentative Model of the Dynamic Behavior of a Society," University of Padua, preprint, 1978.

Further details along the same lines are reported in:

Lepschy, A., and S. Milo, "Historical Event Dynamics and 'A Study of History' by Arnold Toynbee," *Scientia*, 111 (1976), 39–50.


SEMIGROUPS AND WREATH PRODUCTS; THE KROHN–RHODES DECOMPOSITION THEOREM

Sources for background material on finite-state machines are:

Ginsburg, S., *Algebraic Theory of Automata*, Academic, New York, 1968.
Arbib, M., *Machines, Languages and Semigroups*, Academic, New York, 1967.

See also:

Kalman, R., P. Falb, and M. Arbib, *Topics in Mathematical System Theory*, McGraw-Hill, New York, 1969.

The proof of the decomposition theorem is given in:

Krohn, K., and J. Rhodes, "Algebraic Theory of Machines," *Trans. Am. Math. Soc.*, 116 (1965), 450–464.

A more recent account, complete with extensive examples in biology, psychology, and physics, is:

Rhodes, J., "Applications of Automata Theory and Algebra via the Mathematical Theory of Complexity," Lecture Notes, Math Dept., University of California, Berkeley, 1971.

DECOMPOSITION OF ANALYTIC SYSTEMS

The original reference is:

Krener, A., "A Decomposition Theory for Differentiable Systems," *SIAM J. Control Optim.*, 15 (1977), 813–829.

# 4  Complexity

Twinkle, twinkle, little star,
How I wonder where you are!
"1.73 seconds of arc from where I seem to be,"
Replied the star, "because $ds^2 = -[1/2(M/Y)]$
$1\ dr^2 - r^2\ d\theta^2 - [1/2(N/\gamma)]\ dt$."
"Oh," said Arthur, "now I see."
RALPH BARTON, *Twinkle, Twinkle, Little Star*

All depends, then, on finding out these easier problems, and on
solving them by means of devices as perfect as possible and of
concepts capable of generalization.
D. HILBERT

Certainly one of the most overworked words in the systems analysis lexicon
is the adjective "complex." One encounters phrases such as "complex
system," "degree of complexity," "complex problem," ad infinitum upon
perusal of the technical (and expository) systems literature, but very little to
indicate what the author really has in kind when using the terminology.
Extrapolating from the context in which such vague phrases appear, it seems
clear that on a philosophical level, complexity involves notions of nonintuitive system behavior, patterns of connection among subsystems such that
prediction of system behavior is difficult without substantial analysis or
computation, decision-making structures that make the effects of individual
choices difficult to evaluate, and so on. Unfortunately, like the concept of
time, everyone seems to understand complexity until it is necessary to define
it. In short, we can't really define what we mean by a complex system, but
we know one when we see it.

True as the preceding remarks may be, they don't provide much help in
trying to characterize relative types and degrees of system complexity
mathematically. Consequently, our modest goals in this chapter will be to
indicate some of the basic components that must be present in any
mathematical theory of complexity, to provide a few measures of complexity
arising in different contexts, and to show, by example, how the ideas of
complexity can be applied to the study of certain questions arising in applied
systems analysis, particularly in the realm of social decision making. Imper-
fect as this development may be, a theory of system complexity is, in the
words of von Neumann, "a prerequisite to the understanding of learning and
evolutionary processes." Consequently, the system theorist must attempt to
remove the complexity concept from the folklore of systems analysis and
bring it into the realm of developed theory. The goal of this chapter is to
provide background material for such an attempt.

97

The initial sections of this chapter treat the many ingredients that must enter into any reasonable mathematical theory of complexity. Considerations such as hierarchical structure, widely varying time scales, and interaction levels are discussed. Following these introductory sections, we make use of the algebraic results of the preceding chapter and show how *one* theory of complexity can be based upon the theory of finite-state machines. In addition, for those systems described by sets/relations or potential (entropy) functions, we shall discuss alternative approaches to the complexity question in the later sections of the chapter. The overall picture that emerges is that complexity is quite a "complex" business and that there is unlikely to be any uniformly satisfactory mathematical theory. However, if we lower our sights and agree to consider specific models and ask specific questions, then the results of this chapter indicate that something useful and nontrivial can be said.

Since the notion of what constitutes a "complex" system seems so difficult to pin down, one might suspect that there are actually several facets to the complexity issue and that different types of system complexity manifest themselves, depending upon the problem, the analyst, the questions being investigated, and so forth. In this section we wish to outline a few of the more obvious types of complexity and to give some indication of how they arise in the analysis of large-scale systems.

## STATIC COMPLEXITY

Probably the first thought that comes to mind when considering the question of complexity is that a system is complex if its component pieces (subsystems) are put together in an intricate, difficult-to-understand fashion. Such a situation would be a typical example of *static complexity*. Here, we are concerned only with the structure of the system communication channels and the interaction pattern of its component parts, neglecting any dynamical or computational considerations. However, even a measure of a system's static complexity is not a fine enough classification, as several different aspects of connective structure must be accounted for. Among these aspects, we may include

- Hierarchical structure
- Connective pattern
- Variety of components
- Strength of interactions

Let us explore these points in more detail.

By some accounts, the single most overriding consideration in assessing a system's complexity is its hierarchical organization. Presumably, this feeling is generated by the observation that a high degree of complexity implies high rates of information processing by different decision makers and, conversely, the necessity of hierarchical structure to accommodate the processing of data and execution of decisions. Assuming the validity of this proposition, it follows that the number of hierarchical levels in a given system represents a rough measure of its complexity.

As an illustration of the "hierarchy principle," we consider Simon's classic watchmaker problem. Two watchmakers, Chronos and Tempus, manufacture the same precision timepieces in quite different fashions. Each watch consists of 1,000 pieces, and Tempus constructs his sequentially, so that if one is partly assembled and he is interrupted, it immediately falls apart and he must begin again from scratch. On the other hand, Chronos divides the construction into subassemblies of 10 pieces each such that 10 of the subassemblies forms a larger subassembly and a collection of 10 of the larger subassemblies constitutes the watch. Thus, when Chronos is interrupted, he loses only the subassembly on which he is currently working.

Assuming that the probability of an interruption is $p$, it is easy to see that the probability that Tempus completes a watch is $(1-p)^{1,000}$. On the other hand, Chronos has to complete a total of 110 subassemblies, and the probability that he will not be interrupted while completing any one of these is $(1-p)^{10}$. Some fairly straightforward computations with $p = 0.01$ show that it will take Tempus, on the average, about 20,000 times as long to complete a watch as Chronos.

As noted, this elementary example illustrates the basic point that hierarchical structure allows the effect of errors in local decision making to be overcome in overall systems behavior. Since noise, time-lags, and misunderstandings are part of all large-scale processes, it is no surprise that hierarchical organization has naturally evolved as a structure within which large systems may be controlled. Of course, hierarchy may appear in many forms, and what is necessary is to find a decomposition of the system that accounts for its intrinsic complexity. We shall pursue this point later.

## CONNECTIVE PATTERNS

Another vital aspect of the complexity question involves the manner in which the component subsystems of a process are connected. As we have seen in the last chapter, the connectivity structure of a system determines the data paths within a structure and restricts the influence that one part of a system may have upon another. These are clearly system properties affecting any intuitive concept of complexity.

Using the topologically based $q$-analysis idea from Chapter 3, we shall later develop a complexity measure that involves the various $q$-chains of the system and their mutual interrelations. Such a measure will emphasize the geometric, or dimensional, aspect of connectivity.

In another direction, we shall also explore connectivity and complexity from an algebraic viewpoint, taking an internal description of a system as our starting point. For instance, if we have a system described by the linear differential equation

$$x = Fx, \qquad x(0) = c, \tag{4.1}$$

where $F$ is an $n \times n$ matrix, the zero/nonzero pattern of $F$ (its connectivity structure) will surely influence our feeling about how complex the process is. Incidentally, this trivial example illustrates the important point that high dimensionality and high complexity may have little correlation. The system dimension $n$ may be very large, but if $F$ has a particularly simple structure, e.g., diagonal or sparse, we may conclude that Equation (4.1) represents a system of very low complexity, in that its behavior is very easy to predict and to understand. The complexity of a process like Equation (4.1) will have to be studied by a careful examination of how the subsystems interact (i.e., by the connectivity pattern) and not by the dimension of the overall process.

## VARIETY

The semiphilosophical "law of requisite variety," which, in rough terms, asserts that variety in a system's output can be modified only by sufficient variety in its input seems also to be a statement about system complexity. While this principle is of only modest interest when we think of a system as an object that accepts and emits only sequences of numbers, a more catholic view, in which inputs and outputs are general nonnumerical quantities, enhances the scientific interest of the variety law. Identifying complexity with a system's ability to exhibit many different modes of input–output behavior establishes a link between variety and one facet of system complexity. One might term this *control complexity*, since it is a measure of the system's ability to transform variety in its input to variety in the output response.

To illustrate the above idea, we consider the problem of controlling a system $\Sigma$ that is subject to external disturbances. Assume that the controller $C$ has three types of control at his disposal, $\alpha$, $\beta$, and $\gamma$, while there are three types of disturbances 1, 2, and 3 that may be encountered. The behavior of the system falls into one of three categories, $a$, $b$, or $c$, depending upon the combination of disturbance and control that occurs.

Assume that the possibilities are as depicted in the following matrix:

|            |   | α | β | γ |
|------------|---|---|---|---|
|            | 1 | b | a | c |
| Disturbance | 2 | a | c | b |
| Type       | 3 | c | b | a |

For this simple problem, the control set $\{\alpha, \beta, \gamma\}$ and the disturbance set $\{1, 2, 3\}$ each have variety 3, and the table shows that it is always possible for the controller to direct the system to any desired behavior, regardless of the external disturbance. A further basic result from cybernetic theory states that

$$\frac{\text{total variety}}{\text{in behavior}} \geq \frac{\text{disturbance variety}}{\text{control variety}}.$$

The point of this result is that if we always desire the system to exhibit a given mode of behavior in the face of external perturbations, only increased variety in the controlling actions can force down variety in the behavior. This is a rephrasing of Ashby's Law of Requisite Variety: only variety can destroy variety. This thesis is the cybernetic analogue of the Second Law of Thermodynamics and is closely related to the theory of information à la Shannon.

The implications of the above results for studies of complexity are quite clear if we think of complexity as manifesting itself in different behavioral modes of a system. We shall return to these points below.

INTERACTION LEVELS

A final point in the assessment of static complexity is the relative strength of the interactions among various system components and hierarchical levels. In a number of cases, small interaction levels, while theoretically increasing complexity by their presence, may be negligible from a practical point of view, and the practical complexity of the system is much less.

For instance, the three-dimensional system

$$\dot{x}_1 = x_1, \qquad x_1(0) = 1,$$
$$\dot{x}_2 = \quad x_2, \qquad x_2(0) = 1,$$
$$\dot{x}_3 = \qquad\quad x_3 \quad x_3(0) = 1,$$

could logically be assigned complexity 1, since each Jordan block of the coefficient matrix is of size 1. The closely related system

$$\dot{x}_1 = x_1,$$
$$\dot{x}_2 = \quad x_2,$$
$$\dot{x}_3 = \quad \varepsilon x_2 + x_3,$$

with $\varepsilon$ a parameter, would be assigned complexity 2, since the coefficient matrix

$$F = \begin{bmatrix} 1 & 0 & 0 \\ 0 & 1 & 0 \\ 0 & \varepsilon & 1 \end{bmatrix},$$

has its largest Jordan block of size 2 for any $\varepsilon \neq 0$. However, the solution

$$x_1 = x_2 = e^t, \qquad x_3 = e^t + \varepsilon^t e^t,$$

would indicate that for sufficiently small $\varepsilon$ the second system behavior is arbitrarily close to the first. Thus, it is reasonable to assign the same *practical* complexity to both processes upon suitable restriction of $\varepsilon$ (depending upon the application).

CONCLUSION

The preceding remarks support the statement that a system is never universally complex. It may be complex in some respects but not in others, or it may be complex only if used in a certain way. In short, static complexity is a multipronged concept that must be approached from several directions, keeping in mind the objectives of the analysis and the goals of the process.

## DYNAMIC COMPLEXITY

Turning now from connective structure and static considerations, let us consider some complexity issues that arise in connection with a system's dynamical motion or behavior.

RANDOMNESS VERSUS DETERMINISM AND COMPLEXITY

As we have noted, one of the principal intuitive guidelines for considering a process to be complex is that its motion be, in some way, difficult to explain or predict or, equivalently, that the output be a nonsimple (difficult to compute?) function of the input. In general, we can expect that the static considerations just discussed will surely influence the dynamical behavior of a process and, consequently, its dynamic complexity. However, the reverse is not true. A system may be structurally simple, i.e., have a low static complexity, yet its dynamic behavior may be very complex.

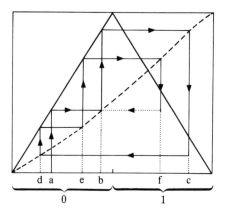

FIGURE 4.1  A dynamically complex process.

As an example of a dynamically complex process, consider the process depicted in Figure 4.1. Here the rule for generating the sequence of points $a, b, c, \ldots$ is to use the legs of the inscribed triangle together with the diagonal of the unit square as "reflecting" barriers, choosing an arbitrary starting point. A typical sequence of abscissa interactions is shown in Figure 4.1.

In the example shown, it can be proved that by associating any point to the left of the midpoint of the base of the triangle with "0" and any point to the right with "1," the sequence of points generated by the above *deterministic* procedure will be mathematically *indistinguishable* from a Bernoulli process with parameter $p = \frac{1}{2}$ (other values of $p$ can be obtained by using a line other than the diagonal of the square).

The preceding result is of enormous philosophical as well as system-theoretic interest since, if we imagine the sequence of 0's and 1's as representing the output of the process, there is no mathematical way to determine whether the internal mechanism transforming the inputs (initial state) into the output (0–1 sequence) is the above deterministic rule or is the observed behavior of a stochastic process. One or the other may be preferred on physical, psychological, or prejudicial grounds, but, short of looking inside the black box, no amount of mathematical manipulations and operations on the input–output sequence will enable one to determine whether or not the basic mechanism is stochastic. Philosophically, examples of the foregoing type cast serious doubt upon the claims of certain extremists that stochastic elements represent *essential* features of physical processes. What can be asserted, of course, is that probability and statistics are *convenient* tools to use in analyzing situations in which a degree of uncertainty is present. However, there is no mathematical reason to believe that the mechanism generating the uncertainty is inherently random; it could equally well be some deterministic process of the above type.

From the viewpoint of dynamic complexity, the process of Figure 4.1 is exceedingly complex, since the observed output is totally random. Thus, given a sequence of past outputs, we have no mathematical procedure that would be better than flipping a fair coin to predict the next output. Clearly, if we interpret dynamic complexity as the ability to predict system behavior, the preceding process is very complex.

TIME SCALES

Another aspect of dynamic complexity that must be considered is the question of different time scales for various parts of the process. One often enounters situations in which some components of a process are changing quite rapidly, while others are fluctuating at a much slower rate. A typical example occurs in the regulation of a water reservoir network where daily (or even hourly) decisions must be made for the release of water from an individual dam, while the overall network input–output flow is decided on a monthly or quaterly basis. Obviously, the fluctuations at the local level are much greater than for the overall network.

Some changes of time scale are reminiscent of the problem we encounter in numerical analysis when we wish to integrate a "stiff" system of differential equations or deal with an ill-conditioned problem. A simple version of ill-conditioning is represented by the linear system

$$\ddot{x} - 25x = 0$$

$$x(0) = 1, \qquad \dot{x}(0) = -5.$$

Theoretically, this problem has the solution

$$x(t) = e^{-5t}.$$

However, if we attempt to determine the solution to this problem numerically, the complementary solution

$$\bar{x}(t) = e^{5t}$$

enters the calculation with a small multiplier $\varepsilon$. Thus, what we actually compute is

$$x^*(t) = e^{-5t} + \varepsilon e^{5t}.$$

For sufficiently small $t$ (or $\varepsilon$), there is no problem; however, if the rounding-off error is too great (large $\varepsilon$) or if we want the solution over too great an interval (large $t$), the true solution is totally dominated by the spurious solution $\bar{x}(t)$.

In other cases, the problem may not come from numerical considerations but may be inherent in the theoretical solution itself. For instance, the "stiff" system

$$\dot{x}_1 = x_1 + 2x_2, \qquad x_1(0) = 0,$$
$$\dot{x}_2 = -10x_2, \qquad x_2(0) = 1,$$

has the solution

$$x_2(t) = -2/11[e^{-10t} - e^t],$$
$$x_2(t) = e^{-10t}.$$

Thus, the first component of the process is changing an order of magnitude faster than the second, and any attempt to compute the trajectory of the system numerically demands that we use an integration step small enough to accurately track the "fastest" component.

The phenomenon of "stiffness" in the system (mechanical engineering terminology) clearly influences the dynamic complexity, since accurate prediction now requires a substantial investment in data-processing resources.

CONCLUSION

The examples just given serve to further underscore the point made earlier that high system dimensionality (either of the state space or number of components) does not necessarily imply high complexity, and vice versa. In general, the two concepts have very little to do with each other, and a naive pronouncement that a system is complex just because it has many components fails to hold up under even superficial analysis. The moral is that total system complexity is much too sophisticated a notion to be describable by such simple-minded approaches as dimensionality.

## COMPUTATIONAL COMPLEXITY

Up to now, we have given a fairly broad, intuitive description of some of the more important facets of complexity. However, there are different complexity theories that are valid for well-defined systems, and these theories are not always naturally related or even compatible with each other.

One such complexity theory involves the construction of Turing machines and their algorithms for generating computable functions. The structure and size of these algorithms form the basis for what has come to be termed "computational complexity," especially in the computer science literature. Unfortunately, the intuitive notions of complexity given above do not have much appeal in the Turing machine context since, in principle, a Turing machine can do virtually everything (as it is assumed to have infinite memory and infinite time): it has infinite complexity!

The situation is somewhat more interesting when we consider only algorithms, independent of machines. For computing a given set of functions, we could distinguish among the algorithms by their *computational complexity*. To determine a complexity level for an algorithm, we must specify all possible computations or algorithms and then show how many steps a given algorithm requires to compute a particular function.

Several mathematical approaches to the problem of computational complexity have been offered, and a number of them are cited in the chapter references. However, the notion of computational complexity is, in general, much too restrictive for system-theoretic work, so we shall have little occasion to make use of the existing results in what follows. The only theoretical point to note for future reference is that in any complexity measure, whenever we "combine" computations, the complexity of the overall computation is bounded by the complexity of the component computations. We shall see the system-theoretic version of this principle in the next section.

## AXIOMS OF SYSTEM COMPLEXITY

Before proceeding to define system complexity by mathematical formulae, it is necessary to list some basic properties that any such measure must satisfy if it is to agree with the main intuitive complexity concepts outlined above. As usual in axiomatic approaches, there may be a lack of uniform agreement on the axioms themselves; however, once the axioms are settled, the mathematics can then proceed to give us concrete measures and insights into the complexity problem.

Since the principal system aspects that any complexity measure must address are hierarchy, connectivity, and dynamic behavior, the complexity axioms we present have been constructed to account for these components of system structure. If $\theta(\Sigma)$ represents any real-valued complexity measure defined on a system $\Sigma$, then we have

*Axioms of Complexity*

1. *Hierarchy*   If $\Sigma_0$ is a subsystem of $\Sigma$, then

$$\theta(\Sigma_0) \leq \theta(\Sigma),$$

i.e., a subsystem can be no more complex than the system as a whole.

2. *Parallel Composition*   If $\Sigma = \Sigma_1 \oplus \Sigma_2 \oplus \ldots \oplus \Sigma_k$, i.e., $\Sigma$ is the parallel composition of the systems $\{\Sigma_i\}$, then

$$\theta(\Sigma) = \max_{1 \leq i \leq k} \theta(\Sigma_i).$$

3. *Serial Composition*　If $\Sigma = \Sigma_1 \otimes \Sigma_2 \otimes \ldots \otimes \Sigma_k$, i.e., $\Sigma$ is the serial composition of the systems $\{\Sigma_i\}$, then

$$\theta(\Sigma) \leq \theta(\Sigma_1) + \theta(\Sigma_2) + \ldots + \theta(\Sigma_k).$$

4. *Feedback Composition*　If there is a feedback operation $\ominus$ from a system $\Sigma_2$ to $\Sigma_1$, then

$$\theta(\Sigma_1 \otimes \Sigma_2) \leq \theta(\Sigma_1) + \theta(\Sigma_2) + \theta(\Sigma_2 \ominus \Sigma_1)$$

(note that Axiom 3 is just a special case of Axiom 4, when there is no feedback loop.)

5. *Normalization*　With respect to the particular mathematical description of a given class of systems, there exists a distinguished subset of systems $\mathscr{S}$ for which

$$\theta(\Sigma) = 0 \quad \text{for all} \quad \Sigma \in \mathscr{S}.$$

In a moment we shall see how these axioms suffice to generate meaningful complexity measures for systems defined in various ways; in fact, in some cases the axioms of complexity uniquely characterize a complexity measure. But first, a few comments on the axioms are in order.

To begin with, we note that the intuitive notions surrounding complexity are taken into account by appeal to more or less standard decomposition results and the axioms. Since any system can be decomposed into a series-parallel or cascade (hierarchical) combination of subsystems (possibly with feedback), Axioms 2–4 account for the connective structure of such a decomposition. Hierarchical aspects are covered by Axiom 1, while dynamical considerations are addressed in Axiom 5. Thus, the axioms of complexity seem reasonable, at least to the extent that no major aspect of complexity is omitted.

The second point to observe is that in at least one important situation (finite-state processes), these axioms are the smallest set for which a unique complexity measure results. Thus, appealing to Occam's razor, we further justify the above axioms.

Finally, we mention that the axioms are particularly convenient for various *algebraic* approaches to the analysis and measurement of complexity. In the next chapter, we shall study some differential-topological aspects of systems, including catastrophe theory and will consider certain questions in the topology of forms. A theory of complexity for topological forms is also of considerable scientific interest; unfortunately, it is not yet clear how to generate the topology of a form by algebraic tools. Thus, either such a procedure must be devised or a new measure of *topological* complexity must be introduced. It may be necessary to modify the preceding axioms in order to carry out such a program successfully.

## COMPLEXITY OF FINITE-STATE MACHINES

From a system-theoretic viewpoint, the most advanced theory of system complexity is for those processes modeled as finite-state machines. We recall from Chapter 3 that any finite-state machine $M$ generates a finite transformation semigroup $(Q, \mathscr{F}^*)$, where $Q$ = the state space of $M$ and $\mathscr{F}^*$ = the semigroup of all transformations on $Q$. We first define complexity in algebraic terms using the wreath product, then relate the definition to machines and the axioms of complexity.

*Definition* 4.1. Let $(X, S)$ be a (right-mapping) semigroup. Then the *group complexity* $\#_G(X, S)$ is defined to be the smallest integer $n$ such that

$$S \mid (Y_n, C_n)w(X_n, G_n)w \dots w(Y_1, C_1)w(X_1, G_1)w(Y_0, C_0)$$

where $G_1, \dots, G_n$ are finite simple groups, $C_0, \dots, C_n$ are finite combinatorial semigroups (flip-flops) and "$w$" denotes the wreath product operation.

Thus, the group complexity of the semigroup $(X, S)$ is the minimal number of alternations of blocks of simple groups and blocks of combinatorial semigroups needed to obtain $(X, S)$. It is important to note that by making use of decomposition results, we could define complexity in terms of phase space decomposition. For instance,

$$\#_G(X, S) = \min \#_G\{T: \ T \text{ is a series-parallel or cascade}$$
$$\text{decomposition of } S\}$$

Since combinatorial semigroups represent machines that do no computation, the basic complexity element is the simple group, which carries out elementary arithmetic operations, such as addition and multiplication. The question now arises as to what the significance of the Krohn–Rhodes theory is. Basically, it tells us to what extent we can decompose a machine into components that are primitive and irreducible and that the solution depends upon the structure of the components and the length of computation. Hence, complexity does not depend only upon the length of the computation chain, but also upon the degree of complication of each component in the chain. Thus, complexity takes account of not only the total number of computations in a chain (the computational aspect) but also the inherent complexity of the submachines hooked together through the wreath product (the structural aspect). Heuristically, the computational part can be represented by the amount of "looping" in a computer program that computes the action of $\mathscr{F}^*$ on $Q$.

Given the definition of group complexity for finite-state machines, we inquire as to its relationship to the earlier axioms of complexity. We answer this by the following result.

*Theorem 4.1.* Let $\theta: M_{\mathscr{F}} \to N$, the nonnegative integers, where $M_{\mathscr{F}}$ is the set of all finite-state machines and $N$ is the nonnegative integers. Assume $\theta$ satisfies the axioms of complexity, with the normalization condition (Axiom 5) being

$$\theta(U_3) = 0, \qquad \theta(D_1) = 0,$$

where $U_3$ is the three-state flip-flop of Chapter 3 and $D_1$ is the delay-1 machine. Then

$$\theta(f) = \#_G(f^S)$$

for all $f \in M_{\mathscr{F}}$. (Note: $f^S$ is the semigroup of the machine f.)

The proof of this basic complexity result may be found in the references cited at the end of the chapter.

## Remarks

1. Theorem 4.1 shows that the group complexity function $\#_G$ is essentially the unique integer-valued function satisfying the complexity axioms under the given normalization. Any other function $\#_{G'}$ satisfying the Axioms is such that $\#_{G'}(f) \leq \#_G(f)$ for all $f \in M_{\mathscr{F}}$.

2. The delay-1 machine is also, along with the flip-flop $U_3$, a combinatorial semigroup. Its action is

$$D_1(a_1, \ldots, a_n) = a_{n-1}, \qquad D_1(a_1) = \text{null},$$

where $\{a_n, a_{n-1}, \ldots, a_1\}$ is any input string.

3. $\theta(f) = 0$ if and only if $f$ is a series-parallel combination of the machines $U_3$ and $D_1$.

4. To see that machines of every level of complexity exist, consider the machine (circuit) $C = (U, Y, Q, \lambda, \delta)$ with

$$U = \{a, b, c\}$$
$$Y = \{0, 1\},$$
$$Q = \{1, 2, \ldots, n\},$$
$$\lambda(i, a) = i + 1 \bmod n, \qquad i = 1, 2, \ldots, n$$
$$\lambda(1, b) = 2,$$
$$\lambda(2, b) = 1,$$
$$\lambda(x, b) = x, \qquad x \neq 1, 2,$$
$$\lambda(1, c) = 2,$$
$$\lambda(y, c) = y, \qquad y \neq 1,$$
$$\delta(q, d) = q \bmod 2, \qquad q \in Q, \qquad d \in U.$$

Using the preceding results, plus some additional algebraic facts from semigroup theory, it can be verified that the above machine has complexity

$$\theta(C) = n - 1$$

for every initial state $q \in Q$.

5. The normalization of $U_3$ and $D_1$ is set up so that these machines form the simplest (least complex) objects in the theory. This is reasonable since neither type of machines does any computation and their actions are completely predictable. Since everyone understands them, they cannot possibly be complex.

This property is reminiscent of information theory when selecting events that have information content zero. The machines $U_3$ and $D_1$ generate regular patterns; they do not yield any surprises. Therefore, their behavior does not produce information. Consequently, if we were able to detect subsystems that behave like flip-flops, we could erase these subsystems without changing the structural complexity associated with other subsystems, nevertheless decreasing the computational complexity in terms of length of computation.

In summary, the complexity of a machine $f$ equals the minimal number of times nonarithmetic and arithmetic operations must be alternated (in series) to yield $f$, when, by convention, only the arithmetic operations are counted.

## EVOLUTION COMPLEXITY AND EVOLVING STRUCTURES

As a somewhat speculative, but highly suggestive, example of the use of complexity, we consider some aspects of evolving organisms. The basic thesis is the *evolution principle*:

An evolving organism transforms itself in such a manner that it maximizes the contact with the complete environment subject to reasonable control and understanding of the contacted environment.

To expand upon the evolution principle, we remark that "contact with the environment" means the memory space needed to simulate the behavior of the organism on a computer or, equivalently, the number of flip-flops required to build a machine to simulate the organism's behavior. The complete environment means all forms of contact, both physical and mental.

By "reasonable control and understanding of the contacted environment," we mean that the complexity of the interaction between the organism and the environment is relatively high or is approximately equal numerically to the value of the present contact. It can be argued that increased control implies increased complexity, and, since complexity is deeply related to understanding (complexity is equivalent to the minimal number of coordinates needed to understand a process), an organism operating at a high complexity in interaction with its environment implies high understanding and ability to act.

Intuitively, one can justify the evolution principle by considering the principal reasons for an organism's failure to survive. First of all, something may happen that the organism doesn't know about and it kills him. For instance, an antiscience English professor walks into an area of high radioactivity, or a baby eats some ant poison. In these cases, some element is suddenly introduced into the environment and this element kills the organism. In short, the *contact* is too limited, and the organism dies as a result.

At the other extreme, the contact may be very high but the complexity is too low and "things get out of hand." For example, two psychoanalysts develop a new theory of madness requiring them to spend many hours alone with previously violent individuals. One of the psychoanalysts is nearly strangled to death but lives and recovers, while the other becomes very remorseful after this violent incident and apparent setback to the theory and eventually commits suicide. In this case, the contact with the environment is high but the complexity, control, and understanding of the situation is too low, resulting in death. Or, a flower may bend toward the sun and, in doing so, become visible from the footpath and be picked by a passing schoolgirl. The contact with the sunlight was increased but the control to avoid being picked after being seen was nonexistent.

Thus, if an organism can increase contact and increase control, understanding, and complexity by nearly the same amount, it will be in all ways better off. The evolution principle formalizes this heuristic argument.

To make the above discussion more precise, we let $E_t$ be the finite-state machine representing the environment at time $t$, while $O_t$ represents the organism. $R_t$ will be the machine denoting the result of $O_t$ interacting with $E_t$. (Recall that the result $R$ of an interaction between two machines is, by definition, equal to the state-output machine

$$R = (U, \text{range } \bar{\delta}, \text{range } \bar{\delta}, \lambda, j),$$

where range $\bar{\delta}$ is some set of representations for the stable loops of the interaction and $j$: range $\bar{\delta} \to$ range $\bar{\delta}$ is the identity map.) Further, we let $C_t \doteq \#(R_t)$ be the number of states of $R_t$ and $c_t \doteq \theta(R_t) + 1$, the complexity function of $R_t$ plus one. Hence, $C_t$ is the *contact number* at time $t$, while $c_t$ is the basic *complexity number*.

Now, we let $h: N^+ \times N^+ \to R^1$ be a map from the cross product of the positive integers to the reals, with the property that if $a$, $b$, $c \in N^+$, $a < c$, $b < c$, then $h(a, b) < h(c, c)$. We call $h$ a *culture function*. The significance of the culture function is that it contains the strategy that the organism will follow as it grows. But we must be more specific.

Intuitively, the purpose of the organism is to keep $c_t$ close to $C_t$ and then to maximize the two nearly equal quantities. But, how should the organism change its strategy if $C_t$ becomes substantially larger than $c_t$? Should it immediately attempt to lower $C_t$ to $c_t$, or should it attempt to bring them both to a midway point, or should it do nothing? The culture function $h$ is what determines the *local* strategy when $C_t - c_t$ is large.

For instance, in a society like Great Britain where a (relatively) large premium is placed upon social propriety, emotional control, duty, and the like, but where there is, opposing this, a strong force for personal advancement, we might have a culture function like

$$h_E(a, b) = a^3 - e^{a-b}.$$

Here the negative term represents a severe penalty for $C_t - c_t$ being too large, while the $a^3$ term represents some attempt to maximize contact $C_t$. In short, $h_E$ represents a repressed but productive culture.

Alternatively, we could consider a culture like the American, which sacrifices all other considerations to economic advancement. It encourages inventiveness and enterprise, while discouraging activities not directly related to economic productivity (e.g., art, music, scholarly endeavor). We might represent this by the culture function

$$h_A(a, b) = a^2 + b^2 - (a - b)^2 = 2ab.$$

Here contact (e.g., enterprise) and understanding (e.g., inventiveness) are rewarded, while contact minus understanding (i.e., uncontrolled activity) is penalized to the same degree. Consequently, $h_A$ represents a bland, immature, but productive culture.

Finally, consider the French society. Here the culture suggests that one should enjoy oneself, manipulate the environment for one's own pleasure, and so on. This could be represented by

$$h_F(a, b) = b.$$

There is no penalty for a large contact minus understanding. The function $h_F$ indicates that one should always increase control and understanding. The culture represented by $h_F$ is a society full of love, sex, talk, and personal striving, idealizing beauty and intellectualism, but rather unproductive.

In summary, the idea behind the British culture function $h_E$ is that there is a cultural force to control oneself, then advance onward; symbolically, first $\rightarrow \leftarrow$, then $\uparrow$. The American function $h_A$ suggests "don't rock the boat." The French function is "don't worry: live; wine, women, and song, and— since this takes money, sexual attractiveness, and so on—manipulate.

The contact function $C_t$, complexity function $c_t$, and culture function $h$ may be used together to suggest a generalized "Hamiltonian of life," which governs evolving organisms. Such a formulation is very close in spirit to

Thom's program for studying morphogenesis, which we shall consider in the next chapter. The reader may find more details of this Hamiltonian formulation in the works cited at the chapter's end.

## CHOICE PROCESSES AND COMPLEXITY

At the level of individual or social choice problems, complexity is related to the ability or inability of human decision makers to make decisions in a consistent or rational manner. In this connection, complexity exhibits a type of uncertainty that cannot be properly treated in terms of probabilities.

One clear sign of complexity entering into decision making is an inability to prove the existence of a function representing preferences for choices. The social choice problem is similar to the problem faced by a chess player when searching for a "satisfactory" strategy to the extent that the decision maker is involved in a problem of combinatorial dimension. To search for all game-theoretic alternatives goes far beyond the computational capabilities of human beings or computers.

In view of the preceding comments, we are led to conclude that it is necessary to depart from hypotheses involving optimizing behavior since such an approach to decision making docs not come to grips with nontrivial choice problems in complicated situations. However, it is not necessary to sacrifice rationality when we abandon optimality since even "limited rationality" may turn out to be a satisfactory decision basis when complexity prevents necessary computations from being carried out.

*Example of a Decision or Search Rule* An individual, as a member of society (or voter), is faced with a "large" market of public goods and is required to choose among different kinds of commodities or services (nuclear energy, missiles, health care, and so on) offered to him for sale by different government agencies at different prices (i.e., tax rates). In order to receive a tax rate quotation (or possibly some other relevant information) from any given agency, the voter must incur some (not necessarily monetary) cost constituting his marginal search cost. The voter's problem is this: Given a certain bundle of public goods that satisfies his aspirations, search for those tax rates such that his final taxes (plus total search costs) will be kept as low as possible.

The above problem can be formalized as follows. Let $t_i$ denote the tax rate quotation of agency $i$. Let $t = (t_1, \ldots, t_n)$ be the tax structure and suppose $t_i \in [0, 1] = I$. Denote by $I^n$ the $n$-dimensional cartesian product of $I$, and define a probability density $F$ on $I^n$ representing the voter's initial belief about what tax rates the agencies are likely to quote. The order of quotations presented to the voter is considered to be irrelevant; thus, for simplicity, it is assumed that $F$ is symmetric, i.e., if $p$ is a permutation of $(1, 2, \ldots, n)$ and if $t^p = (t_{p(1)}, \ldots, t_{p(n)})$, then $F(t) = F(t^p)$.

The setup of this problem enables us to construct a decision rule that tells the voter, for each $i$, whether to stop searching after receiving $i$ quotations or whether to continue searching on the basis of the $i$ quotations he has received. A decision rule is assumed to be a mapping from a set of observations into a set of actions. In this problem, for each $i$ let the set of actions be $A = \{\text{"accept"}, \text{"reject"}\}$, and the set of observations be $O_i = I^i$. Then a decision rule is a sequence of functions $D = (D_1, \ldots, D_{n-1})$, where $D_i \colon O_i \to A$. If $(t_1, \ldots, t_i) \in O_i$, then $D_i(t_1, \ldots, t_i)$ records the voter's decision to either accept the tax rates that have been quoted to him and choose (by vote) the given bundle of public goods presented to him, or to continue searching and reject the tax rates $t_1, \ldots, t_i$.

Now for this kind of problem it is perfectly legitimate to ask what the voter's optimal decision rule is. This question could be answered by the machinery provided in statistical decision theory for finding optimal solutions for search problems. Instead, here we are interested in the basic ill-structuredness of the problem given by the complexity of the decision rule. Thus we proceed to associate with every decision rule $D$ a (computer) program $f_D$ that computes $D$. This permits us to define the complexity of the program by the amount of "looping" between subprograms (computational complexity). Hence, a sequential machine is used as a metaphor for determining complexity of sequential decision rules. This can be further illustrated by elaborating on the problem above by using the sequential machine framework.

Let $U =$ set of observable tax rates = finite subset of $[0, 1]$. Let $Y = \{\text{"stop,"}$ continue to $i+1$, $i = 1, 2, \ldots, n\}$. Then the machine $f_D$ is defined inductively on the length $m$ of the input sequence by

$$D_1(t_1) \quad \text{if} \quad m = 1, \quad \text{or} \quad f_D(t_1, \ldots, t_{m-1}) = \text{"stop"}$$

or

$$D_i(t_1, \ldots, t_m) \quad \text{if} \quad f_D(t_1, \ldots, t_{m-1}) = \text{"continue to } i+1\text{"}.$$

The computational length and the structural complexity of subsystems that are needed for compute $f_D$ reflect a measure of complexity for $f_D$ (equivalently for the decision rule $D$). Obviously, an optimal rule is one that is generally more complex and more expensive; it may also very well be beyond the computational power and sophistication of the voter. Hence the voter facing an ill-structured problem wants to make it well structured by seeking a decision rule that matches his computational ability and sophistication.

## DESIGN VERSUS CONTROL COMPLEXITY

In a previous section, we considered the complexity functions $c_t$, referring to the complexity of interaction between an organism and its environment, and $C_t$, referring to the contact between organism and environment. These notions are closely related to the two basic types of decision-making complexity, which we refer to as *design* and *control* complexity.

Design complexity is the level of complexity of a transformation semi-group when full use is made of the system potential. Control complexity is the specific complexity number that results from computations that keep the system under complete control. A *qualitatively stable* decision rule would be one for which these two numbers coincide. However, in most practical situations the design complexity will exceed the control complexity. In a certain sense, the concepts are naturally associated to programs of "optimization" and problems of "satisficing," respectively. Thus, design complexity pertains to that decision rule that is best in some appropriate sense and, in general, involves some optimality principle. However, the optimal decision cannot be realized given the limited computational resources of the decision maker (control complexity).

We could redefine our evolution complexity relation to be the difference between the design and control complexity. The smaller the difference, the more stable (balanced) the system tends to be. (This notion is closely allied to the concept of *resilience* of a system as understood by ecologists.)

To illustrate the principles involved, consider a typical "tragedy-of-the-commons" situation. A certain finite area of land is given, as is a set of herdsmen. Each herdsman will try to keep as many cattle as possible and will assume that this is equivalent to maximizing his profit. Suppose the marginal utility of adding one more animal to the commons is $+1$ for every herdman; however, the social utility contributed to him is negative (a fraction of $-1$) due to effects of overgrazing or, more generally, the depletion of resources.

The tragedy consists in the incompatibility of individual rationality and social necessity or, in our terms, in the discrepancy between design and control complexity. A breakdown (catastrophe) cannot be avoided unless there are significant changes in the "level of understanding" (due to learning, adaptation, or control) or in the design, by reducing or eliminating external effects. Examples of this type are particularly prevalent in the ecological sphere and, as noted before, are highly suggestive of the elusive resilience concept, which we shall reconsider in the next chapter.

## A PROGRAM FOR PRACTICAL APPLICATIONS OF COMPLEXITY

The main steps to take in a more practical application of complexity would be the following:

  1. Try to find a reasonable analogy between a natural system and an artificial (mathematical) system in finite-state terms.
  2. Compute various "reasonable" transformation semigroups for a given system (using, perhaps, functional equations or relations), taking into account its past history and different possible designs.
  3. Compute the design complexities of the semigroups.
  4. Compute the "rational" level of contact function associated to the "natural" semigroup of transformations.
  5. Compute the control complexity of this "natural" contact function.
  6. Compute those contact functions and complexities that yield stable configurations for particular designs.

The achievement of stable configurations doesn't necessarily mean that the semigroup of transformations for the design is identical with that for the control; it would be sufficient if both had the same relative increase through all finite states.

## POLYHEDRAL DYNAMICS AND COMPLEXITY

Our exposition thus far of complexity measures for systems describable as finite-state machines is not meant to suggest that alternative measures have not been proposed. As we have continually emphasized, the appropriate mathematics in any given situation depends almost exclusively upon the way in which the problem is mathematically formulated. A complexity measure developed with finite-state descriptions in mind may be of no particular use if an alternative characterization of the process is employed. In this section, we consider complexity when the algebraic–topologic description of the process as a simplicial complex is used.

Since the basic algebraic objects of the polyhedral dynamics description are the simplices, we formulate our complexity function in terms of the dimension of the simplices and the interconnection between them. We stress that the following definition of complexity embraces only the *static*, structural complexity of the relation represented by the complex. Dynamic considerations are probable best considered in the light of the finite-state results.

For the polyhedral complexity, we adopt the following version of the axioms of complexity presented earlier:

A. A system consisting of a single simplex has complexity 1.
B. A subsystem (subcomplex) has complexity no greater than that of the entire complex.
C. The combination of two complexes to form a new complex results in a level of complexity no greater than the sum of the complexities of the component complexes.

Note that Axioms A–C implicitly assume that the system under considera-tion is connected at the zero-level, i.e., the structure vector $Q$ has $Q_0 = 1$. If this is not the case, then we compute the complexity function for the disconnected complexes, then use the maximum of these numbers to repres-ent the complexity of the system. Such a procedure is equivalent to consid-eration of the entire system as a parallel combination of its disconnected (at zero-level) components.

A measure that satisfies the preceding axioms and is readily computable from the structure vector $Q$ is

$$\psi(K) = 2\left[\sum_{i=0}^{N} (i+1)Q_i\right]\Big/(N+1)(N+2),$$

where $N = $ dimension of the complex $K$ and $Q_i$ is the $i$th component of the $q$-analysis structure vector $Q$. The factor $2/(N+1)(N+2)$ is introduced purely as a normalization to satisfy Axiom A.

To illustrate the use of the complexity measure $\psi$, consider again the predator–prey example of Chapter 3. The predator relation, $\lambda_{\mathrm{PRD}}$, has the structure vector

$$Q_{\mathrm{PRD}} = (\overset{5}{1}\ 1\ 2\ 3\ 2\ \overset{0}{1}),$$

while the prey relation, $\lambda_{\mathrm{PRY}}$, gives

$$Q_{\mathrm{PRY}} = (\overset{5}{1}\ 3\ 3\ 4\ 2\ \overset{0}{1}).$$

Thus,

$$\psi(\mathrm{PRD}) = \tfrac{11}{7}, \qquad \psi(\mathrm{PRY}) = \tfrac{50}{21},$$

indicating that the prey relation is somewhat more "complex" than the predator relation.

## ALGEBRAIC SYSTEM THEORY AND COMPLEXITY

While the finite-state machine definition of complexity may be extended to the case of finite-dimensional linear systems via some "unnatural" algebraic identification of the semigroup of the linear system, it is somewhat more natural to follow another path. The reason is that the semigroup "realization" of a finite-state linear system is seldom minimal (i.e., canonical). This is not surprising, since the objective of the Krohn–Rhodes theory is to give existence theorems for series-parallel realizations, which are almost always nonminimal. Mathematically, the most elegant way to proceed is via module theory, which, as noted earlier, always leads to minimal realizations. However, the mathematics is a bit beyond the scope of this book, so we shall content ourselves with a complexity discussion at the level of polynomials and linear algebra.

As general motivation for our complexity function, we recall Figure 3.7, depicting the general structure of a linear system, and the discussion of the Realization Theorem of Chapter 3. We saw that any linear dynamical system $\Sigma$ was composed as a direct sum of subsystems $\Sigma_i$, where $\Sigma_i$ was characterized by the $i$th nontrivial factor of the matrix

$$\psi_W W(z),$$

where $W(z) =$ transfer matrix of $\Sigma$ and $\psi_W =$ characteristic polynomial of $\Sigma$. The components $\Sigma_i$ represent the irreducible building blocks of $\Sigma$ and, as a result, we focus our complexity measure on them.

Since the invariant factors of $\psi_W W(z)$ essentially characterize the structure of $\Sigma$, keeping in mind the axioms of complexity, as a measure of system complexity we propose

$$\xi(\Sigma) = \sum_{i=1}^{q} (n - \deg \psi_i + 1) \log (n - \deg \psi_i + 1),$$

where $n = \dim \Sigma$, and $\psi_i =$ the $i$th nontrivial invariant factor of $\psi_W W(z)$. It is relatively easy to verify that the measure $\xi$ satisfies the earlier axioms, with the normalization that the complexity of a cyclic system ($F =$ cyclic) is zero.

It is no accident that the complexity measure $\xi$ bears a strong resemblance to the measure of information content in a string of symbols, since the axioms of complexity are very closely related to the "natural" axioms required of an entropy measure. We shall return to this point later.

An additional point to observe about the measure $\xi$ is that while the emphasis is upon system structure (the $\psi_i$) in defining complexity, dimensionality of the state space also plays a role. Roughly speaking, given two systems with similar cyclic structure, the higher-dimensional system will be more complex. This is an intuitively satisfying aspect of the measure $\xi$.

As an illustration of the above measure, we consider two systems described by the transfer matrices

$$W_1(z) = \text{diag}\left(\frac{1}{z+1}, \frac{1}{z+2}, \frac{1}{z+3}\right),$$

$$W_2(z) = \begin{bmatrix} \dfrac{1}{z} + \dfrac{1}{z^2} & \dfrac{1}{z} + \dfrac{1}{z^2} & \dfrac{1}{z} \\ 0 & 0 & \dfrac{1}{z} \end{bmatrix}.$$

It is readily computed that the matrix $\psi_{W_1} W_1(z)$ has the single invariant factor

$$\psi_1^1 = (z+1)(z+2)(z+3).$$

Hence,

$$\xi(\Sigma_1) = 0.$$

On the other hand, the matrix $\psi_{W_2} W_2(z)$ has the invariant factors

$$\psi_1^2 = z, \qquad \psi_2^2 = z^2.$$

Thus, the complexity of $\Sigma_2$ is

$$\begin{aligned} \xi(\Sigma_2) &= \sum_{i=1}^{2} (n - \deg \psi_i + 1) \log (n - \deg \psi_i + 1) \\ &= (3-1-1) \log (3-1+1) + (3-2+1) \log (3-2+1) \\ &= 3 \log 3 + 2 \log 2. \end{aligned}$$

As expected, the nontrivial cyclic structure of $\Sigma_2$ makes it much more complex than $\Sigma_1$.

## NONLINEAR, FINITE-DIMENSIONAL PROCESSES

The measurement of complexity for a system governed by the *nonlinear* differential equation

$$\dot{x} = f(x, u)$$

is a considerably more difficult problem, principally since there are no convenient, succinct algebraic representations, such as $W(z)$, to characterize the input–output structure of the system. Two approaches suggest themselves.

First, we could approximate the finite-dimensional state space of the process by some discrete state space in a manner analogous to that employed in numerical processes. For instance, the state space $R^n$ could be discretized by truncating the coordinate directions as

$$a_i \le x_i \le b_i, \qquad i = 1, 2, \ldots, n,$$

and then discretizing the finite hyperblock by some grid. We then define the *finite-state* dynamics as that induced by the original continuous system. Having approximated the original problem, we may then employ the finite state complexity results given earlier. We note, however, that it is by no means a trivial task to establish the validity of the discretization process. In one way or another, we must be able to establish the invariance of structure under subdivision and show that the discrete problem converges (in some sense) to the original as the discretization becomes finer and finer.

A second approach is to make use of the decomposition results given in Chapter 3. If the dynamics $f(x, u)$ are analytic in $x$ and continuous in $u$, Krener's theorem gives an analogue to the Krohn–Rhodes theorem. Unfortunately, an analogous complexity theory has not yet been developed for such problems, but there appears to be no major obstacle in extending the finite-state results to the finite-dimensional setting.

## COMPLEXITY AND INFORMATION THEORY

We have already noted some strong connections between classical information theory á la Shannon–Wiener and the concept of system complexity. In fact, some early attempts in biology at quantifying complexity defined it categorically as the number of distinguishable units comprising an organism. Such an approach clearly invites comparison with the information content present in a string of symbols. However, information theory is not really a satisfactory basis upon which to formulate a theory of complexity. We have seen that a system is a holistic object, not the mere aggregate of its parts. Furthermore, the system variables do not act separately, but in conjunction with others to form complex effects. Separate primary variables may not be important, but rather their combination, which correspond to these effects. Information theory, by itself, cannot identify these combinations. Like all statistical theories, it disregards the fact that the relative positions of the elements in a structure may matter. In other words, the numerical frequencies of different elements in a system is not sufficient to explain the phenomena. Information is needed about the manner in which the elements are related.

One interesting approach toward remedying the above deficiency is to appeal to the notion of "similar phenomena." Specifically, one postulates that the original system variables $x_1, x_2, \ldots, x_n$ having independent dimensions are replaced by $P_1, P_2, \ldots, P_k$ made dimensionless by suitable combination of the $x_i$. The number of such dimensionless variables is determined by the theorem that a dimensionally homogeneous equation

$$F = (x_1, x_2, \ldots, x_n) = 0$$

can be expressed in terms of the $P$ variables formed with the $x_i$ such that

$$f(P_1, P_2, \ldots, P_{n-r}) = 0, \qquad r \le m,$$

with $r =$ rank of the dimensional matrix of the $n$ original variables and $m =$ the number of fundamental dimensions, such as mass and length, in the physical system.

Since virtually all laws of physical theory are dimensionally invariant, the dimensionless products $P_i$ can be interpreted as similarity criteria. Thus, we are able to reduce considerably the number of system variables that must be taken into account. At the same time, the usual information-theoretic problem of nonstationarity is also alleviated, since any increments leading to nonstationarity are likely to be much smaller at the macroscopic level (the $P$ variables) than at the microsystem level (the $x$ variables).

The focus of attention will now be on the fundamental relationships governing system behavior, not on the particular models representing the process. Thus, we want to characterize complexity in terms of the invariant properties of the system structure. Since it is important to be able to locate the various sets of system configurations, we introduce a dimensionally invariant discriminant function

$$Y = a_1 P_1 + \ldots + a_k P_k,$$

where the weighting coefficients are determined such that the $t$-statistic or $F$-ratio between various groups (subsystems) is maximized. Thus, we wish to maximize the ratio of the between-group variance to the within-group variance

$$\phi(a_1, \ldots, a_k) = \frac{n_1 n_2}{n_1 + n_2} \frac{(a, d)^2}{(a, Ca)},$$

where $d' = (d_1, d_2, \ldots, d_k)$ is the vector of mean differences on the $k(=n-r)$ dimensionally invariant functions $P_i$, $C$ is the within-group covariance matrix, and $n_1$ and $n_2$ are observations in the two groups.

Let $Y_{lk}^m$ be the value of the $m$th dimensionally invariant discriminant function evaluated for element $k$ of group $l$. The *a posteriori* probability that $k$ belongs to group $l$, when it is actually in group $m$, (the case $k_m$) is given by

$$P_{lmk_m}^{m'} = \frac{P_m \exp(Y_{lmk_m}^{m'})}{\sum\limits_{i=1}^{r} P_i \exp(Y_{lik_m}^{m'})},$$

where the superscript $m'$ denotes the particular discriminant function that leads to maximization of the true probabilities of group membership, $r$ is the total number of groups, and $P_m$ is the *a priori* probability that $k$ is in group $m$.

We propose to define system complexity in terms of information content, i.e., as a measure of the average uncertainty of an element's location. Specifically, the complexity of group $m$ is defined as

$$H_m = \frac{1}{n_m} \sum_{k_m=1}^{n_m} G_{k_m},$$

where

$$G_{k_m} = -\sum_{i=1}^{r} P_{imk_m}^{m'} \log_2 P_{imk_m}^{m'},$$

with $n_m =$ the number of elements in group $m$.

We also measure the *redundancy* of the $i$th group as

$$R_i = 1 - \frac{H_i}{\log_2 r}.$$

## NOTES AND REFERENCES

### INTRODUCTION

One of the first articles to address the question of system complexity directly, and still an excellent starting point for more technical discussions, is:

Simon, H., "The Architecture of Complexity," *Proc. Am. Philos. Soc.*, 106 (1962), 467–482.

See also:

Morin, E., "Complexity," *Int. Soc. Sci. J.*, 26 (1974), 583–597.
Weaver, W., "Science and Complexity," *Am. Sci.*, 36 (1968), 536–544.
Baldwin, M., "Portraits of Complexity," Battelle Monographs, Battelle Memorial Institute, Columbus, Ohio, June 1975.

### STATIC COMPLEXITY

#### Hierarchy

A fine summary of many of the heirarchical aspects of system structure is the book:

Pattee, H., ed., *Hierarchy Theory*, Braziller, New York, 1973.

Material on the construction of reliable machines from unreliable components utilizing hierarchical considerations is discussed in:

Arbib, M., *Brains, Machines and Mathematics*, McGraw-Hill, New York, 1964.

An interesting application of hierarchy theory to the humanities is:

Goguen, J., "Complexity of Hierarchically Organized Systems and the Structure of Musical Experiences," *Int. J. Gen. Syst.*, 3 (1977).

## Variety

The standard work on variety as it relates to system problems is the classic book:

Ashby, W. R., *Introduction to Cybernetics*, Chapman and Hall, London, 1956.

A recent article outlining the gap between Ashby's ideas and the state-variable approaches utilized by engineers is:

Porter, B., "Requisite Variety in the Systems and Control Sciences," *Int. J. Gen. Syst.* 2 (1976), 225–229.

A computer-science-oriented view of the relations between control and complexity is given by:

Yudin, D., and A. Goryashko, "Control Problems and Complexity Theory I, II," *Eng. Cybern.* (USSR), 12 (1974), 10–24. 13 (1975), 1–13.

Recent works on the complexity question for systems described by graphs and relations are:

Nechiporenko, V. I., *The Structural Analysis of Systems*, Sovietskoe Radio Publishing Co., Moscow, 1977 (in Russian).
Gorbatov, V. A. *The Theory of Partially Ordered Systems*, Sovietskoe Radio Publishing Co., Moscow, 1976 (in Russian).

See also:

Ashby, W. R., "Requisite Variety and Its Implications for the Control of Complex Systems," *Cybernetica*, 1 (1953), 83–99.
Porter, B., "Cybernetics and Control Engineering," *J. Dyn. Syst. Meas. Control, Trans. ASME, Ser. G.*, 95 (1973), 349.
Yudin, D. B., and A. P. Goryashko, "Control Problems and Complexity Theory," *Eng. Cybern.* (USSR), 14 (1976), No. 3.

## Interaction levels

Further remarks and examples emphasizing the need to consider interaction levels in a mathematical theory of complexity are given in:

Gottinger, H., "Complexity and Dynamics: Applications of Dynamic System Theory," *IEEE Trans. Syst. Man Cybern.*, SMC 6 (1976), 867–873.
Ashby, W. R., and M. Gardner, "Connectance of Large, Dynamic Cybernetic Systems: Critical Values for Stability," *Nature*, 228 (1970), 784.
Gottinger, H., "Towards an Algebraic Theory of Complexity in Dynamic Systems," *General Systems Yearbook*, XXII (1977), 73–83.

For those readers who are not familiar with the mechanics of the Jordan canonical form of a matrix, two standard references are:

Bellman, R., *Introduction to Matrix Analysis*, McGraw-Hill, New York, 1960.
Gantmacher, F., *Matrix Theory*, Vols. 1 and 2, Chelsea, New York, 1961.

124

## COMPUTATIONAL COMPLEXITY

The theory of computational complexity of algorithms is fairly advanced, compared to a similar theory for large systems. A summary of the current state is found in the books:

Traub, J., ed., *Analytic Computational Complexity*, Academic, New York, 1976.
Karp, R., ed., *Complexity of Computation*, SIAM-AMS Proceedings Vol. 7, American Mathematical Society, Providence, Rhode Island, 1974.

## AXIOMS OF SYSTEMS COMPLEXITY

For a more complete discussion of these axioms, see:

Gottinger, H., "Complexity and Dynamics: Applications of Dynamic System Theory," *IEEE Trans. Syst. Man. Cybern.*, 1976, 867–873.

The following lecture notes should also be consulted.

Rhodes, J., *Applications of Automata Theory and Algebra*, Math. Dept., University of California, Berkeley, 1971.

## CHOICE PROCESSES AND COMPLEXITY

The issue of choice processes and complexity is treated from many different viewpoints in:

Gottinger, H., and W. Leinfellner, eds., *Decision Theory and Social Ethics: Issues in Social Choice*, Reidel, Dordrecht, 1978.

Also of interest in this connection are the papers:

Futia, C., "The Complexity of Economic Decision Rules," Bell Laboratories, Murray Hill, New Jersey, January 1975.
Gottinger, H., "Complexity and Information Technology in Dynamic Systems," *Kybernetes*, 4 (1975), 129–141.

## POLYHEDRAL DYNAMICS AND COMPLEXITY

The results quoted follow:

Casti, J., "Complexity, Connectivity, and Resilience in Complex Ecosystems," in *IFAC Symposium on Bio- and Ecosystems*, Leipzig, Germany, 1977.

## COMPLEXITY AND INFORMATION THEORY

The approach to complexity via information theory follows:

Sahal, D., "System Complexity: Its Conceptions and Measurement in the Design of Engineering Systems," *IEEE Trans. Syst. Man Cybern.*, SMC-6 (1976), 440–445.

125

Alternative views along somewhat the same lines are:

Moshowitz, A., "Entropy and the Complexity of Graphs," *Bull. Math. Biophys.*, 30 (1968), 175–204; 225–240.
Kolmogorov, A., "Three Approaches to the Quantitative Definition of Information," *Prob. Inf. Transmission*, 1 (1965), 1–7.
Cornacchio, J. V., "Maximum Entropy Complexity Measures," *Int. J. Gen. Syst.* 3 (1977), 267–271.

A recent survey summarizing much of the information–theoretic view of complexity is:

Sahal, D., "Elements of an Emerging Theory of Complexity Per Se," *Cybernetica*, 19 (1976), 5–38.

# 5 Stability, Catastrophes, and Resilience

Either the well was very deep, or she fell very slowly, for she had
plenty of time as she went down to look about her, and to wonder
what was going to happen next.
LEWIS CARROLL, *Alice in Wonderland*

Universal Form and Harmony were born of Cosmic Will, and
thence was Night born, and thence the billowy ocean of Space; and
from the billowy ocean of space was born Time—the year ordaining
days and nights, the ruler of every movement.
*Rigveda*, X, 190

You boil it in sawdust: you salt it in glue:
You condense it with locusts and tape:
Still keeping one principal object in view—
To preserve its symmetrical shape.
LEWIS CARROLL, *The Hunting of the Snark*

The most thoroughly cultivated qualitative aspect of large systems historically has been their behavior under various types of external perturbations.
Classically, the perturbations have been assumed to occur in the system's
initial state or in the system's external input, while more recent investiga-
tions have focused upon disturbances in the system structure itself. In either
event, we are interested in knowing whether the behavior of the system will
be substantially altered by unwanted, unknown, or unplanned changes in
operating conditions. When stated in such vague terms, there is little
possibility of saying anything definite (or interesting) about the behavior of
the process; we need to formulate precise questions within a suitable
mathematical framework if progress is to be made.

The aim of the current chapter is to survey some of the major stability
ideas that occupy system theorists and to indicate how various stability
notions arise in practical applications. Since the subject is so vast, we
deliberately deemphasize some of the more classical concepts and concentrate attention upon more modern notions such as resilience, catastrophes,
and pulse processes, referring the reader to the literature for all but the most
basic classical results.

Since we have continually emphasized that a system problem may have
many different, nonequivalent mathematical formulations, stability questions
must also be formulated in corresponding terms. Thus, our presentation will
follow many paths, depending upon the particular description of the problem. Justification for such a seemingly haphazard approach will be found in
the examples that illustrate both application of the theory and the importance of mathematical flexibility in problem formulation.

## EXTERNAL DESCRIPTIONS

For stability considerations, it is most natural to consider the external description of a system in the feedback form

$$e_1 = u_1 - He_2, \qquad (5.1)$$

$$e_2 = u_2 + Ge_1, \qquad (5.2)$$

where the quantities $e_1$, $e_2$, $u_1$, and $u_2$ belong to some extended function space $\tilde{X}$ and where the operators $H$ and $G$ map $\tilde{X}$ into itself.

We can interpret (5.1) and (5.2) as representing the feedback connection

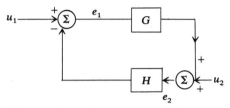

with the operator $G$ being the subsystem in the forward path, $H$ representing the feedback subsystem, and the quantities $u_1$, $u_2$ and $e_1$, $e_2$ being the inputs and errors, respectively. The outputs of the system may be considered to be the quantities $Ge_1$ and $He_2$.

In analyzing Equations (5.1) and (5.2), there are two basic types of questions to be answered, given $u_1$, $u_2$ and some set $U \subseteq \tilde{X}$:

- Does (5.1)–(5.2) have a unique solution in $\tilde{X}$ for $e_1$ and $e_2$ in $\tilde{X}$?
- If (5.1)–(5.2) has any solutions in $\tilde{X}$ for $e_1$, $e_2$ in $\tilde{X}$, do these solutions actually belong to the space $U$?

The first question is that of existence and uniqueness, while the second might be termed the stability problem. Generally speaking, different analytic approaches are used to study these problems, principally techniques from functional analysis.

As an important example of the stability problem, consider the case when $\tilde{X} = U = L_\infty[0, \infty]$, the essentially bounded functions on the half-line. This is the so-called "bounded-input/bounded-output" stability problem, which is of obvious practical interest. Later, we shall present results on this question in terms of properties of the (possibly nonlinear) operators $G$ and $H$.

## INTERNAL DESCRIPTIONS

The most common mathematical description of a dynamical process is a differential equation of the type

$$\dot{x} = f(x, t), \qquad x(0) = c, \qquad (5.3)$$

128

which we have earlier termed an internal description. The classical results of Lyapunov, Poincaré, and others have all been based upon such a description, with the dynamics $f(\cdot, \cdot)$ assuming different forms.

Historically, the first systematic investigation of the stability properties of (5.3) was by Lyapunov, who considered the question: If the origin is an equilibrium point of (5.3), i.e., $f(0, t) =$ for all $t$, and if the system is perturbed by a "small" amount away from the origin ($c \neq 0$), does the future trajectory of the process remain "close" to the origin for all future time? Geometrically, this situation is depicted in Figure 5.1. The basic idea

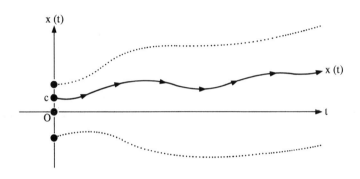

FIGURE 5.1 Lyapunov stability.

is that if the solution starts within a small distance of the origin, it should remain within the slightly larger "tube" indicated by the dotted lines.

A somewhat stronger stability notion would demand that the solution $x(t) \to 0$ as $t \to \infty$, i.e., that the system ultimately return to the equilibrium point. This is the concept of *asymptotic stability* (according to Lyapunov). It is of importance to note that Lyapunov and asymptotic stability are independent concepts, as it is easy to construct examples where one fails and the other holds and vice versa (e.g., the system $\dot{r} = [\dot{g}(\theta, t)/g(\theta, t)]r$, $\dot{\theta} = 0$, where $g(\theta, t) = (\sin^2 \theta/[\sin^4 \theta + (1 - t \sin^2 \theta)^2]) + [1/(1 + t^2)]$ is asymptotically stable but becomes unbounded as the initial state $\theta_0 = \theta(0) \to \pm \pi$—but why?).

As an aside, we observe that the above standard stability issues center upon a *local* neighborhood of an equilibrium point, assumed to be known in advance. Later we shall see that the stability results center upon properties of $f$ in this local neighborhood. Thus, from a practical viewpoint we must calculate all equilibria of $f$ before any of the traditional results may be employed. Such a preliminary calculation may or may not represent a problem, depending upon the structure of $f$. Here we tacitly assume that the equilibria of $f$ are only fixed points. In general, they may be far more complicated objects—limit cycles, vague attractors, and the like.

Associated with each stable equilibrium point is a surrounding open region called its *domain of attraction*. Roughly speaking, the stable equilibrium point acts as a sort of "magnet" to attract any initial state within its domain of attraction (see Figure 2.14).

A substantial part of modern stability theory centers upon how the boundaries and attractor points change as various parts of the system dynamics are changed. In addition, it is of considerable practical importance to be able to describe the boundary of a given equilibrium mathematically. We shall look into some aspects of these questions in later sections.

## STRUCTURAL STABILITY

A feature that characterizes the classical stability notions is that they pertain to *one specific system* and the behavior of its trajectory in the neighborhood of an equilibrium point (attractor or repellor). An entirely different approach is to ask about the behavior of a *family of trajectories* generated by considering all systems "nearby" the nominal system (5.3). In rough terms, (5.3) would be called *structurally stable* if the topological character of the trajectories of all nearby systems are the same as that of (5.3).

An elementary example of the structural stability idea, the damped harmonic oscillator, has already been considered in Chapter 2. Mathematically, difficulties arise in making the notion of a "nearby system" precise, as well as in characterizing what we mean by a trajectory being *equivalent*, or topologically similar, to another trajectory.

Bifurcation theory, and its currently fashionable variant catastrophe theory, is also close in spirit to the structural stability concept. In bifurcation analysis, we generally assume that the system dynamics depend upon some parameters—i.e., $f = f(x, t, a)$, where $a$ is a vector of parameters—and ask about the character of equilibria as the parameters change. For instance, the system

$$\dot{r} = r(a - r^2),$$

$$\dot{\theta} = 1,$$

with $x_1^2 + x_2^2 = r^2$, $\theta = \tan^{-1} x_2/x_1$, has only the equilibrium $r = 0$ for $a < 0$. This equilibrium corresponds to a stable focus (see Figure 5.2). However, for $a > 0$ the equilibrium $r = 0$ becomes an unstable focus and a new equilibrium $r = \sqrt{a}$ emerges. This new equilibrium is a stable limit cycle, with radius growing as $\sqrt{a}$. The point $a = 0$ represents what is termed a Hopf bifurcation point (note the appearance of the center from a stable focus as the parameter $a$ passes through the critical value $a = 0$).

Catastrophe theory addresses the question of when a change in the system parameters causes a given point in phase space to shift from the domain of

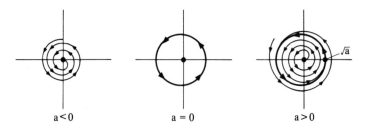

FIGURE 5.2   Hopf bifurcation point.

attraction of a given equilibrium to that of another. The simplest case is one in which all system equilibria are fixed points derivable from a potential function, the so-called "elementary" theory. More complicated equilibria, like periodic orbits or Lorenz attractors, require analysis beyond the scope of this volume. The "catastrophes" occur for those parameter values that cause the system to shift from one attractor region to another. We shall examine these issues in more depth in a later section, which will also make some of the connections between catastrophe theory, bifurcation analysis, and structural stability more precise.

## CONNECTIVE STABILITY AND RESILIENCE

An interesting hybrid stability concept, joining the classical Lyapunov ideas with the combinatorial–topological approach to be described below, is the notion of *connective stability*. Here we are concerned with the question of whether an equilibrium of a given system remains stable (in the Lyapunov sense) irrespective of the binary connection pattern between system states. In other words, we begin with the system (5.3) as before and then define an *interconnection matrix* $E = [e_{ij}]$ such that

$$e_{ij} = \begin{cases} 1, & \text{if variable } x_j \text{ influences } x_i, \\ 0, & \text{otherwise,} \quad i, j = 1, 2, \ldots, n. \end{cases}$$

The equilibrium $x = 0$ is then connectively stable if it is Lyapunov stable for *all* possible interconnection matrices $E$.

Connective stability is of considerable practical interest, since in many processes the presence or absence of a given connection is not always clear because of equipment malfunctioning, model uncertainty, stochastic disturbances, and the like. Such situations are particularly prevalent in models in areas such as economics, biology, and energy. In particular, we shall give a detailed analysis of an ecological problem in a later section, after presentation of the main theoretical results in connective stability.

An aspect of stability that has received considerable attention, especially in ecological circles, is the notion of *resilience*. On an intuitive level, there seems to be a general consensus that resilience is some measure of a system's ability to absorb external disturbances without dramatic consequences for either its transient or steady-state behavior. On the surface, this sounds very much akin to structural stability and, indeed, there is substantial overlap between the two. However, as actually envisioned by practitioners, the concept of resilience is somewhat broader, since a satisfactory resilience measure must somehow combine perturbations to the actual dynamics with disturbances to the trajectory of a fixed process. Unfortunately, the theory is still in its formative stages and only provisional definitions and results are available. A sketch of some of the more interesting ideas will be given below.

## GRAPHS AND PULSE PROCESSES

We have already seen that many interesting systems are profitably modeled by graphs or, more generally, by simplicial complexes. Such representations of complex processes are particularly convenient when the precise numerical relationships between system components required for an internal description are not available. The question arises as to how stability considerations fit into such a framework.

To fix ideas, consider a process described by a signed directed graph $G$. Here $\{u_1, u_2, \ldots, u_N\}$ are the vertices and we assume that each arc of $G$ has either a plus or minus sign attached to it, indicating a positive or negative connection between the vertices of the arc. A simple example of such a signed digraph for electrical energy demand is given in Figure 5.3. For

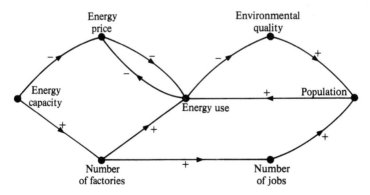

FIGURE 5.3 Signed digraph for electrical energy demand.

example, population increase results in increasing energy use, hence the arc from population to energy use has a plus attached to it. On the other hand, increasing energy use tends to reduce environmental quality, resulting in a minus on the appropriate arc, and so on. Similar graphs have been useful in analyzing a variety of problems in urban transport, naval manpower systems, health care delivery, air pollution, and coastal recreation facilities.

In passing, we note that cycles in a signed digraph correspond to feedback loops; deviation-amplifying cycles are *positive feedback* loops, while deviation-counteracting cycles correspond to *negative feedback* loops. For example, the cycle

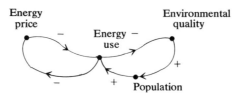

is deviation-counteracting since increased price reduces use, which increases environmental quality, resulting in increased population, which then uses more energy, thereby reducing the price. In general, we note the rule:

*A cycle is deviation-amplifying if and only if it has an even number of minus signs; otherwise, it is deviation-counteracting.*

While the signed digraph is a powerful tool for analyzing many problems, it contains a number of simplifications, the most important being that some effects of variables on others are stronger than other effects. In other words, we need not only a plus or minus on each arc, but also some indication of the numerical strength of the relationship. Thus, we arrive at the notion of a *weighted* digraph, a special case of the weighted relation introduced in the study of simplicial complexes. An even more general concept is to think of each vertex in the graph as having a numerical level and of the strength of connection between two vertices $u_i$ and $u_j$ as being a function $f(u_i, u_j)$. Allowing each vertex to have a time-dependent value leads to the concept of a *pulse process* in $G$.

Denote the value of vertex $u_i$ at time $t$ as $v_i(t)$, $i = 1, 2, \ldots, N$; $t = 0, 1, \ldots$. Assume that the value $v_i(t+1)$ depends upon $v_i(t)$ and upon the vertices adjacent to $u_i$. Thus, if $u_j$ is adjacent to $u_i$ and if $p_j(t)$ represents the change in $u_j$ at time $t$, then the effect of this change on $u_i$ at time $t+1$ will be assumed to be $\pm p_j(t)$, depending upon the sign of the arc joining $u_i$ and $u_j$. More generally, for a weighted digraph we have the rule

$$v_i(t+1) = v_i(t) + \sum_{j=1}^{N} f(u_j, u_i)p_j(t), \tag{5.4}$$

where $f(u_i, u_j)$ denotes the weight of the connection between vertices $u_i$ and $u_j$. A *pulse process* on a digraph $G$ is defined by the rule (5.4), together with the vector of initial vertex values $v(0)$ and the vector $p(0)$ of outside pulses on each vertex at time 0. Of particular importance are the so-called *simple* pulse processes for which $p(0)$ has only one nonzero entry.

While there are many fascinating questions surrounding pulse processes, our considerations in this chapter focus primarily upon stability of both the values and the pulses as the system's history unfolds. More specifically, we say that a vertex $u_i$ is *value stable* if the sequence $\{|v_i(t)|: t = 0, 1, \ldots\}$ is bounded. Similarly, $u_i$ is *pulse stable* if the sequence $\{|p_i(t)|: t = 0, 1, \ldots\}$ is bounded. The weighted digraph is pulse (value) stable if each vertex is. The reader will note the strong similarity in spirit between these stability concepts and the bounded-input/bounded-output stability discussed above for systems given in external form, although the two system descriptions are fundamentally quite different. Before leaving the graph-theoretic issue of pulse and value stability, we should point out that the simple graph

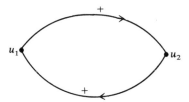

shows that pulse stability does not imply value stability, although the converse is true (why?).

## INPUT–OUTPUT STABILITY

Returning now for a more detailed examination of some questions posed above, we consider the external system description discussed in the section on external descriptions (p. 127). We shall have to use a bit of mathematical terminology to describe our results here. For the reader unversed in Banach and Hilbert spaces, it suffices to consider the space $X$ below to be $R^n$. Our initial concern is to obtain conditions on the operators $G$ and $H$ that ensure that bounded system inputs yield bounded outputs. The basic results in this area fall into two categories: small-gain-type theorems and passivity conditions. These two approaches are just about the only general methods that have proved successful to date for tackling problems of nonlinear feedback stability.

To illustrate the kind of results to be expected, we present the following theorem.

*Small-Gain Theorem.   Let G and H map the extension $\tilde{X}$ of a Banach space X over $[0, \infty]$ into itself. Let $x_T(\cdot)$ denote the truncation of a function $x \in X$ to $[0, T]$. Then the feedback system*

$$e_1 = u_1 - He_2,$$
$$e_2 = u_2 + Ge_1,$$

$$(5.5)$$

*is stable if there exist constants $k_1$, $k_2$, $m_1$, and $m_2$ such that*

$$\|(Gx)_T\| \leq k_1 \|x_T\| + m_1,$$

$$\|(Hx)_T\| \leq k_2 \|x_T\| + m_2$$

*with $k_1 k_2 < 1$. Here $\|\cdot\|$ denotes the norm in X.*

The physical interpretation of this small-gain result is very simple: if $G$ and $H$ correspond to stable subsystems, then if either $G$ or $H$ is sufficiently small with respect to the stability margin of the other system, then the overall feedback system will also be stable. Essentially, the theorem provides an explicit quantitative bound in place of the qualitative phrase "sufficiently small." Specifically, the overall system is stable if the product of the subsystem gains is less than one. In classical feedback terminology, this corresponds to a positive "return difference."

The practical advantage of the small-gain theorem is that the criterion is easy to apply, since the gains $k_1$ and $k_2$ can usually be estimated quite easily. Also, if the condition $k_1 k_2 < 1$ is not satisfied, we can usually determine what sort of "compensation" should be applied in order to make it hold. We should further note that the type of stability that the small-gain theorem ensures depends upon the particular Banach space $X$. Thus, if $X = L_2[0, \infty]$, for example, then satisfaction of the conditions of the theorem guarantees $L_2$-stability. In particular, we capture the bounded-input/bounded-output situation by taking $X = L_\infty[0, \infty]$.

The simplest example of the small-gain theorem is that in which $G$ and $H$ are both linear time-invariant operators, i.e.,

$$(Gx)_T = \int_0^T g(T-s)x(s)\,ds,$$

$$(Hx)_T = \int_0^T h(T-s)x(s)\,ds,$$

in which case it is easy to see that with $X =$ continuous functions on $[0, T]$, the conditions of the theorem will be satisfied if

$$\left(\sup_{0 \leq r \leq T} |g(r)|\right)\left(\sup_{0 \leq r \leq T} |h(r)|\right) < 1.$$

We note, in passing, that when $G$ is a linear time-invariant operator and $H$ is memoryless, the small-gain theorem leads to the circle criterion of Popov.

By restricting the space $X$ to be a Hilbert space, i.e., a Banach space in which the norm $\|\cdot\|$ is derived from an inner product, we can obtain a different stability result.

*Passivity Theorem.* Let $X$ be a real Hilbert space on $[0, \infty]$ with inner product $\langle \cdot, \cdot \rangle$. Then the system (5.5) is stable if there exist constants $k$, $m_1$, $m_2$, $m_3$, $\delta$, and $\varepsilon$ such that

$$\langle (Gx)_T, (Gx)_T \rangle \le k \langle x_T, x_T \rangle + m_1,$$

$$\langle x_T, (Gx)_T \rangle \ge \delta \langle x_T, x_T \rangle + m_2,$$

$$\langle x_T, (Hx)_T \rangle \ge \varepsilon \langle (Hx)_T, (Hx)_T \rangle + m_3,$$

*and*

$$\delta + \varepsilon > 0.$$

In electrical circuit terminology, the physical meaning of the passivity theory is that $u_1$ and $e_1$ are voltage functions, $G$ is an admittance operator, $u_2$ and $e_2$ are current functions, and $H$ is an impedance operator. Then the above inequalities mean that $G$ has a conductance level of at least $\delta$, $H$ has a conductance level of at least $\varepsilon$, and the system is stable if the effective conductance levels of $G$ and $H$ add up to a positive number.

Before moving on to other types of stability results, we note that both the small-gain and passivity theorems provide only *sufficient* conditions for stability of a nonlinear feedback system. Many workers have studied methods for obtaining *instability* criteria, as well as multiplier methods to extend the main ideas sketched above. Since most of these results are too technical for an introductory book of this sort, we shall not elaborate upon them other than to mention their existence and to provide references for the interested analyst.

## INTERNAL MODELS AND STABILITY

Historically, the mathematical, as contrasted with the metaphysical, discussion of stability began with systems of differential equations and addressed the issue of whether a given equilibrium point of the system was stable with respect to perturbations of the initial conditions. Various problems associated with classical mechanics and the stability of planetary orbits (the famous "three-body" problem) gave rise to a number of questions that were finally formalized by the work of Lyapunov, Poincaré, and others around the turn of the century. Since the main issue in Lyapunov-type stability is whether a system will return to a given equilibrium after an arbitrarily long time following an initial disturbance, we present the two most basic results in this direction, referring to the references for the myriad extensions, generalizations, and refinements.

Let us first consider the linear case, when the internal system model is described by the set of differential equations

$$\dot{x} = Fx, \qquad x(0) = x_0 (\neq 0). \tag{5.6}$$

Here $F$ is an $n \times n$ constant matrix, and it is assumed that the characteristic polynomial of $F$ is known as

$$\psi_F(z) = a_0 z^n + a_1 z^{n-1} + \ldots + a_{n-1} z + a_n.$$

We shall be concerned about the asymptotic stability of the equilibrium point $x = 0$.

Since the solution of Equation (5.6) is

$$x(t) = e^{Ft} x_0,$$

it is evident that an arbitrary nonzero initial disturbance $x_0$ will be returned to the origin as $t \to \infty$ if and only if the characteristic roots of $F$ all have negative real parts. As these roots are precisely those of $\psi_F(z)$, we are concerned with the problem of deciding whether the roots of $F$ lie in the left-half plane on the basis of the properties of the coefficients of $\psi_F(z)$.

Such a criterion, developed in the late 1800s by the British mathematicians Routh and Hurwicz, is described in the following theorem.

*Routh–Hurwicz Theorem.* *The polynomial $\psi_F(z)$ has all of its roots with negative real parts if and only if*

1. *All $a_i > 0$, $i = 0, 1, \ldots, n$*
2. *The $n \times n$ array*

$$A = \begin{bmatrix} a_1 & a_0 & 0 & 0 & \ldots & 0 & 0 \\ a_3 & a_2 & a_1 & a_0 & \ldots & 0 & 0 \\ a_5 & a_4 & a_3 & a_2 & \ldots & 0 & 0 \\ \cdot & & & & & \cdot & \cdot \\ \cdot & & & & & \cdot & \cdot \\ \cdot & & & & & \cdot & \cdot \\ 0 & 0 & 0 & 0 & \ldots & a_{n-1} & a_{n-2} \\ 0 & 0 & 0 & 0 & \ldots & 0 & a_n \end{bmatrix}$$

*has only positive leading minors.*

As a result of the Routh–Hurwicz result, it is a relatively straightforward algebraic task to check the stability of the origin for a linear system *if* the characteristic polynomial of $F$ is known. For example, the damped harmonic oscillator, described by the second-order system

$$\ddot{x} + b\dot{x} + cx = 0,$$

$$x(0) = c_1, \qquad \dot{x}(0) = c_2,$$

can easily be seen to generate the array

$$A = \begin{bmatrix} b & 1 \\ 0 & c \end{bmatrix}.$$

Thus, applying the Rough–Hurwicz result, we see that the initial disturbance will "die out" if and only if

1. $b > 0$, $c > 0$
2. $bc > 0$,

i.e., if and only if the "damping" coefficient $b$ performs a positive damping effect (generates friction).

Unfortunately, the requirement that $\psi_F(z)$ be known is a serious obstacle in many cases, especially when the order of the system $n$ is large. It would be preferable in such cases to have a test for stability that could be applied directly to the elements of $F$ itself. Such a procedure was developed by Lyapunov and is based upon the simple physical notion that the equilibrium point of a system is asymptotically stable if all trajectories of the process beginning sufficiently close to the equilibrium point move so as to minimize a suitably defined "energy" function with the local minimal energy position being at the equilibrium point itself.

We first consider application of the preceding idea to the general non-linear equation

$$\dot{x} = f(x), \qquad x(0) = x_0 \tag{5.7}$$

and then specialize to the linear case where $f(x) = Fx$. We make the assumption that $f(0) = 0$ and that the function $f$ is continuous in a neighborhood of the origin.

The mathematical features of an energy function are embodied in the following definition.

*Definition 5.1.* A function $V(x)$ is called a *Lyapunov* (energy) *function* for the system (5.7) if

1. $V(0) = 0$
2. $V(x) > 0$ for all $x \neq 0$ in a neighborhood of the origin
3. $dV(x)/dt < 0$ along trajectories of (5.7)

The basic result of Lyapunov is the celebrated Lyapunov Stability Theorem:

*Lyapunov Stability Theorem. The equilibrium $x = 0$ of the system (5.7) is asymptotically stable if and only if there exists a Lyapunov function $V(x)$ for the system.*

To apply the above result to the linear system (5.6), we choose the candidate Lyapunov function

$$V(x) = (x, Px),$$

where $P$ is an (as yet) unknown symmetric matrix. In order that $V(x)$ be a Lyapunov function for the system, we must have

$$\frac{dV}{dt} = (\dot{x}, Px) + (x, P\dot{x})$$

$$= (x, (F'P + PF)x) < 0.$$

This implies that the equation

$$F'P + PF = -C$$

is solvable for any matrix $C > 0$.

Furthermore, conditions (1) and (2) imply that $P$ must be positive definite. Hence, we have the result that the origin is asymptotically stable for (5.6) if and only if the equation

$$F'P + PF = -C$$

has a solution $P > 0$ for every $C > 0$.

It should not be assumed, however, that the quadratic form chosen for $V(x)$ is the only possibility for a Lyapunov function for the linear system (5.6). To illustrate this point, consider the economic problem of modeling $n$ interrelated markets of $n$ commodities (or services) that are supplied from the same or related industries. If $x(t)$ denotes the vector of commodity prices at time $t$, a classical model for the situation is

$$\dot{x}(t) = Ax(t),$$

where $A = [a_{ij}]$ is an $n \times n$ constant matrix. When all commodities are gross substitutes, $A$ is a Metzler matrix, i.e., $a_{ij}$ satisfies

$$a_{ij} \begin{cases} <0, & i = j \\ \geq 0, & i \neq j. \end{cases}$$

The question of whether or not prices are stable in such a situation was addressed in 1945 by Metzler with the following classic result: "The Metzler system $\dot{x} = Ax$ is stable if and only if the leading minors of $A$ satisfy the condition

$$(-1)^k \det \begin{bmatrix} a_{11} & a_{12} & \cdots & a_{1k} \\ a_{12} & a_{22} & \cdots & a_{2k} \\ \cdot & & & \\ \cdot & & & \\ \cdot & & & \\ a_{k1} & a_{k2} & \cdots & a_{kk} \end{bmatrix} > 0$$

for all $k = 1, 2, \ldots, n$."

The proof of the above result is a consequence of choosing the Lyapunov function

$$V(x) = \sum_{i=1}^{n} d_i |x_i|,$$

with $d_i > 0$, constants to be specified. Suitable choice of the $d_i$, together with the Metzlerian property of $A$ shows that $V(x)$ is indeed a Lyapunov function for the system. Hence, by the Lyapunov stability theorem, the origin is an asymptotically stable equilibrium point of the system.

A class of nonlinear problems to which the Lyapunov stability theorem is especially easy to apply are those in which the nonlinear terms are assumed to be "small" perturbations of a dominant linear part. It is reasonable to suppose, for example, that if the system dynamics are

$$\dot{x} = Fx + h(x), \qquad x(0) = x_0, \tag{5.8}$$

with $F$ a stability matrix (i.e., it has all its characteristic roots in the left-half plane), then the equilibrium $x = 0$ will be asymptotically stable if the initial disturbance $x_0$ and the nonlinear perturbation $h(x)$ are not too large. The mathematical formalization of this intuitively clear result is the following theorem.

*Poincaré–Lyapunov Theorem. Let the system (5.8) satisfy the following conditions:*

1. *$F$ is a stability matrix*
2. *$h(\cdot)$ is a continuous function of $x$ such that $h(0) = 0$ and $\|h(x)\|/\|x\| \to 0$ as $\|x\| \to 0$*
3. *$\|x_0\| \ll 1$.*

*Then the equilibrium $x = 0$ is asymptotically stable.*

One of the difficulties with using the preceding result is condition (3)—the requirement that the initial disturbance be "sufficiently small." How small depends, in general, on the strength of the nonlinearity $h$ and the magnitude of the real part of the characteristic root of $F$ nearest the imaginary axis.

In an attempt to eliminate condition (3) and obtain a sufficient condition for global stability, we must strengthen our hypotheses about the system dynamics. The Russian mathematician Krasovskii provided such a result as follows:

*Krasovskii's Theorem.   The equilibrium solution $x = 0$ of the nonlinear system $\dot{x} = f(x)$ is asymptotically stable in the large if there exists a constant $\varepsilon > 0$ such that the matrix $J(x) + J'(x)$ has characteristic values less than $-\varepsilon$ for all $x$, where $J(x)$ is the Jacobian matrix of the function $f$, i.e.,*

$$[J(x)]_{ij} = \frac{\partial f_i}{\partial x_j}.$$

The proof of Krasovskii's theorem is an easy corollary of the Lyapunov stability theorem using the Lyapunov function $V(x) = (x, (J(x) + J'(x))x)$.

As an illustration of application of the Lyapunov stability theorem, let us consider an RLC electrical circuit with parametric excitation. The dynamics of such a process are described by the equation

$$\ddot{x} + a\dot{x} + b(t)x = 0,$$

where $a > 0$, $b(t) = b_0(1 + f(t))$, $b_0 \geq 0$, and $f(t)$ is a bounded function. Here $x$ is the voltage across the resistor, $a$ the resistance and $b(t)$ is the time-varying capacitance. The above equation is equivalent to the system

$$\dot{x}_1 = x_2$$
$$\dot{x}_2 = -b(t)x_1 - ax_2$$

and we are interested in studying the stability of the equilibrium $x_1 = x_2 = 0$.

Consider the energy function

$$V(x_1, x_2) = \frac{1}{2}\left(x_2 + \frac{ax_1}{2}\right)^2 + \left(\frac{a^2}{4} + b_0\right)\frac{x_1^2}{2}.$$

It is easily verified that

1. $V(x_1, x_2) \geq 0$
2. $V(x_1, x_2) = 0$ if and only if $x_1 = x_2 = 0$
3. $dV/dt = (-a/2)x_2^2 - (b - b_0)x_1x_2 - (ab/2)x_1^2$

Thus, the origin will be asymptotically stable if $dV/dt < 0$ in some neighborhood of the origin. However, this will indeed be the case if for some $\alpha > 0$, we have

$$\varepsilon^2 b_0 f(t)^2 - a^2(1 + \varepsilon f(t)) \leq -\alpha < 0,$$

which will certainly be satisfied if $\varepsilon$ is small enough.

Thus, for sufficiently small $\varepsilon$, we can conclude asymptotic stability of the origin. This result can be interpreted in the following way. There are two opposing forces at work in the problem: a parametric excitation proportional to $\varepsilon$ and a load, the damping force $a\dot{x}$. Satisfying the above inequality amounts to choosing the resistance $a$ large enough for the load to absorb all the energy provided by the excitation. In this case, the origin is stable. If the load is not large enough, we may expect the energy balance of the system to increase and the origin to become unstable.

While there are many more fascinating aspects to the stability problem as outlined above, we can but scratch the surface in a monograph of this size. Thus, we urge the interested reader to consult the chapter references for many more details, while we move on to a discussion of some recent stability concepts that appear to be particularly well suited to systems analysis studies.

## CONNECTIVE STABILITY

In practical problems it is often difficult to specify the system interconnections with total certainty since it is frequently the case that the presence or absence of a direct connection between one subsystem and another cannot be measured or can be measured only with low precision. One approach to the study of such situations is to assume that the connections are random variables, subject to some known distribution functions. Statistical methodology may then be employed to answer various probabalistic questions about the system's dynamical behavior. Here we wish to employ an alternative approach, using no *ad hoc* statistical arguments, to study stability characteristics of systems whose interconnections are not precisely known. As noted in an introductory section, this approach is called "connective" stability.

Consider a dynamical process whose internal description is

$$\dot{x} = A(x, t)x, \qquad x(0) = x_0, \qquad (5.9)$$

where $x$ is the system state vector, $A$ is a continuous matrix function of its arguments for all $t \geq 0$, and all $x \in R^n$. To study the connective aspects of the situation, we write the elements of $A$ as

$$a_{ij}(x, t) = -\delta_{ij}\psi_i(x, t) + e_{ij}\psi_{ij}(x, t),$$

where $\delta_{ij}$ is the Kronecker delta symbol (i.e., $\delta_{ij} = 1$ if $i = j$, 0 otherwise) and the $\psi_i$, $\psi_{ij}$ are continuous functions of their arguments. The elements $e_{ij}$ are the components of the system *connection matrix E* and satisfy

$$e_{ij} = \begin{cases} 1, & \text{if variable } x_j \text{ influences } \dot{x}_i. \\ 0, & \text{otherwise} \end{cases}$$

The concept of connective stability is then given in Definition 5.2.

142

*Definition 5.2.* The equilibrium state $x = 0$ of (5.9) is *connectively asymptotically stable in the large* if and only if it is asymptotically stable in the large for all interconnection matrices $E$.

To obtain practical tests for connective stability, we impose additional conditions on the functions $\psi_i$ and $\psi_{ij}$. Assume that there exist constants $\alpha_i > 0$, $\alpha_{ij} \geq 0$ such that

1. $\psi_i(x, t) \leq \alpha_i$
2. $|\psi_{ij}(x, t)x_j| \leq \alpha_{ij} |x_j|$, $i, j = 1, 2, \ldots, n$

holds for all $x \in R^n$ and all $t \geq 0$.
   Further, define the matrix $\bar{A} = [\bar{a}_{ij}]$ as

$$\bar{a}_{ij} = -\delta_{ij}\alpha_i + e_{ij}\alpha_{ij}, \qquad i, j = 1, 2, \ldots, n.$$

Then we have the following basic result.

*Connective Stability Theorem.* The equilibrium state $x = 0$ of (5.9) is *connectively asymptotically stable in the large* if and only if the matrix $\bar{A}$ satisfies the condition

$$(-1)^k \det \begin{bmatrix} \bar{a}_{11} & \bar{a}_{12} & \cdots & \bar{a}_1 \\ \bar{a}_{21} & \bar{a}_{22} & \cdots & \bar{a}_2 \\ \cdot & & & \\ \cdot & & & \\ \cdot & & & \\ \bar{a}_{k1} & \bar{a}_{k2} & \cdots & \bar{a}_{kk} \end{bmatrix} > 0, \qquad k = 1, 2, \ldots, n.$$

*Remarks*

1. The condition on the principal minors of $\bar{A}$ is referred to as the Sevestyanov–Kotelyanskii condition in the stability theory literature. Economists will recognize the matrix $\bar{A}$ as a Hicks matrix.
   2. If the bounds on $\psi_i$ and $\psi_{ij}$ do not hold for all $x \in R^n$, but only in some region $M \subset R^n$, then we must localize the above result to $M$.

To study the size of the region of connective stability, define the set of numbers $\{d_i\}$ such that

$$|a_{jj}| - d_j^{-1} \sum_{i=j} d_i |a_{ij}| \geq \varepsilon > 0.$$

Also, let the number $\{u_i\}$ be such that

$$M \supset \{x \varepsilon R^n : |x_i| < u_i, i = 1, 2, \ldots, n\},$$

i.e., the $u_i$ define a hypercube in $R^n$ contained in $M$.

In terms of the above quantities, it can be shown that the region

$$\left\{ x \varepsilon R^n : \sum_{i=1}^{n} d_i |x_i| < \min_i d_i u_i \right\}$$

is a region of connective asymptotic stability for the system (5.9).

Thus, in rough terms, we see that obtaining the largest region of connective stability is equivalent to finding numbers $d_i$ satisfying the above inequality such that the smallest $d_i$ is as large as possible.

As an indication of the use of the connective stability theorem, we consider the following model of a four-species predator–prey problem. The dynamical equations are

$$\dot{x}_1 = a_1 x_1 + b_1 x_1 x_2 - D_1(x_1) + D_3(x_3),$$

$$\dot{x}_2 = a_2 x_2 + b_2 x_2 x_1 - D_2(x_2) + D_4(x_4),$$

$$\dot{x}_3 = a_3 x_3 + b_3 x_3 x_4 - D_3(x_3) + D_1(x_1),$$

$$\dot{x}_4 = a_4 x_4 + b_4 x_4 x_3 - D_4(x_4) + D_2(x_3),$$

where the variable $x_i(t)$ represents the population of the $i$th species, $D_i(x_i)$ is the dispersal rate for the $i$th species, and the $a$'s and $b$'s are constants. It is physically reasonable to assume that the functional forms for the $D_i(\cdot)$ are

$$D_i(x_i) = x_i f_i(x_i),$$

which we shall assume for the remainder of our analysis. Our goal will be to determine conditions on the constants $a_i$, $b_i$ and the functions $f_i(x_i)$ that ensure connective stability of the origin.

Under the structural assumption on $D_i(x_i)$, the system dynamics assume the form (5.9), with

$$A(x, t) =$$

$$\begin{bmatrix} a_1 + b_1 x_2 - f_1(x_1) & 0 & f_3(x_3) & 0 \\ 0 & a_2 + b_2 x_1 - f_2(x_2) & 0 & f_4(x_4) \\ f_1(x_1) & 0 & a_3 + b_3 x_4 - f_3(x_3) & 0 \\ 0 & f_2(x_2) & 0 & a_4 + b_4 x_3 - f_4(x_4) \end{bmatrix}$$

Thus, the interconnection matrix for the problem is

$$E = \begin{bmatrix} 1 & 0 & 1 & 0 \\ 0 & 1 & 0 & 1 \\ 1 & 0 & 1 & 0 \\ 0 & 1 & 0 & 1 \end{bmatrix},$$

while the functions $\psi_i$ and $\psi_{ij}$ are

$$\psi_1 = -(a_1 + b_1 x_2 - f_1(x_1)), \qquad \psi_2 = -(a_2 + b_2 x_1 - f_2(x_2)),$$

$$\psi_3 = -(a_3 + b_3 x_4 - f_3(x_3)), \qquad \psi_4 = -(a_4 + b_4 x_3 - f_4(x_4)),$$

$$\psi_{13} = f_3(x_3), \qquad\qquad\qquad \psi_{24} = f_4(x_4),$$

$$\psi_{31} = f_1(x_1), \qquad\qquad\qquad \psi_{42} = f_2(x_2),$$

all other $\psi_{ij} = 0$.

To apply the theorem, we must first find constants $\alpha_i$, $\alpha_{ij} \geq 0$ such that

$$a_1 + b_1 x_2 - f_1(x_1) \leq -\alpha_1 < 0,$$

$$a_2 + b_2 x_1 - f_2(x_2) \leq -\alpha_2 < 0,$$

$$a_3 + b_3 x_4 - f_3(x_3) \leq -\alpha_3 < 0,$$

$$a_4 + b_4 x_3 - f_4(x_4) \leq -\alpha_4 < 0,$$

$$|f_1(x_1)| \leq \alpha_{31}, \qquad |f_2(x_2)| \leq \alpha_{42},$$

$$|f_3(x_3)| \leq \alpha_{13}, \qquad |f_4(x_4)| \leq \alpha_{24}.$$

The Hicks conditions of the connective stability theorem will then be satisfied if and only if

1. $\alpha_1 > 0$,
2. $\alpha_1 \alpha_2 > 0$,
3. $\alpha_1 \alpha_3 > \alpha_{13} \alpha_{31}$,
4. $\alpha_1 \alpha_2 \alpha_3 \alpha_4 + \alpha_{13} \alpha_{31} \alpha_{24} \alpha_{42} > \alpha_1 \alpha_3 \alpha_{24} \alpha_{42} + \alpha_2 \alpha_4 \alpha_{13} \alpha_{31}$.

Thus, conditions (1)–(4) define a region in the $(x_1, x_2, x_3, x_4)$ state space for which the origin is asymptotically stable for all perturbing $f_i$ (i.e., for all dispersal rates) and all $a_i$, $b_i$. Further results and extensions of the above analysis can be found in the papers cited in the chapter references.

## HOPF BIFURCATIONS

The connective stability results provide criteria that system parameters must satisfy if the equilibrium at the origin is to be asymptotically stable for all interconnections between various subsystems. However, when one of the system parameters varies to a critical level so that the basic theorem no longer applies, it is natural to inquire as to what type of transformation of the origin such a parameter change represents. Basically, we are concerned with those critical values of the sytem parameters at which the equilibrium point changes its qualitative character (e.g., attractor → center, attractor → repellor).

In the simplest possible version of such a "bifurcation" problem, only one parameter is allowed to vary. We have already seen an example of this type of problem above where we briefly considered the concept of structural stability. The principal result for such classes of problems was given by Hopf in the 1940s, following up on earlier work of Andronov and Poincaré. We shall consider the two-dimensional case, where the system dynamics are

$$\dot{x}_1 = f_1(x_1, x_2, \mu), \qquad x_1(0) = x_1^0$$
$$\dot{x}_2 = f_2(x_1, x_2, \mu), \qquad x_2(0) = x_2^0.$$

The $n$-dimensional case is slightly more complicated, but the main results remain basically unchanged.

The main result telling us about the changes in system stability behavior as $\mu$ varies is the Hopf bifurcation theorem.

*Hopf Bifurcation Theorem (in $R^2$). Assume that the functions $f_1$ and $f_2$ are at least four times differentiable in each argument and that $f_1(0, 0, \mu) = f_2(0, 0, \mu) = 0$ for all real $\mu$. Further, assume that the matrix*

$$J(f) = \begin{bmatrix} \dfrac{\partial f_1}{\partial x_1} & \dfrac{\partial f_1}{\partial x_2} \\ \dfrac{\partial f_2}{\partial x_1} & \dfrac{\partial f_2}{\partial x_2} \end{bmatrix}_{(x_1, x_2) = (0, 0)}$$

*has two distinct, complex conjugate characteristic values $\lambda(\mu)$ and $\bar{\lambda}(\mu)$ such that for $\mu > 0$, Re $\lambda(\mu) > 0$. Also, assume*

$$\frac{d}{d\mu}[\text{Re}\,(\lambda(\mu))]\big|_{\mu=0} > 0.$$

*Then:*

1. *There is a twice-differentiable function $\mu: (-\varepsilon, \varepsilon) \to R$ such that the initial point $(x_1^0, 0, \mu(x_1^0))$ is on a closed orbit of period $2\pi/|\lambda(\mu)|$ with radius growing as $\sqrt{\mu}$ for $x_1^0 \neq 0$, $\mu(0) = 0$.*
2. *There is a neighborhood $U$ of $(0, 0, 0)$ in $R^3$ such that any closed orbit in $U$ is one of the above.*
3. *Furthermore, if $0$ is an attractor when $\mu = 0$, then $\mu(x_1^0) > 0$ for all $x_1^0 \neq 0$ and the orbits are attracting.*

*Remark* A closed orbit in $R^2$ is any point $x^*$ such that $x(t) = x(t+T) = x^*$ for some $T > 0$. In particular, equilibrium points are closed orbits.

The Hopf theorem shows that the system trajectories may change character as $\mu$ departs from 0 and that the type of change depends upon the real part of the characteristic value of the system Jacobian matrix $J(f)$ at the origin. Conclusion (1) simply states that an equilibrium at the origin will "bifurcate" into a closed orbit of a certain size proportional to $\sqrt{\mu}$. If the origin was an attracting fixed point when $\mu = 0$, then conclusion (2) states that in a sufficiently small neighborhood of the origin (in $x_1 - x_2 - \mu$ space), the closed orbit that arises out of the fixed point will itself be attracting.

In short, the Hopf bifurcation theorem is concerned with the birth of closed orbits from fixed-point equilibria and the resultant dynamical behavior as the parameter $\mu$ passes through the critical value $\mu = 0$. For the planar system considered here, the closed orbits can only represent periodic solutions to the system under study. In higher dimensions, the situation is far more complex.

*Example: Lienard's Equation* A well-known nonlinear differential system that often occurs in simple models of oscillatory phenomena, such as population dynamics or electrical circuits, is the simple Lienard-type equation

$$\dot{x}_1 = x_2,$$
$$\dot{x}_2 = -x_1 + \mu x_2 - x_2^3.$$

We study this equation as the parameter $\mu$ varies from negative to positive values.

We easily verify that the origin $x_1 = x_2 = 0$ is an equilibrium point of the system for all $\mu$. Furthermore,

$$J(f) = \begin{bmatrix} 0 & 1 \\ -1 & \mu - 3x_2^2 \end{bmatrix}$$
$$= \begin{bmatrix} 0 & 1 \\ -1 & \mu \end{bmatrix}$$

at $x_1 = x_2 = 0$. The characteristic values of $J$ are

$$\tfrac{1}{2}[\mu \pm \sqrt{\mu^2 - 4}].$$

Consider values of $\mu$ such that $|\mu| < 2$. In this case $\lambda(\mu) \neq 0$. Further, for $-2 < \mu < 0$, $\operatorname{Re} \lambda(\mu) < 0$, for $\mu = 0$, $\operatorname{Re} \lambda(\mu) = 0$, and for $0 < \mu < 2$, $\operatorname{Re} \lambda(\mu) > 0$. Also,

$$\frac{d}{d\mu} \operatorname{Re} \lambda(\mu)\big|_{\mu=0} = \tfrac{1}{2} > 0.$$

Thus, all conditions for the Hopf bifurcation theorem apply and we conclude that there is a one-parameter family of closed orbits in a neighborhood of the origin.

To find out whether these orbits are stable and if they occur for $\mu > 0$, we must employ techniques beyond the scope of this book since the origin is not an attracting fixed point; hence, conclusion (c) of the theorem does not apply. As it turns out, however, for this equation, the periodic orbits are indeed attracting and bifurcation does take place for $\mu > 0$.

We note that a minor extension of this example also covers the general Van der Pol equation

$$\ddot{u} + f(u, \mu)\dot{u} + g(u) = 0,$$

through the change of variable $x_1 = u$, $x_2 = \dot{u} + f(u, \mu)$. Here we convert the Van der Pol equation to the general Lienard equation

$$\dot{x}_1 = x_2 - f(x, \mu)$$
$$\dot{x}_2 = -g(x_1),$$

which can also be handled by the Hopf theorem. Hence, we can conclude that the Van der Pol equation also has stable oscillations for $\mu > 0$ arising from the bifurcation of a fixed point at the origin.

## STRUCTURALLY STABLE DYNAMICS

A vital part of the analysis of a differential equation model of a dynamical process is the decision as to whether small perturbations of the system dynamics can result in qualitatively different behaviors. We have already noted this problem as that of *structural stability*. In this section, we wish to present some elementary results characterizing structurally stable systems. Since all mathematical models of physical phenomena contain simplifications, errors, and other departures from reality, the importance of structural stability as a cornerstone for effective modeling cannot be overemphasized.

We consider the two dynamical processes

$$\dot{x}_1 = F_1(x_1, x_2),$$
$$\dot{x}_2 = F_2(x_1, x_2),$$
\qquad\qquad (I)

$$\dot{x}_1 = G_1(x_1, x_2),$$
$$\dot{x}_2 = G_2(x_1, x_2),$$
\qquad\qquad (II)

defined in the disc $D: x_1^2 + x_2^2 \leq 1$. Further, we assume that the vectors $(F_1, F_2)$ and $(G_1, G_2)$ are not tangent to the boundary of $D$ and that they always point to the interior of $D$. The original definition of structural stability of the system (I) was given by Pontryagin and Andronov in the following form:

*Definition 5.3.* The differential equation (I) is said to be *structurally stable* if there is a $\delta > 0$ such that whenever the differential equation (II) is such that

$$|F_i - G_i| < \delta, \qquad \left|\frac{\partial(F_i - G_i)}{\partial x_j}\right| < \delta, \qquad i, j = 1, 2$$

at all points in $D$, then there is a homeomorphism (1–1, onto, continuous) $h: D \to D$, which maps trajectories of (I) onto trajectories of (II) and preserves the orientation of these trajectories.

In other words, (I) is structurally stable when, for (I) and (II) close enough, the trajectories of (I) can be continuously deformed onto those of (II), preserving the direction of the flow.

To give practical conditions for testing the structural stability of a given equation, we need a few other notions.

*Definition 5.4.* A *singularity* of the differential equation (I) is a point $(x_1^*, x_2^*)$ such that $F_1(x_1^*, x_2^*) = F_2(x_1^*, x_2^*) = 0$. The singularity is called *hyperbolic* if the characteristic values of the matrix

$$J = \begin{bmatrix} \dfrac{\partial F_1}{\partial x_1} & \dfrac{\partial F_1}{\partial x_2} \\[2ex] \dfrac{\partial F_2}{\partial x_1} & \dfrac{\partial F_2}{\partial x_2} \end{bmatrix}_{(x_1^*, x_2^*)}$$

have nonzero real part. A hyperbolic singularity may be a *sink, saddle point,* or *source*, depending upon whether $J$ has 2, 1, or 0 characteristic roots with negative real part.

In the neighborhood of a hyperbolic singularity, the system trajectories can look like one of the following:

Sink          Saddle point          Source

Finally, consider a closed orbit $\gamma$ of the differential equation (I). Through a point $p$ on $\gamma$ we pass a small line segment $\sigma$ transversal to the trajectory along the orbit (see Figure 5.4.). Following trajectories of (I) through points

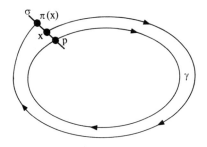

FIGURE 5.4   The Poincaré map.

$x$ on $\sigma$, we get the *Poincaré map* $\pi$

$$\pi : \sigma \to \sigma$$

defined for all $x \in \sigma$ sufficiently close to $p$.

Analogous to the definition of a hyperbolic singularity, we have the notion of a hyperbolic closed orbit.

*Definition 5.5.*   The closed orbit $\gamma$ is said to be *hyperbolic* if $|d\pi/dx|_{x=p} \neq 1$.

Note that when $|d\pi/dx|_{x=p} < 1$, then $\gamma$ is a stable limit cycle and the trajectories spiral toward $\gamma$. If $|d\pi/dx|_{x=p} > 1$, then $\gamma$ is an unstable limit cycle, and if $|d\pi/dx|_{x=p} = 1$, all trajectories near $\gamma$ are closed.

With the foregoing definitions in hand, we can finally state the basic result of Andronov and Pontryagin.

*Structural Stability Theorem (in the disc).*   *The differential equation* (I) *is structurally stable if and only if*

1. *The singularities of* (I) *are hyperbolic.*
2. *The closed orbits of* (I) *are hyperbolic.*
3. *No trajectory of* (I) *connects saddle points.*

Note that condition (1) implies that there are only a finite number of singularities, while (2) and (3) together imply there are only a finite number of closed orbits.

In Figure 5.5 we show that phase portrait of two differential systems, one that is structurally stable and one that is not. However, we emphasize that it is never possible to guarantee that a differential equation is structurally stable just by looking at its phase portrait. For example, assume that the origin is one of the singularities of a structurally stable system (I), while the system (II) obtained by multiplying both components of (I) by $(x_1^2 + x_2^2)$ has

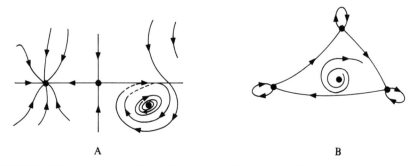

FIGURE 5.5  A, Structurally stable system; B, structurally unstable system.

exactly the same phase portrait but fails to be structurally stable since at the origin the singularity of (II) is not hyperbolic (both characteristic roots are zero).

*Example: Classical Lotka–Volterra System*  The prototypical model for a deterministic one-predator/one-prey system with continuous growth is the Lotka–Volterra system

$$\frac{dH}{dt} = H(t)[a - \alpha P(t)],$$

$$\frac{dP}{dt} = P(t)[-b + \beta H(t)],$$

where $H(t)$ and $P(t)$ are the populations of prey and predators, respectively, while the parameters $a$ and $b$ relate to the birth and death rates of $H$ and $P$. The parameters $\alpha$ and $\beta$ account for the interaction between species. For obvious physical reasons, we confine our attention to the region $H \geq 0$, $P \geq 0$, and all parameters are positive. (We recapture the setting of the structural stability theorem by suitably scaling $H$ and $P$ to lie within that part of the unit disc in the first quadrant.)

The physically interesting system equilibrium point is

$$H^* = b/\beta, \qquad P^* = a/\alpha.$$

Evaluating the Jacobian matrix

$$J = \begin{bmatrix} a - \alpha P & -\alpha H \\ \beta P & -b + \beta H \end{bmatrix}$$

at $(H^*, P^*)$, we find that the characteristic values of $J$ at the singularity are the purely imaginary numbers

$$\lambda = \pm i(ab)^{1/2}.$$

Thus, the singularity is *not* hyperbolic. Consequently, the classical Lotka–Volterra model is not structurally stable, as condition (1) of the theorem is violated.

In some intuitive discussions of structural stability, one sees the statement that "a system is structurally stable if all nearby systems exhibit the same qualitative behavior." The preceding example shows that once we make the notions of "nearby," "same," "qualitative," and "behavior" precise, the concept takes on a slightly different look, since all trajectories of the system are closed orbits, with the equilibrium point $(H^*, P^*)$ being topologically a center. Furthermore, any nearby system arising out of a change in the system parameters $a$, $b$, $\alpha$, $\beta$ will exhibit exactly the same sort of behavior. Thus, on intuitive grounds we may be led to conclude that the system is structurally stable. It is geometrically clear, however, that the trajectories of nearby systems cannot be continuously mapped onto each other; hence, the system is not structurally stable according to Definition 5.3, and this is borne out, of course, in the fact that the system singularities are not all hyperbolic. The moral is that intuitive notions and precise definitions do not always mix, and when doing mathematics we must stick to the definitions. The above case suggests that a different definition of structural stability may be in order.

For a time it was hoped that structural stability would be a property shared by almost all differential systems (that is, that the structurally stable systems would form an open, dense set in the set of all systems). This, in fact, is the case in dimension one or two. However, Smale and Williams have shown that the reverse is true in higher dimensions, so there is no general assurance that unstable systems can be arbitrarily closely approximated by structurally stable ones if the phase space is of dimension $n \geq 3$. Fortunately though, there do exist broad classes of $n$-dimensional systems for which structural stability can be established. The simplest and best known are Morse–Smale differential systems which exhibit only a finite number of singularities and closed orbits. Others, like the Anosov systems, have a very complicated geometrical structure due to the fact that they possess infinitely many closed orbits. An account of these systems will be given in a later section.

## CATASTROPHE THEORY

A facet of the structural stability–bifurcation theory circle of questions that has attracted much recent attention and publicity is "catastrophe" theory. Basically, the theory may be interpreted as a partial answer to the question: In a $k$-parameter family of functions, which local types do we typically meet? The same mathematical machinery also addresses the converse question: Given a function, what does a family that contains it look like, close to the given function?

The importance of the above questions for practical model building follows from the fundamental assumption underlying the use of elementary catastrophe theory, namely, that the system under investigation is goal-oriented, even if the analyst is not aware of precisely what the goal may be. In short, the system is governed by gradient-type dynamics and is attempting to minimize (locally) some cost function. If the decision maker has $k$ control parameters $\alpha_1, \alpha_2, \ldots, \alpha_k$, at his disposal, the system outputs will assume those steady-state values $x_1^*, x_2^*, \ldots, x_n^*$ such that some function

$$f(x_1, x_2, \ldots, x_n; \alpha_1, \alpha_2, \ldots, \alpha_k)$$

is locally minimized. By analogy with classical mechanics, the function $f$ is termed a *potential* (or *energy*) function for the system. In general, the steady-state values $x_i^*$ will depend upon the choice of the parameters $\alpha$, hence

$$x_i^* = x_i^*(\alpha), \qquad i = 1, 2, \ldots, n,$$

and the idea of "catastrophe" enters when we consider a discontinuous change in the values of $x_i^*$ as a result of a smooth change in the controls $\alpha$.

Clearly, there are infinitely many systems of the above type (one for each function $f$). However, many of these become the same if we make a change of coordinates in the space of input and output variables $\alpha$ and $x$. The easiest way to weed out insignificant changes is to concentrate on those properties of energy functions that are topological only (actually, we allow only smooth, i.e., infinitely differentiable, functions $f$ and smooth coordinate changes). The basic theorem of catastrophe theory, that of Thom, then enables us to classify all smooth potential functions topologically. As we shall see, the most remarkable feature of this theorem is that the classification depends only upon the number of control variables $k$ (assuming that it is finite).

The importance of Thom's theorem for applications is that, in general, we do not know the relevant function $f$; we only assume that the system dynamics are governed by such a potential. Then, the theorem justifies our consideration of one of a small, finite number of "canonical" potentials as models for the process, safe in the knowledge that the "true" function $f$, whatever it may be, differs from the canonical model only by coordinate changes. In addition, the theorem guarantees structural stability of the canonical model. Hence, the true model must exhibit the same topological character as the canonical model. Before giving a statement and discussion of Thom's result, let us examine a simple special case.

Consider the family of functions in $R^2$ depending upon a single parameter

$\alpha \in R$, given by

$$f(x_1, x_2; \alpha) = x_1^3 - \alpha x_1 - x_2^2.$$

The critical points of $f$ are located at $x_1^*(\alpha)$, $x_2^*(\alpha)$ and are defined by the equations

$$\frac{\partial f}{\partial x_1} = 3x_1^2 - \alpha = 0, \qquad \frac{\partial f}{\partial x_2} = -2x_2 = 0.$$

Thus, the manifold of critical points, $M_f$, lies in the plane $x_2 = 0$ along the curve $3x_1^2 - \alpha = 0$ in the $(x_1, \alpha)$-plane in $R^3$. We examine the critical points of $x_1^3 - \alpha x_1$ for various values of $\alpha$.

As depicted in Figure 5.6, there are two critical points of $x_1^3 - \alpha x_1$ for $\alpha > 0$: a parabolic-type maximum where $x_1$ is negative and a parabolic-type

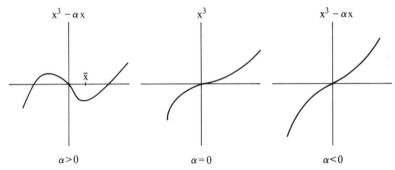

FIGURE 5.6   Behavior of $x^3 - \alpha x$ for various $\alpha$ values.

minimum at some point $\bar{x} > 0$. As $\alpha$ decreases, these two critical points merge into a single degenerate cubic critical point when $\alpha = 0$, and thereafter there are no critical points of $x_1{}^3 - \alpha x_1$ for $\alpha < 0$.

The projection of $M_f$ into the $\alpha$ space

$$\psi: M_f \to R^k$$

$$(x^*(\alpha), \alpha) \mapsto \alpha$$

is called the *catastrophe* map of the family $f(x; \alpha)$. For most values of $\alpha$, $M_f$ provides a local covering of the control space $R^k$, perhaps with several sheets. However, where $\psi$ is singular, the number of sheets can change abruptly. That is, there is a *coalescence* or *bifurcation* of critical points of $f$ at some value $\alpha = \hat{\alpha}$. Such a singular point is called a *catastrophe* point of family $f(x; \alpha)$.

In the above example, it is clear that $f(x_1, x_2; \alpha) = x_1^3 - \alpha x_1 - x_2^2$ has a catastrophe point at $\hat{\alpha} = 0$. It is important to note that any small perturbation of $f$ yields a new function family $\tilde{f}(x_1, x_2; \alpha)$ which must necessarily have a catastrophe point somewhere near $\hat{\alpha} = 0$, and near the catastrophe $M_{\tilde{f}}$ has the same qualitative nature in its covering of the $\alpha$-axis as does $M_f$ near $\hat{\alpha} = 0$. This situation, the "fold" catastrophe, is depicted in Figure 5.7.

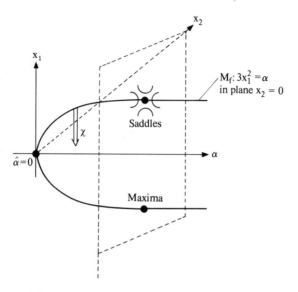

FIGURE 5.7   The fold catastrophe.

We are now ready to state the main theorem of catastrophe theory as discovered by Thom and clarified and elaborated by E. Zeeman:

*Thom–Zeeman Theorem.   For each $k \leq 5$ and $n \geq 1$ there is an open, dense set of $C^\infty$-potential functions $\mathcal{F}$ such that*

1. *$M_f$ is a differentiable $k$-manifold smoothly embedded in $R^{n+k}$.*
2. *Each singularity of the catastrophe map $\psi: M_f \rightarrow R^k$ is locally equivalent to one of a finite number of standard types called elementary catastrophes. The number of types is*

| $k$ | 1 | 2 | 3 | 4 | 5 | $\geq 6$ |
|---|---|---|---|---|---|---|
| No. of types | 1 | 2 | 5 | 7 | 11 | $\infty$ |

.

3. *The map $\psi$ is structurally stable at each point of $M_f$ with regard to small perturbations of $f$ in $\mathcal{F}$. Further, there exists a canonical form for $f(x; \alpha)$ near each point $(x^*, \alpha) \in M_f$ as given in Table 5.1.*

*Remarks*

1. Here $C^\infty$-equivalence of two maps means that if

$$\psi: M \rightarrow N, \qquad \psi': M' \rightarrow N',$$

TABLE 5.1   Canonical Forms for $f(x;\alpha)$

| $k$ | $n$ | Canonical Form for $f(x;\alpha)$ | Name |
|---|---|---|---|
| 1 | 1 | $x_1^3 + \alpha x_1$ | Fold |
| 2 | 1 | $x_1^4 + \alpha_1 \dfrac{x_1^2}{2} + \alpha_2 x_1$ | Cusp |
| 3 | 1 | $\dfrac{x_1^5}{5} + \alpha_1 \dfrac{x_1^3}{3} + \alpha_2 \dfrac{x_1^2}{2} + \alpha_3 x_1$ | Swallowtail |
| 4 | 1 | $\dfrac{x_1^6}{6} + \alpha_4 \dfrac{x_1^4}{4} + \alpha_1 \dfrac{x_1^3}{3} + \alpha_2 \dfrac{x_1^2}{2} + \alpha_3 x$ | Butterfly |
| 3 | 2 | $x_1^3 + x_2^3 + \alpha_3 x_1 x_2 - \alpha_1 x_1 - \alpha_2 x_2$ | Hyperbolic umbilic |
| 3 | 2 | $x_1^3 - 3x_1 x_2^2 + \alpha_3(x_1^2 + x_2^2) - \alpha_1 x_1 - \alpha_2 x_2$ | Elliptic umbilic |
| 4 | 2 | $x_1^2 x_2 + x_2^4 + \alpha_3 x_1^2 + \alpha_4 x_2^2 - \alpha_1 x_1 - \alpha_2 x_2$ | Parabolic umbilic |
| 5 | 1 | $x_1^7 + \alpha_1 x_1^5 + \alpha_2 x_1^4 + \alpha_3 x_1^3 + \alpha_4 x_1^2 + \alpha_5 x_1$ | Wigwam |
| 5 | 2 | $x_1^2 x_2 - x_2^5 + \alpha_1 x_2^3 + \alpha_2 x_2^2$ $+ \alpha_3 x_1^2 + \alpha_4 x_2 + \alpha_5 x_1$ | Second elliptic umbilic |
| 5 | 2 | $x_1^2 x_2 + x_2^5 + \alpha_1 x_2^3 + \alpha_2 x_2^2$ $+ \alpha_3 x_1^2 + \alpha_4 x_2 + \alpha_5 x_1$ | Second hyperbolic umbilic |
| 5 | 2 | $1 \pm (x_1^3 + x_2^3 + \alpha_1 x_1 x_2^2 + \alpha_2 x_2^2$ $+ \alpha_3 x_1 x_2 + \alpha_4 x_2 + \alpha_5 x_1)$ | Symbolic umbilic |

then $\psi$ and $\psi'$ are *equivalent* if there exist diffeomorphisms (1–1, onto, $C^\infty$) $h$ and $k$ such that

$$k^{-1}\psi'h = \psi.$$

2. Roughly speaking, structural stability of $\psi$ at each point of $M_f$ means that given a point of $M_f$, there is some neighborhood of $f$ in $\mathscr{F}$ such that each function in the neighborhood has a catastrophe map that is equivalent to $\psi_f$.

3. The infinite number of nonequivalent catastrophe maps for $k \geq 6$ may be eliminated by a weaker notion of equivalence. However, the finite, $C^\infty$-classification for small $k$ is most important in practice and is mathematically the most appropriate setting for the problem.

## SOME CATASTROPHE-THEORETIC EXAMPLES

To illustrate the wide range of potential applications of the preceding theorem, we present several examples in this section, from both the physical and the social sciences.

### URBAN PROPERTY PRICES

An increasingly evident problem in many urban areas is the rapid increase in property prices, particularly for residential housing. Here we discuss a simplified model of this process, using catastrophe theory to help model the observed discontinuities of the property price cycle.

Let $r$ represent the real rate of change of housing prices in a particular urban market. In the first approximation, we assume that there are two types of buyers who are interested in this sort of property and that the combined level of their activities in the property market dictates $r$. Call these buyers *consumers* and *speculators*. The former are interested in a wide range of attributes of the housing bundle and their demand is strongly price-elastic, especially in volatile or cyclical markets. Speculators, on the other hand, are overwhelmingly concerned with short-term (and often highly leveraged) capital gains. Since the two groups have fundamentally different objectives, time horizons, and price elasticities, they may reasonably be thought of as disjoint sets of investors. If $D_c$ represents the demand for property by consumers and $D_s$ the demand by speculators, then the global behavior of property prices may in this simple case be as depicted in Figure 5.8.

Increasing either $D_c$ or $D_s$ tends to increase $r$, but the key to catastrophic rises and falls lies with the speculators: changes in $D_c$ for constant $D_s$ cause only smooth changes in $r$. Suppose the process starts at $O$ in the $D_c$–$D_s$ space. There are then two possibilities for passage through the cusp region and back to $O$, the paths $OPQRO$ and $OPQSO$. The first corresponds to a spurt of speculative demand causing, after a short lag, a jump in prices from $P$ to $Q$, followed by a profit-taking sell-off by speculators with only moderate increase in consumer demand, triggering a collapse of prices at $R$. This sort of process is characteristic of the high-frequency components of $r$ and is quite typical in speculative markets. The demand by consumers for market intervention is related to both the magnitude of $r$ and the amplitude of these relatively short-term "boom-and-bust" cycles. Slowing the frequency of the $OPQRO$ cycle may be an appropriate response under such conditions, if it allows $D_c$ to build up sufficiently at $Q$ to drive the return path around the cusp through $S$. Rapid and distressing falls in price are thus avoided. This observation illustrates, if crudely, the fast-time/slow-time behavior divergence that is characteristic of dynamic catastrophe-theoretic models.

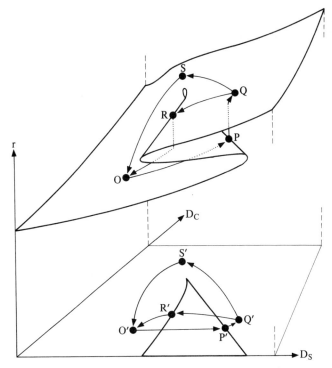

FIGURE 5.8 Catastrophe manifold for urban property prices.

Governments interested in orderliness and stability in housing markets—
low and viscous $r$—usually regulate $D_c$ and $D_s$ by tightening or loosening
the supply of money—that is, by raising or lowering interest rates. We now
show how the butterfly catastrophe, a generalization of the cusp, enables us
to upgrade the urban property price example by including time dependence
as well as interest rate changes in the catastrophe manifold. It will be seen
that inclusion of these important factors generates the possibility of a third
mode of stable behavior for $r$, a type of "compromise" rate of change of
prices.

For the butterfly $(k = 4, n = 1)$, the canonical form for the potential is
given by

$$f(\alpha, x) = \frac{x^6}{6} + \tfrac{1}{4}\alpha_1 x^4 + \tfrac{1}{3}\alpha_2 x^3 + \tfrac{1}{2}\alpha_3 x^2 + \alpha_4 x,$$

where $\alpha \in R^4$, $x \in R$. The associated catastrophe surface $M$ is the four-
dimensional surface given by

$$\frac{\partial f}{\partial x} = x^5 + \alpha_1 x^3 + \alpha_2 x^2 + \alpha_3 x + a_4 = 0.$$

The surface $M \subset R^5$, and the bifurcation set $\beta \subset R^4$. We draw two-dimensional sections of $\beta$ to show how it generalizes the cusp. When the *butterfly factor* $\alpha_1 > 0$, the $x^4$ term swamps the $x^6$ term and we obtain the cusp. The effect of the *bias* factor $\alpha_2$ is merely to bias the position of the cusp. When the butterfly factor $\alpha_1 < 0$, then the $x^4$ term conflicts with the $x^6$ term and causes the cusp to divide into three cusps enclosing a pocket. This pocket represents the emergence of a compromise behavior midway between the two extremes represented by the upper and lower surfaces of the cusp.

To employ the butterfly catastrophe in the urban property price setting, we let the bias factor represent the interest rate $i$, while the butterfly factor is the negative of time, $-t$. Thus, normalizing the nominal interest rate at $i = 0$, we have the picture given in Figure 5.9.

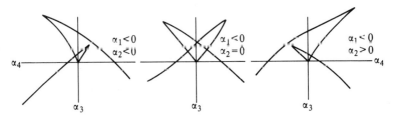

FIGURE 5.9  Two-dimensional sections of the butterfly catastrophe.

Figure 5.10 shows that an increase in speculative demand coupled with a sufficiently high consumer demand will lead to a control space trajectory intersecting the interior pocket of intermediate $r$, rather than resulting in a dramatic jump to the upper or lower surfaces of $M^2$. As the previous diagrams showed, manipulation of the interest rate $i$ influences both the size and position of this pocket of intermediate behavior, thereby theoretically preventing catastrophic jumps or drops in property price rates—but at a price in secular inflation.

LAKE POLLUTION

A problem that often arises is to explain (model) the severe fluctuations during short time periods in phytoplankton biomass in small eutrophic lakes. Here we exhibit a dynamical model of this process utilizing the cusp catastrophe, since several characteristics of observed phytoplankton dynamics suggest the appropriateness of a catastrophe-theoretic model.

We consider the total biomass of all algal species in the lake as the system output variable $x$. In most lakes, and particularly in those in which blue-green algae are dominant, phosphate is the limiting nutrient. Thus, the

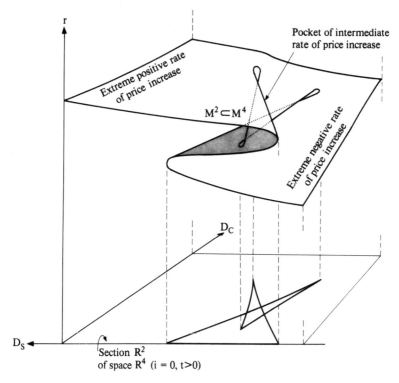

FIGURE 5.10   The butterfly catastrophe.

soluble phosphate concentration will be modeled as one of the control variables, $\alpha_1$. As a surrogate measure of light and temperature in the lake, we consider one of the phytoplankton genera, *Anabaena*. Observations show that algal die-offs are preceded by an accumulation of *Anabaena* on the surface, which is caused by the tendency of that algae to form gas vacuoles and float when exposed to low light intensities. Furthermore, fluctuations in soluble phosphate concentration appear to be inversely correlated with phytoplankton concentration. Thus, we choose our second control variable $\alpha_2$ to be *Anabaena* concentration.

The equation for the change in phosphate concentration is based upon the fact that algae incorporate phosphate at a rate proportional to the concentration of algae during the bloom. When die-off occurs, phosphate is precipitated to the bottom of the pond in the algal cells and is not released until after the bloom–die-off sequence is completed. Thus, the soluble phosphate concentration will exponentially tend to the equilibrium level measured in the pond.

To formulate the equation governing *Anabaena* concentration, we note that *Anabaena* growth rate will be controlled only by the number of *Anabaena* cells present, while the decrease in intrinsic growth rate will also be controlled by the concentration of other algae because of competition for nutrient.

Finally, the equation for the total algal concentration follows from the logistic-type model discussed at greater length in the next section.

Putting the preceding remarks together, and using the canonical cusp equation for the output variable $x$, we obtain the following system of equations to model the process.

$$\dot{x} = -(c_1 x^3 - c_2 \alpha x + c_3 \alpha_2),$$

$$\dot{\alpha}_1 = -c_4 x(\alpha - a_0)$$

$$\dot{\alpha}_2 = c_5 \alpha_1 \alpha_2 - c_6 \alpha_2 x,$$

where $c_1, \ldots, c_6$ are rate constants and $a_0$ is the equilibrium phosphate level.

Using some experimental data obtained on a catfish pond in Alabama (USA), the above equations were numerically integrated to simulate the eutrophication cycle. The constants used were

$c_1 = 3.10 \, (\mu g \, Chl/ml)^{-2}(time)^{-1}, \qquad c_2 = 0.60 \, (\mu g \, P/ml)^{-1}(time)^{-1},$

$c_3 = 0.05 \, (time)^{-1}, \qquad c_4 = 1.00 \, (\mu g \, Chl/ml)^{-1}(time)^{-1},$

$c_5 = 1.35 \, (\mu g \, P/ml)^{-1}(time)^{-1}, \qquad c_6 = 1.95 \, (\mu g \, Chl/ml)^{-1}(time)^{-1},$

$a_0 = 0.$

The initial values were $x_0 = 0.02$, $\alpha_1^0 = 1.28$, $\alpha_2^0 = 0.11$.

The results of the experiment are given in Figures 5.11–5.13. The agreement between the data and the above model is fairly good for *Anabaena* and algal concentration except for the large dip in the fifth time period. This dip corresponds to an increase in average wind velocity (according to the data source) and could be the result of increased vertical or horizontal mixing, thereby removing algal cells from the top layer of the pond at the measuring station. Thus, the simulation provides a deterministic envelope within which such stochastic processes as weather can influence the algal bloom–die-off cycle.

The agreement for soluble phosphate concentration is less exact; the discrepancy between the model and data may have several possible sources. For instance, the measurement of phosphate concentration may have failed to detect dissolved fertilizers because of their location in time and space, as measurements were taken only every 1–3 days and at a single location in the pond. Alternatively, the model may be incorrect and in need of reformulation. Only further experimentation that monitors phosphate concentration more closely will determine the overall validity of the model.

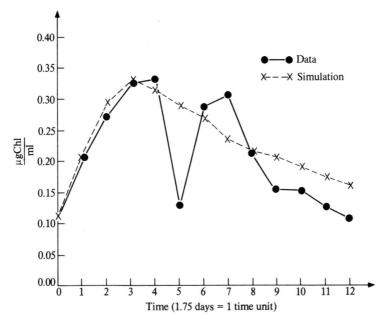

FIGURE 5.11 Trajectories of control and state variables plotted against data: total algae ($\psi$). (Source of data: Parks *et al.*, 1975.)

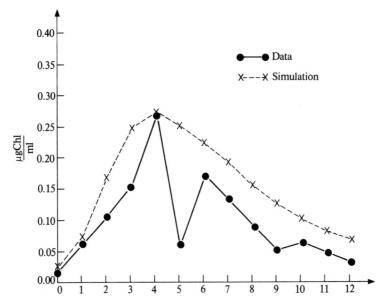

FIGURE 5.12 Trajectories of control and state variables plotted against data: *Anabaena* ($\alpha_2$) (Source of data: Parks *et al.*, 1975.)

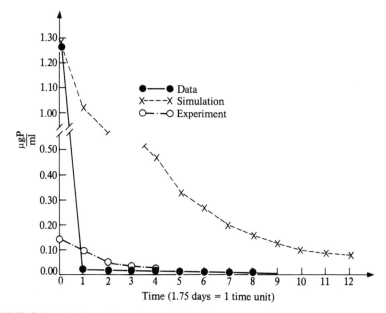

FIGURE 5.13 Trajectories of control and state variables plotted against data: environmental phosphate ($\alpha_1$). (Source of data: Parks *et al.*, 1975.)

## THE CUSP CATASTROPHE AND THE LOGISTIC EQUATION

A criticism often leveled at the use of catastrophe theory to model physical phenomena is that no physical consideration is given to the use of the standard (canonical) equation to describe the output equation. Here we wish to show that for many growth processes in which the classical logistic equation makes sense, the canonical cusp catastrophe is a logical choice for modeling the process.

The logistic equation, which is widely used in population biology to model population increase (or decrease) in an environment with an upper limit on carrying capacity, has the form

$$\dot{x} = (a - dx)x,$$

where $a$ is the intrinsic rate of growth (without the limited carrying capacity) and $d$ is the contribution of one population unit to the decrease in intrinsic growth rate due to density effects. Clearly, when $ax = dx^2$, the population stops growing.

One of the assumptions of the logistic model is that the decrement in intrinsic growth rate for each member of population added is linear in $x$. Although experimental evidence seems to confirm this relationship for many species and environments, certain combinations of species and environments may exist in which density effects are more important and in which the decrement in intrinsic growth rate may be proportional to the *square* of the population. For instance, in the lake pollution problem just discussed, nutrient influx from external sources is minimal, which increases competition for available nutrient even when the available nutrient is at a high level. In addition, *Anabaena* is known to secrete a substance toxic to other algae that would rapidly limit phytoplankton growth at higher densities.

Modification of the logistic equation to fit the above situation results in the new equation

$$\dot{x} = (a - dx^2)x.$$

Adding the effect of removal of species from the environment by death, we have

$$\dot{x} = (a - dx^2)x - b,$$

or

$$\dot{x} = -(x^3 + ax + b),$$

(upon setting $d$ equal to unity). Thus, a simple, logical extension of the logistic model leads immediately to the canonical equation for the cusp catastrophe.


## PULSE AND VALUE STABILITY

In the section on graphs and pulse processes (p. 131), we introduced the concept of pulse stability for a weighted digraph. Now we wish to take up the problem of determining algebraic tests for pulse and value stability, as well as consider certain questions relating stability of the graph to its topological structure.

The central idea in the development of stability tests for graphs is the concept of the characteristic values of a weighted digraph. To make this more precise, we define the *adjacency* matrix $A$ of a graph $G$ as follows

$$a_{ij} = f(u_i, u_j), \qquad i, j = 1, 2, \ldots, n,$$

where $u_1, u_2, \ldots, u_n$ are the vertices of $G$ and $f(\cdot, \cdot)$ is the weight function. The characteristic values of $G$ are then defined to be the characteristic values of $A$.

The connection between the value of each vertex at time $t$, $v_j(t)$, the change in value $p_j(t)$, and the adjacency matrix of $G$ is given in the next result.

*Pulse Process Theorem.* In a simple pulse process starting at vertex $u_i$, we have

$$p_j(t) = [A^t]_{ij}$$

*and*

$$v_j(t) = v_j(0) + [I + A + A^2 + \ldots + A^t]_{ij},$$

*where A is the adjacency matrix of the digraph and* $[\cdot]_{ij}$ *denotes the* $(i, j)$ *entry of the corresponding matrix.*

As an illustration of this result, consider the simple digraph

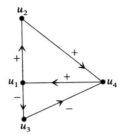

Here the adjacency matrix $A$ is

$$A = \begin{bmatrix} 0 & 1 & -1 & 0 \\ 0 & 0 & 0 & 1 \\ 0 & 0 & 0 & -1 \\ 1 & 0 & 0 & 0 \end{bmatrix}.$$

Assume that a simple pulse process starts at vertex $u_1$ at time $t = 0$, with $v_i(0) = 0$, $i = 1, 2, 3, 4$. A simple calculation shows that

$$A^2 = \begin{bmatrix} 0 & 0 & 0 & 2 \\ 1 & 0 & 0 & 0 \\ 1 & 0 & 0 & 0 \\ 0 & 1 & -1 & 0 \end{bmatrix},$$

$$I + A + A^2 = \begin{bmatrix} 1 & 1 & -1 & 2 \\ 1 & 1 & 0 & 1 \\ 1 & 0 & 1 & -1 \\ 1 & 1 & -1 & 1 \end{bmatrix}.$$

Since the pulse process begins at vertex $u_1$, we have $p_3(2)$ given by the $(1, 3)$ entry of $A^2$, i.e., $p_3(2) = 0$. Similarly, $v_1(2) = v_1(0) + [I + A + A^2]_{1,1} = 0 + 1 = 1$. These results are clearly in agreement with the pulse process theorem.

Our main objective is to relate the concepts of pulse and value stability to the adjacency matrix $A$. No general necessary and sufficient condition seems to be known at present. However, if we assume that the digraph $G$ has *distinct* characteristic values (a generic condition), then we can state the pulse stability theorem:

*Pulse Stability Theorem.   Suppose G is a weighted digraph with distinct characteristic values. Then G is pulse-stable under all simple pulse processes if and only if every characteristic value of G has a magnitude of, at most, unity.*

As a result of the above theorem, we see that to test for pulse stability, we need only calculate the characteristic root of $A$ of largest magnitude. If it lies outside the unit circle, then $G$ is not pulse-stable; otherwise, $G$ is pulse-stable.

Value stability is determined by making use of the pulse stability result just cited. The precise test is given by the following theorem:

*Value Stability Theorem.   The weighted digraph G is value-stable under all simple pulse processes if and only if G is pulse-stable under all simple pulse processes and unity (1) is not a characteristic value of G.*

Thus, we see that value and pulse stability are both determined by examination of the characteristic roots of the graph $G$, i.e., the roots of the adjacency matrix $A$.

*Example: Control of Insect Pests*   Consider the problem of controlling insect pests in a cultivated field by spraying insecticides. We let $P_1$ denote a crop plant that is limited because of crowding, $H_1$ a pest herbivore that eats $P_1$, $W$ a specialized insect that kills only $H_1$, $G$ a generalized predatory insect that eats both $H_1$ and $H_2$ (another herbivore), $P_2$ another plant, and $I$ the insecticide. A signed digraph representing this situation is shown in Figure 5.14.

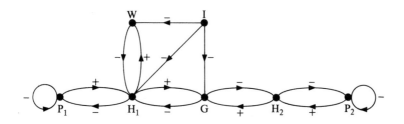

FIGURE 5.14   Signed digraph for insect control.

Note that the sign on arc $(x_i, x_j)$ represents the effect of a change in $x_i$ on the *rate* of change in $x_j$.

The adjacency matrix $A$ for the digraph (Figure 5.14) is

$$
A = \begin{array}{c} \\ P_1 \\ H_1 \\ W \\ G \\ H_2 \\ P_2 \\ I \end{array}
\begin{array}{c}
\begin{array}{ccccccc} P_1 & H_1 & W & G & H_2 & P_2 & I \end{array} \\
\left[\begin{array}{ccccccc}
-1 & 1 & 0 & 0 & 0 & 0 & 0 \\
-1 & 0 & 1 & 1 & 0 & 0 & 0 \\
0 & -1 & 0 & 0 & 0 & 0 & 0 \\
0 & -1 & 0 & 0 & -1 & 0 & 0 \\
0 & 0 & 0 & 1 & 0 & -1 & 0 \\
0 & 0 & 0 & 0 & 1 & -1 & 0 \\
0 & -1 & -1 & -1 & 0 & 0 & 0
\end{array}\right]
\end{array}
$$

The characteristic roots of $A$ are

$$\{-0.119 \pm 1.85i, -0.335 \pm 1.03i, -0.762, -0.328, 0\}.$$

Thus, the largest root has magnitude greater than 1 and, as a result of the pulse stability theorem, the graph of Figure 5.14 is *not* pulse- or value-stable. Such a result could have been predicted from inspection of Figure 5.14 since there are many deviation-amplifying cycles, e.g., $G \rightarrow H_2 \rightarrow P_2 \rightarrow H_2 \rightarrow G$.

If a given digraph is not pulse-stable, it is of obvious interest to know what kind of structural changes would be stabilizing. In other words, we would like to be able to classify stable graphs according to their *structural* characteristics, since we could then determine stabilizing strategies by making those structural changes that would transform the given graph into a stable structure. Unfortunately, no general results of this type yet exist. However, certain specific classes of digraphs often appearing in practice have been studied and useful results obtained. We refer the reader to the chapter references for more details.

## RESILIENCE OF DYNAMICAL PROCESSES

The problem of responsiveness of a system to perturbations in its state or parameters has already been alluded to a number of times in earlier sections. In rough terms, the "resilience" of a dynamical process is a measure of how capable the system is of absorbing disturbances without changing its basic behavior. Clearly, there is far too much vagueness in the foregoing "nondefinition," and in the following sections we shall attempt to formulate the resilience concept in a consistent mathematical fashion. We should note at the outset, however, that there is by no means universal agreement among practitioners on exactly what a resilience measure should consist of. While there are many points of contact between resilience and the notions of structural stability, bifurcation theory, catastrophe theory, connective stability, and the other concepts discussed earlier, no one of these topics seems to capture the entire essence of the resilience idea, at least as it is understood by workers in ecology, where the concept, or at least the terminology, seems to have arisen. Thus, our treatment will necessarily be a tentative and somewhat personal mathematical assessment of how the resilience ideas can be formulated mathematically and thereby brought into the domain of objective, rather than philosophical, systems analysis.

As with the other stability concepts of this chapter, a specific mathematical formulation of system resilience is dependent upon the type of mathematical formulation used to describe the system. Since the work done thus far on resilience has all been based on systems described by ordinary differential equations, we shall also focus on this area. Other system descriptions in terms of graphs, input–output relations, and so on, while intuitively having their own resilience notions, have not been sufficiently studied to justify their inclusion here. In fact, as will be seen below, study of the resilience concept is still at the definitional level, even for a differential equation model, and no real mathematical *results* are yet available. It is to be hoped, however, that the "right" definitions will quickly yield useful, applicable theorems.

We begin with a system $\Sigma$ described by the set of differential equations

$$\dot{x} = f(x, a) + g(t), \qquad x(0) = x_0, \qquad (\Sigma)$$

and assume that the origin is an equilibrium point when no outside disturbances are acting, i.e., $f(0, a) = 0$ for all $a$ when $g(t) \equiv 0$. Here $a$ is a vector of system parameters. In the context of the foregoing setup, the principal ingredient of the resilience idea is to ask either (a) under what conditions the disturbance function $g(t)$ can cause the system state $x(t)$ to leave the domain of attraction $D$ of the origin or (b) what variation in the parameters $a$ will result in a modification of the boundary of $D$, $\partial D$, such that the system state shifts to the domain of an attractor other than the origin.

A naive approach to the first problem would be to measure the resilience of the system by the nearest approach of $x(t)$ to $\partial D$ during the time history of the process (assuming $g(t) \equiv 0$, $a = a^*$ for all $t \geq 0$). The objections to such an approach are primarily practical, rather than mathematical: namely, the minimal distance of $x(t)$ from $\partial D$ is a rather poor indicator of how severe a perturbation $\Sigma$ can absorb with leaving $D$. The reason is that the disturbance necessary to push $\Sigma$ out of $D$ depends not only upon the magnitude of the disturbance but also upon its direction. In geometrical terms, we might imagine the situation depicted in Figure 5.15. Here the

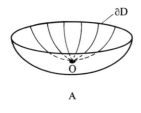
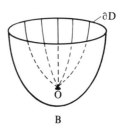

FIGURE 5.15    Potential well for $\Sigma$.

region $D$ can be thought of as a potential "well" (as is the basis for the Lyapunov theory). In Figure 5.15A, $D$ is a shallow well, and, consequently, even if $x(t)$ always remains far from $\partial D$, it is relatively easy to move the system beyond $\partial D$. On the other hand, if $D$ has the shape depicted in Figure 5.15B, then even if $x(t)$ is always near $\partial D$, a substantial disturbance is needed to push $\Sigma$ over the edge into the domain of attraction of another equilibrium.

The above considerations indicate that resilience is not an intrinsic property of $\Sigma$, but that it depends upon $\Sigma$ *and* the class of admissible perturbations. As a trivial illustration of this point, we note that if the minimal distance of $x(t)$ from $\partial D$ is $\alpha$ and $\|g(t)\| < \alpha$ for all $t$, then $\Sigma$ will "absorb" *all possible* disturbances, i.e., $\Sigma$ is infinitely resilient to disturbances from this class. On the other hand, if the *maximal* distance of $x(t)$ from $\partial D$ is $\beta$ and if $\|g(t)\| > \beta$ for all $t$, then the same system $\Sigma$ is unable to absorb *any* perturbation, i.e., $\Sigma$ is totally nonresilient with respect to the given class of perturbations. Thus, without at least an implicit agreement on the class of admissible disturbances, the resilience concept is a rather empty one.

Since we have seen that both the magnitude and direction of the disturbing force $g(t)$ must be taken into account when formulating a resilience measure, let us consider the following approach to the problem. At each time $t$, we construct the direction vector from $x(t)$ to the point on $\partial D$ that is nearest to $x(t)$ (see Figure 5.16). The vector $v(t)$ is constructed from the known vector $x(t)$, (obtained perhaps through numerical integration) and the vector $d(t)$ (which is known since we assume $\partial D$ has been calculated). Thus, $v(t) = d(t) - x(t)$. If we now assume that $g(t)$ is a "pulse" disturbance at time $t$—i.e., $g(t) = \mu\delta(t-s)$, where $\mu$ is a vector indicating the magnitude and direction of the pulse—we may attempt to determine whether or not the pulse will drive the system beyond $\partial D$ by comparing the vectors $\mu$ and $v(t)$. As noted, the question will be decided by whether or not $\mu$ is of sufficient magnitude and acting in the right direction to move $x(t)$ beyond $\partial D$. (Here we may neglect the free dynamics $f(x)$ since we have assumed that $g(t)$ is a single "delta-function" input.)

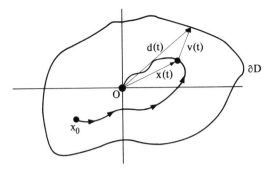

FIGURE 5.16   State-space behavior of $\Sigma$.

If we introduce the magnitude function $m$ as

$$m(t) = \|\mu\| - \|v(t)\|,$$

and the direction function $\theta$ as

$$\cos \theta(t) = \frac{(\mu, v(t))}{\|\mu\| \|v(t)\|},$$

where $(\,,)$ denotes vector inner product and $\|\cdot\|$ is the euclidean norm, then we see that the resilience of $\Sigma$ at time $t$ can be semiquantitatively characterized as follows:

*Low* resilience:   when $m(t) \geq 0$ and $\cos \theta(t) \cong 1$
*High* resilience:   when $m(t) < 0$ or $\cos \theta(t) < 0$.

In other words, $\Sigma$ is resilient with respect to the pulse disturbance $\mu$ at time $t$ if the magnitude of $\mu$ is too small or if $\mu$ pushes $x(t)$ *away* from $\partial D$. Conversely, if $\mu$ is of higher magnitude than $v(t)$ and drives $x(t)$ towards $\partial D$, then we are justified in saying that $\Sigma$ is of low resilience.

The considerations just discussed provide a basis for a systematic mathematical approach to the resilience question as it relates to external perturbations of the state $x(t)$. Continuously acting disturbances or a combination of pulses can easily be accommodated within the foregoing setup through routine mathematical adjustments similar to those employed in probability theory when passing from discrete to continuous or mixed distribution functions. In such cases, of course, we will also have to account for the free dynamics $f(x)$ in assessing the resilience of $\Sigma$ to a given class of disturbance.

## RESILIENCE AND CATASTROPHES

Direct external influence on the state is one way in which a system may shift its position from the domain of one attractor to that of another. The

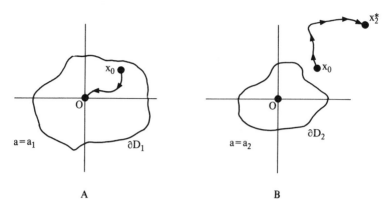

FIGURE 5.17    Domains of attraction of the origin.

preceding section examined this point in some detail. Now we consider the second way in which the system may move to another attractor region: changes in the dynamics themselves by variation of the system parameter vector $a$.

Consider the situation shown in Figure 5.17. Here we see that when the parameter vector $a = a_1$, the initial state $x_0$ lies within the region bounded by $\partial D_1$ and the system tends to the origin. If the vector $a$ shifts to $a = a_2$, then the *same* initial state $x_0$ now lies outside the region bounded by $\partial D_2$ and the ultimate fate of the system is to end up at $x = x_2^*$, an equilibrium far removed from 0. It is easy to imagine a situation where $x_0$ is very near $\partial D_1$, in which case even a slight change in the vector $a$ may deform $\partial D_1$ enough to cause $x_0$ to lie within the attractor region of a different equilibrium.

As we have observed in an earlier section, the situation just described lies at the basis of (elementary) catastrophe theory à la Thom–Zeeman, wherein we explicitly recognize that the equilibria (in this case $x_2^*$ and the origin), as well as their respective attractor boundaries $(\partial D_1, \partial D_2)$, depend (smoothly) upon the parameter vector $a$. Thus, an intimate connection exists between the catastrophe map $\chi$ described in the section on catastrophe theory and the concept of system resilience, since, in an intuitive sense, the closer the initial parameter setting $a$ is to a singularity of $\psi$, the less resilient the system is (to changes in $a$).

Keeping in mind the above considerations, we may formulate a measure of resilience by considering the magnitude and direction of change in the vector $a$ needed to drive $a$ through a singularity of $\chi$ (see Figure 5.18 for the cusp). Since the arguments are much the same as those given in the last section, we shall omit them for brevity, noting that, as before, the resilience concept is fairly vacuous unless we first agree upon the class of admissible changes in $a$. In Figure 5.18, for any $a$, we construct the vector $v$ from $a$ to

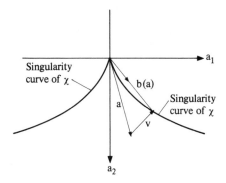

**FIGURE 5.18**  Singularity curves for the cusp catastrophe.

the nearest singularity of $\chi$ and compare $v$ with the allowable changes in $a$ in order to measure the resilience of $\Sigma$ for the given $a$, relative to the admissible perturbations.

*Example: Stock Market*  As a simple illustration of the above argument, consider an elementary stock market model in which the output (state) variable is the rate of change of some market index (e.g., the Dow–Jones averages), while the input variables $a_1$ and $a_2$ represent the excess demand for stock by fundamentalists and the fraction of speculative money in the market (chartists), respectively. The details behind such a model are given in the paper cited in the chapter notes. Modeling the situation using the cusp catastrophe yields the picture shown in Figure 5.19.

Now assume that the units have been selected so that the above model is the *canonical* cusp catastrophe discussed above (pp. 151–155)—that is, the bifurcation set in the input space $C$ is such that

$$a_2 = 5.67 a_1^{2/3},$$

or

$$27 a_1^2 - 4 a_2^3 = 0.$$

These equations are obtained from the canonical cusp potential

$$f(x_1, \alpha_1, \alpha_2) = \frac{x_1^4}{4} + \frac{\alpha_1}{2} x_1^2 + \alpha_2 x_1$$

by the fact that along the cusp lines we must have

$$\frac{\partial f}{\partial x} = 0, \qquad \frac{\partial^2 f}{\partial x 2} = 0.$$

Using these equations, we can eliminate $x$ and obtain the stated result.

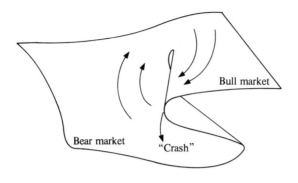

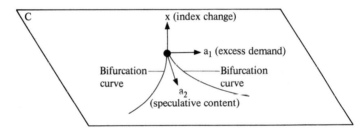

FIGURE 5.19   Cusp model of a stock market.

Assume that the initial parameter vector $a$ is such that the fundamentalist excess demand is 0.1 and the fraction of speculative money in the market is 0.58, i.e., $a = (0.1, 0.58)$. The point nearest to $a$ on the bifurcation curve is

$$b(a) = (0.3, 0.44).$$

Thus, the vector $v(a)$ is

$$v(a) = (0.2, -0.133).$$

Since $v(a)$ represents the *change* in $a$ needed to cross the bifurcation curve, we see that the stock market described by the parameter vector $a$ is nearly *twice* as resilient to changes in $a_1$, fundamentalist demand, as to changes in $a_2$, speculative action.

The preceding catastrophe-theoretic interpretation and analysis of resilience is, of course, restricted to those situations in which the hypotheses underlying elementary catastrophe theory are satisfied:

• The system dynamics $f(\cdot)$ are smooth, i.e., $C^\infty$ functions of $x$ and $a$ and of gradient type.

• The number of components in the parameter vector $a$ is no greater than five.

• The system equlibria are only fixed points: $\Sigma$ has no limit cycles, Lorenz attractors, or more exotic types of steady-state behavior. In other words, only "elementary" catastrophes can occur.

If any (or all) of the above conditions are violated, it may still be possible to analyze resilience employing structural stability concepts other than catastrophe theory. We shall now briefly examine some possibilities.

## MORSE–SMALE SYSTEMS AND RESILIENCE

For systems of dimension $\leq 2$, we have already discussed the problem of structural stability (pp. 147–151). From the past few sections, it is clear that some of the basic ideas underlying the idea of resilience are closely allied to structurally stable systems, since a critical ingredient in assessing resilience is determining whether the dynamics remain "essentially unchanged" under the influence of disturbances to the process. Structural stability of vector fields is one way to analyze this question, since the original system and its perturbed version can be thought of as qualitatively the same if they have similar phase portraits. In this section, we will make the idea of structural stability for vector fields more precise, as well as examine a large class of systems arising in practice whose dynamics are structurally stable. These are the so-called Morse–Smale systems, and the results we present provide a partial generalization of the structural stability theorem, given for the disc in the section on structural stability to the case of $n$-dimensional systems.

We begin with $M$, an $n$-dimensional $C^\infty$-manifold ($M$ is a topological space that in a neighborhood $U$ of each point $m$ looks like $R^n$). Thus, we can perform differential calculus in a consistent manner on $M$ (see Figure 5.20), with the coordinate map $\alpha: M \rightarrow R^n$ being $C^\infty$. Simple examples of manifolds are $R^n$, spheres, tori, and open subsets of $R^n$.

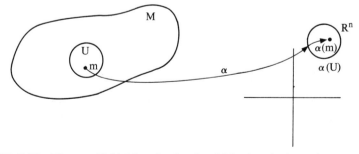

FIGURE 5.20   The manifold $M$ and a local neighborhood of a point $m$.

A $C^1$-vector field (or differential equation) on $M$ is an assignmnent of a tangent vector $v(x)$ to each point $x \in M$, such that the vectors $v(x)$ vary smoothly (in a $C^1$ way).

The concept of "similar phase portraits" for two vector fields $v$ and $w$ is captured by the following definition.

*Definition 5.6.* Two vector fields $v$ and $w$ are *topologically conjugate* if there is a 1-1, onto, continuous map $h$ taking directed solution curves of $v$ onto directed solution curves of $w$.

Thus, if $v$ and $w$ are topologically conjugate, they will have the same number of equilibrium points, the same number of periodic orbits, and the same general qualitative behavior.

We now explain "nearby" vector fields by putting a topology on the space $V(M)$, the $C^1$-vector fields on $M$. We say that $v$ and $w$ are close if they are pointwise close and so are their first derivatives. Precise definitions are a bit unwieldy, so we shall refer the reader to the chapter references for details. The idea of nearness of vector fields allows us to define structural stability.

*Definition 5.7.* A vector field $v \in V(M)$ is *structurally stable* if there is a neighborhood $N(v)$ in $V(M)$ such that each $w \in N(v)$ is topologically conjugate to $v$.

The main problem in structural stability is to find necessary and sufficient conditions for a vector field to be structurally stable.

*Examples*

1. *Simple harmonic oscillator* We have already seen (intuitively) that this elementary system described by the dynamics

$$\ddot{x} = -x$$

has a phase portrait consisting of concentric circles in the $(x, \dot{x})$ phase plane. This vector field is not structurally stable, since any vector field topologically conjugate to $v$ has only periodic orbits, and we can always tilt the arrows of $v$ (see Figure 5.4) slightly toward the origin to obtain a nearby vector field with a nonperiodic orbit.

2. *Van der Pol equation* Here the vector field $v$ is defined by the equations

$$\dot{x}_1 = x_2$$
$$\dot{x}_2 = -\varepsilon(x_1^2 - 1)x_2 - x_1, \qquad \varepsilon > 0.$$

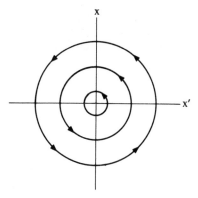

FIGURE 5.21  Phase portrait for simple harmonic oscillator.

The system has one periodic orbit, and every orbit outside it moves toward it and every orbit inside spirals out toward the periodic orbit (see Figure 5.22). Thus, this equation is structurally stable for all $\varepsilon > 0$.

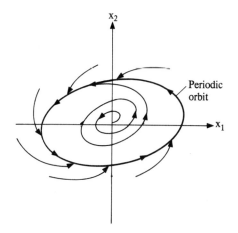

FIGURE 5.22  Phase portrait for the Van der Pol equation.

The most important class of structurally stable vector fields, the Morse–Smale systems, are characterized by the following conditions:

• $v(x)$ has finitely many equilibrium points, i.e., points $x$ such that $v(x) = 0$ and each such point is hyperbolic.
• $v(x)$ has finitely many periodic orbits and each such orbit is hyperbolic.
• The stable and unstable manifolds of equilibrium points and periodic orbits meet transversely when they intersect (this means no tangency is allowed between stable and unstable manifolds).

- The nonwandering points of $\Sigma$ are just the equilibrium points, together with the points on the periodic orbits. (Note: A point $x \in M$ is nonwandering if for each open neighborhood $U$ of $x$ and each $T > 0$, there exists a $t > T$ such that $x(t) \in U$ if $x(0) \in U$. In other words, any solution curve of $\Sigma$ that starts in $U$ eventually returns to $U$ infinitely often.)

In the section on structural stability, we gave necessary and sufficient conditions for structural stability in the case $M = $ two-dimensional disc. In actual fact, the following stronger result is true: if dim $M = 2$, then the structurally stable systems on $M$ coincide with the Morse–Smale systems. If dim $M > 2$, then there may be other structurally stable vector fields on $M$, in addition to the Morse–Smale systems.

The idea of resilience as considered in this book is clearly related to the structural stability ideas just given. However, there are some notable differences that it is of some value to list:

1. Structural stability is concerned with the entire phase portrait of the system; resilience is usually involved only with positive time asymptotic behavior.

2. Perturbations in resilience analysis generally do not involve varying the vector field $v$ over a whole neighborhood in $V(M)$. We generally assume that a submanifold $P$ of $V(M)$ is given such that $\Sigma \in P$ and the only variations in $\Sigma$ will also belong to $P$. We might think of $P$ as described by a finite set of parameters contained in $\Sigma$, and we change (perturb) $\Sigma$ by varying these perturbations.

3. While structural stability is too strong a concept for resilience, because of (1) and (2), the related concept of $\Omega$-stability, wherein we impose topological conjugacy only on the nonwandering points of $\Sigma$, is too weak. The reason is that $\Omega$-stability implies nothing about structural changes in the boundary of the domain of attraction of the nonwandering points.

The foregoing considerations suggest the following provisional definition of a resilient system $\Sigma$.

*Definition 5.8.* Assume that the continuous-time system $\Sigma$ is described by the differential equation $\dot{x} = f(x)$ and that $P$ is a submanifold of $C^1$ vector field on $M$ such that $f \in P$. Then $\Sigma$ is called *resilient* if

1. There is a neighborhood $U$ of $f$ in the $C^1$-topology such that all systems $\Sigma'$ defined by vector fields $f' \in U \cap P$ have the same number (finite) of attractors.

2. For each attractor $A_i$ of $\Sigma$ and each nearby system $\Sigma'$, we have a finite

set $a_i(\Sigma')$ of attractors of $\Sigma'$ and the maps

$$\Sigma' \to \bigcup_i a_i(\Sigma')$$

and

$$\Sigma' \to \bigcup_i \bar{B}_i(\Sigma')$$

are continuous with the $C^1$-topology on $U \cap P$ and with the Hausdorff metric on $A_i$ and $\bar{B}_i$. Here $\bar{B}_i = $ closure of the attractor region for $A_i$.

The foregoing definition of resilience is constructed so that an attractor of $\Sigma$ can "split" into several nearby attractors in $\Sigma'$ and not destroy the resilience of the system. This is reasonable since such a splitting should not change the asymptotic behavior of the system in any essential way.

*Example* The system

$$\dot{x} = \mu x - \varepsilon x^3, \qquad \varepsilon > 0, \tag{5.10}$$

would be resilient in the above sense to variations of $\mu$ about $\mu = 0$, even though the stable fixed point for $\mu < 0$ splits into one unstable and two stable points at $\mu = 0$. The main issue to note is that the two attracting points are still close together.

Resilience of a system, as just defined, is a qualitative property: $\Sigma$ is or is not resilient with respect to perturbations within the submanifold $P$. If we look for a numerical expression attempting to measure the degree of resilience of $\Sigma$, several possibilities suggest themselves, depending upon the particular situation. Let us examine some of the possibilities:

*Minimal Resilience* Here we are concerned about the range of perturbations within the manifold $P$ that do not induce qualitative changes in the behavior of $\Sigma$. Basically, this is the concept of resilience discussed in earlier sections.

One mathematical formalization of minimal resilience is to assume that we are given a metric $d(\cdot, \cdot)$ defined on the "parameter manifold" $P$ and let

$$S_P = \{\Sigma' \in P: \Sigma' \text{ is } not \text{ resilient by Definition 5.8}\}.$$

Then we define minimal resilience of $\Sigma$ by

$$R_{\min}(\Sigma) = d(\Sigma, S_P).$$

Thus, $R_{\min}(\Sigma)$ is the distance from the system $\Sigma$ to the nearest (in the sense of $d$) non-resilient system $\Sigma'$ in $P$.

178

*Speed Resilience*  A measure of resilience more in line with standard sensitivity analysis is to consider the "speed" with which the boundaries of the attractor regions change when $\Sigma$ is perturbed to $\Sigma'$ within $P$. Clearly, a very sensitive dependence of basin boundaries does not correspond to an intuitive sense of resilience, even if the system $\Sigma$ is structurally stable, i.e., more than just resilient.

A measure of speed resilience is provided by

$$R_{\text{speed}}(\Sigma) = 1/\lim_{h\to 0} \frac{1}{h} \sup_{\Sigma' \in P_h} \sup_i [d(A_i, A_i'), d(\bar{B}_i, \bar{B}_i')],$$

where $P_h$ is a ball of radius $h$ in $P$ about $\Sigma$, $A_i$ and $\bar{B}_i$ as above.

Note that $R_{\text{speed}}(\Sigma)$ may be 0 even if $\Sigma$ is resilient if the location of attractors or basins depends non-differentiably on the parameters. For example, the system (5.10) is resilient but has $R_{\text{speed}}(\Sigma) = 0$.

*Volume Resilience*  The size of the region in state space corresponding to a "desired" attractor region can also be used as a resilience measure since a large reduction in the size of a particular basin is almost as catastrophic as its complete disappearance. One measure of volume sensitivity resilience is

$$R_v = \lim_{h\to 0} \frac{1}{h} \sup_{\Sigma' \in P_h} |v(B) - v(B')|,$$

where $B$ is the desired basin, $B'$ the corresponding basin for $\Sigma'$, and $v(\cdot)$ a function measuring volume.

We note that volume resilience should be viewed with caution since in high-dimensional models $(n > 2)$, the basins will often have a complicated structure and may contain a large volume while the boundary could still be close to each point in the basin.

As a concluding remark, we see that in relation to catastrophe theory, resilience presents a twofold extension: attractors much more complicated than fixed points are taken into account, and we concern ourselves explicitly with the properties of the domains of attraction. We now turn our attention to various means of inducing or enhancing stable or resilient behavior in system dynamics.

## AN ECOLOGICAL EXAMPLE OF RESILIENCE: THE BUDWORM PROBLEM

All of the preceding notions concerning resilience and dynamical processes cannot possibly be appreciated in the abstract. The joy, as always, is in the details, and for these we turn to an important ecological system, the spruce budworm. The budworm is an insect pest that periodically destroys vast areas of forest in northeastern North America. From a system-theoretic viewpoint, the dynamics of the budworm outbreaks are interesting because they exhibit the rapid fluctuations and multiple time-scales characteristic of catastrophe theory models. In this section, we show how the cusp catastrophe can be used to characterize some of the resilience aspects of the budworm ecosystem.

The dynamics of budworm growth and die-off can be expressed by the following third-order system

$$\frac{dB}{dt} = \alpha_1 B \left( 1 - \frac{B(\alpha_3 + E^2)}{\alpha_2 SE^2} \right) - \frac{\alpha_4 B^2}{\alpha_5 S^2 + B^2},$$

$$\frac{dS}{dt} = \alpha_6 S \left( 1 - \frac{\alpha_7 S}{\alpha_8 E} \right),$$

$$\frac{dE}{dt} = \alpha_9 E \left( 1 - \frac{E}{\alpha_7} \right) - \alpha_{10} \frac{BE^2}{S(\alpha_3 + E^2)},$$

where $B(t)$ is the budworm density, $S(t)$ is the amount of forest foliage available, and $E(t)$ is a variable characterizing the "energy reserve" in the forest, i.e., the condition of health of the leaves and branches in the forest. The parameters $\alpha_1$ to $\alpha_{10}$ represent various birth and death constants, rate of removal of budworm by predation, and so on. The general question to be asked about the foregoing model is: what combination of parameter values cause low-equilibrium budworm densities to shift rapidly to high equilibrium levels, or, conversely, what parameter values enable one to move high budworm levels back to low equilibrium levels?

To answer the above question, we examine the equilibrium levels of $B$, $S$, and $E$. Call these quantities $\bar{B}$, $\bar{S}$, $\bar{E}$. After a moderate amount of algebraic manipulation of the above equations, we find that the equilibrium budworm level $\bar{B}$ satisfies the cubic equation

$$-\alpha_1(\alpha_3 + \bar{E}^2)\bar{B}^3 + \gamma\alpha_1\alpha_2\bar{E}^3\bar{B}^2$$
$$-[\gamma^2\alpha_1\alpha_5\bar{E}^2(\alpha_3 + \bar{E}^2) + \gamma\alpha_2\alpha_4\bar{E}^3]\bar{B}$$
$$+ \gamma\alpha_1\alpha_2\alpha_5\bar{E}^5 = 0,$$

where we have set $\gamma = \alpha_8/\alpha_7$. In order to bring this equation into standard form for the cubic, we must eliminate the quadratic term. This is accomplished through the change of dependent variable

$$\bar{B} \rightarrow y + \frac{\gamma\alpha_2\bar{E}^3}{3(\alpha_3 + \bar{E}^2)},$$

giving the new cubic equation in y

$$y^3 + ay + b = 0,$$

where

$$a = \frac{[\gamma^2 \alpha_1 \alpha_5 \bar{E}^2 (\alpha_3 + \bar{E}^2) + \gamma \alpha_2 \alpha_4 \bar{E}^3 - \gamma^2 \alpha_1^2 \alpha_2^2 \bar{E}^6}{\alpha(\alpha_3 + \bar{E}^2)},$$

$$b = \frac{\left\{ \dfrac{-(\frac{2}{27}) \gamma^3 \alpha_1 \alpha_2^3 \bar{E}^9}{(\alpha_3 + \bar{E}^2)^2} + \gamma \alpha_2 \bar{E}^3 \dfrac{[\gamma^2 \alpha_1 \alpha_5 \bar{E}^2 (\alpha_3 + \bar{E}^2) + \gamma \alpha_2 \alpha_4 \bar{E}^3]}{3(\alpha_3 + \bar{E}^2)} - \gamma^3 \alpha_1 \alpha_2 \alpha_5 \bar{E}^5 \right\}}{\alpha_1 (\alpha_3 + \bar{E}^2)}$$

Since the equilibrium level of budworm $\bar{B}$ is related to the variable y through the elementary transformation above, we see that the canonical cusp geometry, which governs the behavior of y as a function of a and b, also governs $\bar{B}$ and enables us to synthesize the entire equilibrium behavior of $\bar{B}$ into one picture, Figure 5.23. The cusp geometry tells us that no discontinuities in $\bar{B}$ can occur if $a \geq 0$, i.e., if

$$3[\gamma \alpha_1 \alpha_5 (\alpha_3 \bar{E}^2)^2 + \alpha_2 \alpha_4 \bar{E}(\alpha_3 + \bar{E}^2)] - 5\gamma \alpha_1 \alpha_2^2 \bar{E}^4 \geq 0.$$

For example, if the forest energy reserve is low ($\bar{E} \approx 0$), then we see that no budworm outbreaks will occur since the above expression will always be nonnegative. On the other hand, for high values of $\bar{E}$ ($\bar{E} \approx 1$), realistic ranges of the various parameters indicate that no combination of values can ensure against possible budworm outbreaks. However, this does not mean that outbreaks necessarily will occur, since the value of the variable b also

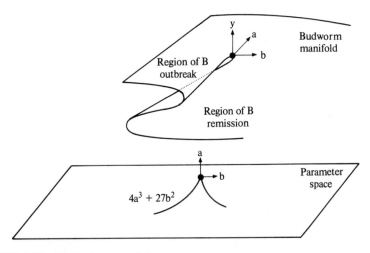

FIGURE 5.23  Budworm manifold.

plays a role in determining whether or not the critical branch of the cusp curve has been crossed.

What is important about the above example is that it enables us to see that it is the combination of system parameters given by $a$ and $b$ that count insofar as the budworm discontinuities are concerned. It seems unlikely that any amount of physical insight and intuition into the budworm process would enable one to conjecture that it is just this combination of parameters and no other that provides the relevant information, but it is so. In addition, once the parameters $a$ and $b$ have been obtained, the well-studied cusp geometry tells us that the critical branches in $(a - b)$-space, where discontinuities can occur, satisfy the equation

$$4a^3 + 27b^2 = 0.$$

Thus, we have a definite algebraic expression involving all the system parameters, albeit in a highly complicated way, which gives us a complete picture of the entire equilibrium behavior of budworm as a function of the system parameters.

The moral of the above story is that physically meaningful variables and mathematically convenient variables are usually two quite different objects and the successful analysis of a given situation quite often hinges on being able to find an appropriate transformation from one to the other. In the above situation, it was fortunate that $\bar{B}$ already satisfied a cubic equation, so that only the trivial transformation from $\bar{B}$ to y was needed to obtain the convenient mathematical form. More generally, a somewhat more complex transformation would be needed. This is one of the challenges inherent in successful use of catastrophe theory for the analysis of system problems.

## STABILITY, CONTROL, AND FEEDBACK DECISIONS

Interesting as the above stability considerations are, they relegate the analyst to the role of a passive observer—no provision is made for the modification of undesirable system behavior by application of external inputs, or controls, chosen by the decision maker. Conceptually, allowance for externally chosen controls in the system model shifts the role of the analyst from that of a passive observer to that of an active "interventionist." Philosophically and psychologically, this is a quantum leap forward to a substantially different view of the system, as already noted in Chapter 1. In the following sections we wish to show that the provision for regulation also represents a major methodological discontinuity in our approach to the analysis of the system and naturally leads to one of the keystone ideas of modern system theory—the concept of *feedback*.

To introduce the main idea of stability via feedback control, consider the state variable description of $\Sigma$:

$$\dot{x}(t) = f(x(t), u(t)), \qquad x(0) = c, \qquad (\Sigma)$$

where, as usual, $x$ is a vector function representing the state of $\Sigma$, and where the control $u(t)$ is a vector function *at the disposal of the decision maker*. In general, physical, social, or resource constraints will be such that the admissible control functions $u(t)$ must lie in some set of functions $U$; thus, $u \in U$. If we now assume that the uncontrolled system (i.e., when $u(t) \equiv 0$) has an undesirable behavior, the question arises of whether the system trajectory $x(t)$ can be improved (in some sense) by application of controlling inputs from $U$. Clearly, this question must be made more precise if it is to be attacked mathematically.

The most classical way to approach the above control question is to ask whether $\Sigma$ can be stabilized by application of controls from $U$. In general, we assume that the equilibria of the uncontrolled system are *not* asymptotically stable in the Lyapunov sense and we attempt to stabilize the system using the control function $u(t)$. The simple scalar linear example

$$\dot{x} = fx + u(t), \qquad x(0) - c,$$

with $f > 0$ shows that, in general, it is not possible to stabilize using controls of the form $u(t)$ since the representation

$$x(t) = ce^{ft} + \int_0^t e^{f(t-s)} u(s)\, ds$$

shows that no bounded function $u(t)$ can be found to "cancel out" the effect of the growing exponential $ce^{ft}$ for all possible values of $c$, the initial disturbance.

A control law of the form $u = u(t)$ is called "open-loop" in the control literature, since the decision (control) is not a function of the current state of the process $x(t)$, but only of the current time $t$. One of the basic precepts of modern (post-1950) control theory has been that *control is a function of state*—that is, the control law $u$ should possess the structure

$$u(t) = u(x(t), t).$$

Such laws are called *feedback control laws*, since the state of the system is observed and then "fed back" to the decision maker, who then makes his decision based upon the system's behavior as characterized by the state $x(t)$. The two conceptually different views are characterized in Figure 5.24.

To see the profound mathematical difference feedback control can make, consider again the scalar linear problem discussed a moment ago. We saw that no bounded open-loop control law could make the origin asymptotically

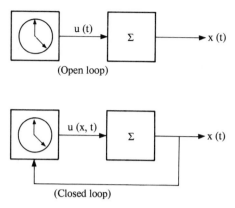

(Open loop)

(Closed loop)

FIGURE 5.24   Open-loop versus closed-loop control.

stable if $f > 0$. Now consider the simple linear feedback law

$$u(x, t) = kx(t),$$

where $k$ is a constant such that $k > f$. Using this law, the closed-loop dynamics are

$$\dot{x} = (f - k)x(t), \qquad x(0) = c,$$

and we see that the origin is asymptotically stable for all initial perturbations $c$. As shall be noted in a moment, this result is a special case of one of the foundational results of linear system theory, the pole-shifting theorem.

At this point it may be appropriate to inquire into the physical difference between open- and closed-loop control laws. While we shall be more precise in a moment, here the two types of laws may be contrasted by noting that the open-loop laws attempt to *force* the system *externally* into a different behavioral mode without changing the relationship between the system states in the uncontrolled mode, i.e., without modifying the connections between the state variables. On the other hand, closed-loop, or feedback, laws change the behavior of the system by actually changing the dynamics $f(\cdot, \cdot)$, itself. Thus, the feedback law rearranges the connections between the state variables and, as a consequence, changes the system trajectory $x(t)$ by actually changing the topology of $\Sigma$.

## LYAPUNOV STABILITY AND POLE-SHIFTING

The simple example of the last section shows that for scalar linear systems, it is possible to alter the characteristic value (and, hence, the stability properties) of the system arbitrarily by employment of a linear feedback control law. Now let us inquire into the possibility of extending this result to multidimensional systems.

Assume that the system is described by the set of linear differential equations

$$\dot{x} = Fx + Gu, \qquad x(0) = c,$$

where $x$ is an $n$-dimensional state vector, $u$ an $m$-dimensional control vector, and $F$ and $G$ are constant matrices of sizes $n \times n$ and $n \times m$, respectively. Utilization of the feedback control law

$$u(t) = -Kx(t),$$

where $K$ is a constant $m \times n$ matrix, clearly generates the closed-loop system dynamics

$$\dot{x} = (F - GK)x, \qquad x(0) = c,$$

and our problem is reduced to consideration of the following question: Given $F$ and $G$, can we always find a constant matrix $K$ such that $F - GK$ has its characteristic values located at prespecified points in the complex plane? Remarkably enough, the answer to this question is yes under very modest assumptions about the matrices $F$ and $G$. The next result details the whole story.

*Pole-Shifting Theorem.* *Assume that the pair of matrices $(F, G)$ is completely reachable, i.e., the $n \times nm$ matrix*

$$\mathscr{C} = [G \,|\, FG \,|\, \ldots \,|\, F^{n-1}G]$$

*is of rank $n$. Then, given an arbitrary set of complex numbers $\Lambda = \{\lambda_1, \lambda_2, \ldots, \lambda_n\}$, it is always possible to find a constant matrix $K$ such that the characteristic values of $F - GK$ coincide with the set $\Lambda$.*

## Remarks

1. The reachability condition on $(F, G)$ is a generic property. Thus, "almost all" linear systems satisfy this hypothesis.

2. If the set $\Lambda$ is symmetric, i.e., $\lambda \in \Lambda$ implies $\bar{\lambda} \in \Lambda$, then the entries of $K$ may be taken to be real. In general, $K$ must be complex.

3. The name "pole shifting" comes from the engineering literature, where the characteristic roots of $F$ are often interpreted as the "poles" of the rational transfer function matrix for the system $\Sigma$. The theorem states that if $\Sigma$ is reachable, then these poles may be arbitrarily altered by linear feedback.

The practical importance of the pole-shifting theorem cannot be overemphasized, since it implies considerable flexibility in the design of any system.

The designer need not worry about designing certain stability characteristics into the system, as any unstable behavior manifested by the system may be arbitrarily changed by application of an appropriate feedback control law.

*Example: Equilibrium in Group Interaction*  Let us consider a formal model of social interaction developed by G. Homans and treated mathematically by H. Simon. The system contains four variables:

1. The intensity of interaction (or communication) among members of a group, $T(t)$
2. The amount of friendliness (or group identification) among group members, $I(t)$
3. The total amount of activity carried on by a member of the group, $W(t)$
4. The amount of activity imposed on the group by its external environment (the amount required for its survival), $P(t)$

For purposes of this example, we shall assume that the variables $I$, $W$, and $T$ represent the *deviation* of interaction, friendliness, and so on, from some desired, or ideal, level $(I = W = T = 0)$ and that the system has been disturbed from the ideal level by some perturbation. Our problem will be to see if it is possible to stabilize the interaction process by manipulation of the external environment $P$.

By translating Homans' verbal postulates about the interrelations of the above variables, a plausible mathematical model of the interaction process is provided by the following differential equations

$$\frac{dI}{dt} = b(T - \beta I),$$

$$\frac{dW}{dt} = c_1(I - \gamma W) + c_2(P - W),$$

and the algebraic relation

$$T = a_1 I + a_2 W.$$

The parameters $a_1$, $a_2$, $c_1$, $c_2$, $\gamma$, $\beta$, and $b$ represent various interaction strengths and proportionality constants. The first equation may be roughly interpreted as saying that friendliness will increase or decrease as the amount of interaction is disproportionately large or small relative to the existing level of friendliness. Similar interpretations can be given to the other equations.

A small amount of algebraic manipulation of the above model soon reduces it to the standard form

$$\dot{x} = Fx + Gu,$$

where

$$F = \begin{bmatrix} b(a_1 - \beta) & ba_2 \\ c_1 & -(c_1\gamma + c_2) \end{bmatrix}, \qquad G = \begin{pmatrix} 0 \\ c_2 \end{pmatrix},$$

$$x = \begin{pmatrix} I \\ W \end{pmatrix}, \qquad u = P.$$

For the sake of definiteness, let us assume that

$$c_1\gamma + c_2 < b(a_1 - \beta)$$

so that the characteristic roots of $F$ are unstable. We ask whether we can find a linear feedback based upon measurement of friendliness and group activity that will move the roots to the left half-plane; in other words, we seek a law

$$P(t) = -(k_1 I + k_2 W)$$

to stabilize $\Sigma$. This question is clearly a weak version of the pole-shifting problem, with the set $\Lambda$ being any collection of numbers in the left half-plane.

To study the question posed above, we must first check the reachability of $\Sigma$. It is easily checked that the reachability matrix $\mathscr{C}$ is

$$\mathscr{C} = \begin{bmatrix} 0 & ba_2 c_2 \\ c_2 & -c_2(c_1\gamma + c_2) \end{bmatrix},$$

which has rank 2 if and only if

$$ba_2 c_2 \neq 0.$$

The pole-shifting theorem guarantees that if $ba_2 c_2 \neq 0$, then there is no mathematical obstacle to finding a feedback law $P$ that will stabilize the system to any desired degree. If $\Sigma$ is already stable, we can use the law $P$ to enhance the stability by moving the roots of $F$ farther into the left half-plane.

The main deficiency of the pole-shifting theorem is that, as it stands, it applies only to linear systems. However, its applicability can be substantially extended by appeal to the Poincaré–Lyapunov stability theorem (p. 139). There we saw that if the system was described by

$$\dot{x} = Fx + h(x), \qquad x(0) = c,$$

where $\|c\|$ sufficiently small and $\|h(x)\|/\|x\| \to 0$ as $\|x\| \to 0$, then the system's asymptotic stability is determined by its linear part, i.e., by $F$. Thus, if we add a control term to the above system, obtaining

$$\dot{x} = Fx + h(x) + Gu, \qquad x(0) = c,$$

the conclusions of the pole-shifting theorem may be employed to move the roots of $F$ to desired locations, thereby ensuring the stability of the system. Furthermore, the condition on $\|c\|$, which depends upon the root of $F$ of the largest real part, can be considerably weakened by "shifting" this largest root far into the left half-plane. The connections between this result and some of the resilience notions considered earlier are evident.


## BIFURCATION CONTROL

Now let us consider the problem of arranging suitable feedback control so that the nonlinear system

$$\dot{x} = f(x, u, a), \qquad x(0) = c$$

has no bifurcation points for any values of the parameter vector $a$. In other words, we wish to choose a control

$$u(t) = u(x(t)),$$

so that the closed-loop dynamic

$$\dot{x} = f(x, u(x), a)$$

has no bifurcation points for any value of $a$. For the sake of definiteness in what follows, let us assume that $f(0, 0, a) = 0$ for all $a$.

In general, the above problem is unsolved, and we must content ourselves with some sufficient conditions for such a "bifurcation-free" control law. These conditions will be seen to be an almost trivial consequence of the following version of the global implicit function theorem.

*Global Implicit Function Theorem.* Let

$$f: E^n \times E^m \times E^k \to E^n$$

*be a continuously differentiable map. Then there exists a unique continuously differentiable map*

$$g: E^n \times E^m \times E^k \to E^n$$

*such that* $g(y, u, a) = x$ *for all* $x, y \in E^n$, $u \in E^m$, $a \in E^k$, *satisfying* $f(x, u, a) = y$, *provided that*

1. $\det[\partial f/\partial x] \neq 0$ *at each* $(x, u, a) \in E^n \times E^m \times E^k$,

*and*

2. *for each* $u \in E^m$, $a \in E^k$,

$$\|f(x, u, a)\| \to \infty \quad as \quad \|x\| \to \infty$$

Basically, the implicit function theorem tells us sufficient conditions under which the equation

$$f(x, u, a) = y$$

has a *unique* solution for $(x, u, a, y)$ in the entire region $E^n \times E^m \times E^k \times E^n$: If the Jacobian matrix of $f$ does not become singular in the region of interest and if $f$ satisfies the growth condition (2), then $f$ is globally invertible.

To apply the global implicit function theorem to the problem of bifurcation control, we simply observe that, by assumption, $f$ has an equilibrium point at the origin. Furthermore, if we find a control law $u(x)$ so that $[\partial f/\partial x]$ is nonsingular in the entire $(x, u, a)$ region and $f(x, u(x), a)$ satisfies the growth condition (2) for all $a$, then we can conclude that there are no equilibria other than the origin and, consequently, no bifurcation points. In short, such a control law $u(x)$ ensures that no perturbations in $a$ will result in the equilibrium at the origin bifurcating into a qualitatively distinct type of system behavior. The foregoing analysis, simple as it is, may very well lie at the heart of the successful use of linearization techniques for control system design.

A more difficult problem is to design controllers that do not allow the characteristic roots of the linearized system to cross the imaginary axis. For the *canonical* catastrophe models, the problem is easily resolved, however, since the behavior of these models is well understood. For instance, the canonical cusp model is

$$\dot{x} = -(x^3 + \alpha_1 x + \alpha_2).$$

Consequently, a negative feedback law for the control variable $\alpha_2$ results in

$$\alpha_2 = -(K_1 x + K_0),$$

with $K_1$, $K_2$ constants. Such a feedback law has the effect of changing $\alpha_1 \to \alpha_1 - K_1$, and by choosing $K_1$ so that $\alpha_1 > 0$ we can ensure that no discontinuous "jumps" from one attractor region to another will occur. For noncanonical models, however, where physical variables are employed rather than canonical coordinates, the control parameters are often nonlinear functions of the physical variables, and in such cases a feedback law on $x$ has the effect of changing more than one control parameter in the canonical model. In these situations, the design of bifurcation-free control laws is more complicated, although we clearly have a well-defined methodology to employ. Reference to more work along these lines can be found in the chapter notes.

## CONTROLLED RESILIENCE

In earlier sections, we have characterized the resilience of a dynamical process in several different ways. However, all of the various definitions required a resilient system to "persist" in its original behavior when subjected to disturbances of varied sorts. Since stability is our leitmotiv, let us now examine the question of global asymptotic stability (in the Lyapunov sense) for a system in which we allow for uncertainties in the dynamics, in the system parameters, and, possibly, in the control actions themselves. As a further novel twist, we shall not follow conventional probabalistic lines and assume that some statistical properties of the uncertainties are given *a priori*: rather, we assume *nothing* about the uncertainties other than that they are bounded. Our goal will be to develop a feedback control law that guarantees global asymptotic stability for *any* disturbance in the system, i.e., for any bounded uncertainty. Clearly, if we regard global asymptotic stability as the behavioral trait that must be preserved in the face of external disturbances, then a system governed by the above type of feedback law would indeed be resilient! An approach to resilience along these lines is another manifestation of the remark made earlier that it may not be necessary to design stability into a system at the beginning, as whatever stability properties we want can usually be arranged by employment of suitable feedback loops.

Since the problem just posed requires a fair amount of technical detail for satisfactory resolution in the general case, we shall examine only the linear version here, relegating the nonlinear case to the references. Fortunately, the same basic results carry over to the nonlinear situation, but with considerably more mathematical preliminaries. So, let us consider the system described by the linear dynamics

$$\dot{x} = Ax + Bu + Cv, \qquad x(0) = c,$$

where $u$ is an $m$-dimensional control vector, $v$ is an $l$-dimensional vector of disturbances, and $A$, $B$, and $C$ are constant matrices of appropriate size. Furthermore, we assume that $A$ is a stability matrix and that the elements of $A$ and $B$, as well as the disturbances may be known only in the sense that we possess upper and lower bounds for their values. As noted, our problem is to determine a feedback control law $u = u(x)$ such that the system is globally asymptotically stable for all bounded disturbances $v$ and all admissible matrices $A$ and $B$.

Under reasonable but technically complicated assumptions about the uncertainties in $A$, $B$, and disturbances $v$, it can be shown that the $i$th component of a stabilizing nonlinear feedback law is given by

$$u_i(x) = \begin{cases} -\rho_i(x)\,\mathrm{sgn}\,[(b_i, Px)], & x \notin N_i, \\ \varepsilon\{y_i \in R : |y_i| \le \rho_i(x)\}, & x \in N_i, \end{cases}$$

where $P$ is the solution of the matrix Lyapunov equation

$$PA + A'P + Q = 0, \qquad Q > 0, \quad \text{arbitrary,}$$

$b_i$ is the $i$th column of the matrix $B$, $\rho_i(x)$ is a function that depends upon the bounds of the uncertainties in $A$, $B$ and the disturbance $v$, $(\cdot, \cdot)$ denotes the usual inner product, and $\mathrm{sgn}\,[\cdot]$ is the signum function. The set $N_i$ is defined as

$$N_i = \{x \in R^n : (b_i, Px) = 0\}.$$

Thus, using the feedback law $u(x)$, the linear system can be shown to be asymptotically stable for all bounded uncertainties in the matrices $A$, $B$, and bounded disturbance $v$. The details of this result, together with the necessary information to calculate the multiplier functions $\rho_i(x)$ can be found in the papers cited in the chapter references.

*Example: Stabilization of a Macroeconomy*   To illustrate use of the above stability result, we examine the problem of stabilizing an economy with unknown, and possibly unknowable, characteristics. We shall postulate a very simple model to indicate the basic approach, although there appears to be no difficulty in extending the model by incorporating more state variables or more controls.

Let $y(t)$ and $\bar{y}(t)$ represent the actual and target "aggregate" demand levels at time $t$. They are assumed to be evaluated at some constant price. In order to allow for an upward trend of target demand level $\bar{y}(t)$, while imposing a growth limit upon it, we postulate the simple form

$$\bar{y}(t) = y^\infty(1 - e^{at}), \qquad y^\infty > 0, \qquad a < 0.$$

For determination of aggregate demand $y(t)$, we assume the dynamic relation

$$\frac{dy}{dt} = ay(t) + k_\mu u(t) + r_g g(t) + r_y,$$

$$y(0) = y_0.$$

Here

   $u(t)$ = index of the "tightness" of the money market (related to a control term)
   $g(t)$ = index of government fiscal policy
   $k_\mu$ = "policy" multiplier for the monetary policy index, $k_\mu > 0$
   $r_g$ = policy multiplier for the fiscal policy index, $r_g > 0$
   $r_y$ = forcing term (external)

The multiplier $r_g$ and the external forcing term $r_y$ may depend, in an unknown fashion, upon $u(t)$ and $y(t) - \bar{y}(t)$.

It should be noted that the term $r_y - ay^\infty$ may represent any stimulating or depressing force acting on the aggregate demand rate. We assume only that this term has known bounds, i.e.,

$$r_y^- \le r_y \le r_y^+.$$

To reflect delay in the response between government monetary policy and lending operations of commercial banks, we postulate that the aggregate demand responds to an exponentially "smoothed" monetary policy index $u(t)$, rather than to the *current* monetary policy indicator, $m(t)$. We allow the smoothing coefficient $r_\mu$ to be an unknown function of $u(t)$ and $y(t) - \bar{y}(t)$, supposing only that its bounds are known. Thus,

$$r_\mu^- \le r_\mu \le r_\mu^+, \qquad \gamma_\mu^+ > 0.$$

Thus, we have the equation for $u(t)$

$$\frac{du}{dt} = r_\mu(m(t) - u(t)), \qquad u(0) = u_0.$$

Fiscal controls appear in the form of tax provisions and rates as well as in decisions about government spending. Uncertainty in the effects of fiscal controls comes from the policy multiplier $r_g$, which depends in some unknown way upon $u(t)$ and $y(t) - \bar{y}(t)$. Again, we assume only that bounds for $r_g$ are given. Hence,

$$r_g^- \le r_g \le r_g^+.$$

Turning to control capabilities, we assume the following:

The fiscal control $g(t)$ is bounded, for each $t$, between $g^-$ and $g^+$, where $g^- < 0 < g^+$.

The monetary control $m(t)$ is bounded between $m^- |u(t)|$ and $m^+ |u(t)|$, $m^- < 0 < m^+$.

Thus, what constrains the actions of the monetary authority is the rate of expansion or contraction relative to the accumulated actions of the past.

Finally, we postulate two "resource" constraints:

1. *Adequacy of fiscal capability*

$$\max\{|r_y^- - ay^\infty|, |r_y^+ - ay^\infty|\} < r_g^- \min\{|g^-|, g^+\}$$

2. *Adequacy of monetary capability*

$$\frac{r_\mu^+ - r_\mu^-}{2r_\mu^-} < \min\{|m^-|, m^+\}$$

In (1), where the bounds on the "noise" $r_y - ay^\infty$ are compared with the bounds on fiscal capability, only the weakest policy multiplier $r_g^-$ is relevant; the value of $r_g^+$ is of no consequence. In (2), what is important is the range of sudden changes in the lag-in-effect, $(r_\mu^+/r_\mu^-) - 1$, compared with the range of monetary control flexibility.

Under the conditions (1) and (2), the stability results cited earlier can be employed to show that there exist policy rules, i.e., fiscal and monetary controls $g(t)$ and $m(t)$, that depend upon the observed state ($u(t)$ and $y(t) - \bar{y}(t)$) of the economy, such that the origin is uniformly asymptotically stable *regardless* of the initial state ($\mu_0, y_0 - \bar{y}_0$) and uncertainties $r_g, r_y, r_\mu$. In particular,

$$\lim_{t \to \infty} u(t) = 0, \qquad \lim_{t \to \infty} (y(t) - \bar{y}(t)) = 0.$$

The structure of the stabilizing feedback policy is depicted in Figure 5.25.

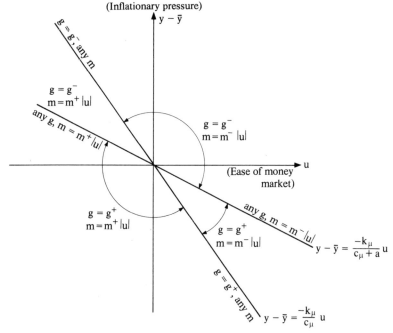

FIGURE 5.25  Stabilizing feedback law for macroeconomy ($c_\mu = \frac{1}{2}(r_\mu^+ + r_\mu^-)$).

We also observe that the control law prescribed by Figure 5.25 is *robust* in the sense that only the *mean* uncertainty $c_\mu$, not any of the bounds, need to be known in order to implement the feedback. Of course, a check of control capabilities requires knowledge of the uncertainty bounds, but these may be conservative.

Before concluding this example, it is worthwhile to note that if, as is done above, one can characterize monetary control as control with uncertain lag and fiscal control as control with uncertain effectiveness, then fiscal control is more fundamental in the sense that it can be shown that stability can be achieved depending *only* upon adequacy of fiscal capability. For instance, the control law

$$m = 0, \qquad g = g^- \quad \text{if} \quad y(t) - \bar{y}(t) > 0,$$

$$m = 0, \qquad g = g^+ \quad \text{if} \quad y(t) - \bar{y}(t) < 0,$$

will suffice to ensure stability if fiscal resources are adequate. On the other hand, given the assured stabilizability of the economy, monetary neutralism is justified or not depending on adequacy of monetary capability—that is, depending on the predictability of the delay in effect of monetary control relative to the flexibility available to the monetary authority in pursuing expansive or contractive policies.

## OBSERVATIONS

The feedback control laws discussed in the preceding sections all rely upon complete knowledge of the system state for their implementation. In many, if not most, large systems, such complete information is not available, and various means must be employed to estimate the state. Since a detailed treatment of this problem would take us beyond the scope of this short monograph, we only note here that many of the techniques developed in optimal estimation theory over the past 20 years or so can be used to advantage for such state estimation. We note, in particular, the Kalman filter and Luenberger observers in this regard. References to the details of these and other techniques are found in the chapter notes.

## NOTES AND REFERENCES

Historically, it appears that the first mathematical study of system stability was stimulated by the work in celestial mechanics in the seventeenth century. The problem of stabilizing a mechanical system via feedback control dates back at least as far as the work by Maxwell on governors for the Watt steam engine. For some of the original papers, see the collections:

Bellman, R., and R. Kalaba, eds., *Mathematical Trends in Control Theory*, Dover, New York, 1964.
Aggarwal, J., and M. Vidyasagar, eds., *Nonlinear Systems: Stability Analysis*, Dowden, Hutchinson and Ross, Stroudsburg, Pennsylvania, 1977.

### EXTERNAL DESCRIPTIONS

The basic results for nonlinear feedback systems of the external (input–output) type were presented in the works by Sandberg and Zames cited below, which ushered in the use of functional-analytic tools to study system stability properties.

Sandberg, I. W., "On the $L_2$-Boundedness of Solutions of Nonlinear Functional Equations," *Bell Syst. Tech. J.*, 43 (1964), 1581–1599.
Zames, G., "On the Input/Output Stability of Time-Varying Nonlinear Feedback Systems—I, II," *IEEE Trans. Autom. Control*, AC-11 (1966), 228–238, 465–476.

INTERNAL DESCRIPTIONS

The classical theory of Lyapunov stability is covered in detail in the books:

Hahn, W., *Stability of Motion*, Springer, New York, 1967.
Lasalle, J., and S. Lefschetz, *Stability by Lyapunov's Direct Method with Applications*, Academic, New York, 1961.

For a concise summary of the main points, see

Casti, J., *Dynamical Systems and Their Applications: Linear Theory*, Academic, New York, 1977, Chapter 7.
Arnol'd, V., *Ordinary Differential Equations*, MIT Press, Cambridge, 1973.

STRUCTURAL STABILITY

One of the best introductory works on qualitative stability is the text:

Hirsch, M., and S. Smale, *Differential Equations, Dynamical Systems and Linear Algebra*, Academic, New York, 1974.

CONNECTIVE STABILITY AND RESILIENCE

The concept of connective stability has been extensively studied by D. Siljak in many different contexts. A representative survey of much of this work may be found in the papers:

Siljak, D., "Stability of Large-Scale Systems under Structural Perturbations," *IEEE Trans. Syst. Man Cybern.*, SMC-2 (1972), 657–663.
Siljak, D., "Connective Stability of Competitive Equilibrium," *Automatica* 11 (1975), 389–400.

The concept of connective stability appears to have arisen initially in connection with certain questions in equilibrium economics. See:

Quirk, J., and R. Saposnik, *Introduction to General Equilibrium Theory and Welfare Economics*, McGraw-Hill, New York, 1968.
Arrow, K., and F. Hahn, *General Competitive Analysis*, Holden-Day, San Francisco, 1971.
Newman, P. "Some Notes on Stability Conditions," *Rev. Econ. Stud.* 72 (1959), 1–9.

GRAPHS AND PULSE PROCESSES

Pulse processes in graphs and the stability concepts associated with them are treated in:

Roberts, F. *Discrete Mathematical Models*, Prentice-Hall, Englewood Cliffs, New Jersey, 1976.

For interesting applications to energy problems, see:

Roberts, F., and T. Brown, "Signed Digraphs and the Energy Crisis," *Am. Math. Monthly*, 82 (1975), 577–594.

Roberts, F., "Building and Analyzing an Energy Demand Signed Digraph," *Environ. Planning*, 5 (1973), 199–221.

## INPUT–OUTPUT STABILITY

The small-gain theorem and the passivity theorem are treated in the paper:

Zames, G., and P. Falb, "Stability Conditions for Systems with Monotone and Slope-Restricted Nonlinearities," *SIAM J. Appl. Math.*, 6 (1968), 89–108.

Under some circumstances the two theorems are equivalent. For conditions see:

Anderson, B. D. O., "The Small-Gain Theorem, the Passivity Theorem and their Equivalence," *J. Franklin Inst.*, 293 (1972), 105–115.

## INTERNAL MODELS AND STABILITY

A magnificent exposition of the Lyapunov theory, together with numerous applications and further extensions, is the classic paper:

Kalman, R., and J. Bertram, "Control System Analysis and Design via the Second Method of Lyapunov—I, II," *J. Basic Eng. Trans. ASME*, 82 (1960), 371–393, 394–400.

See also the book:

Bellman, R. *Stability Theory of Differential Equations*, McGraw-Hill, New York, 1953,

as well as the works cited under *Internal Descriptions*, above.

## CONNECTIVE STABILITY

See the papers by Siljak cited under *Connective Stability and Resilience* for details of the proofs of the connective stability results.

The ecosystem example is taken from:

Casti, J. "Connectivity and Stability in Ecological and Energy Systems," WP-75-150, International Institute for Applied Systems Analysis, Laxenburg, Austria, November 1975.

## HOPF BIFURCATION

An outstanding summary of the current state of knowledge regarding the Hopf bifurcations, including a translation of Hopf's original paper, is:

Marsden, J., and M. McCracken, *The Hopf Bifurcation and its Applications*, Springer, New York, 1976.

STRUCTURALLY STABLE DYNAMICS

An introduction to notions of structural stability is given in the article:

Peixoto, M. "Generic Properties of Ordinary Differential Equations," in *Studies in Ordinary Differential Equations*, J. Hale, ed., Mathematical Association of America, Washington, D.C., 1977.

The initial work in the subject is:

Andronov, A., and L. Pontryagin, "Systemes Grossier," *Dok. Acad. Nauk SSSR*, 14 (1937), 247–251.

A good summary of the recent work is contained in the volume:

Peixoto, M. ed. *Dynamical Systems*, Academic, New York, 1973.


CATASTROPHE THEORY

The already classic work on catastrophe theory is the book:

Thom, R., *Structural Stability and Morphogenesis*, Addision-Wesley, Reading, Massachusetts, 1975.

A fascinating collection of recent reprints on *applied* catastrophe theory is:

Zeeman, E. C., *Catastrophe Theory: Selected Papers 1972–77*, Addison-Wesley, Reading, Massachusetts, 1977.

See also the book:

Poston, T., and I. Stewart, *Catastrophe Theory and Its Applications*, Pitman, London, 1978.

A recent expository article for the mathematically inclined is:

Golubitsky, M. "An Introduction to Catastrophe Theory and its Applications," *SIAM Rev.*, 20 (1978), 352–387.

For some adverse views on the topic, see:

Sussman, H., and R. Zahler, "Catastrophe Theory As Applied to the Social and Biological Sciences: A Critique," *Synthese* 37 (1978), 117–216.


SOME CATASTROPHE-THEORETIC EXAMPLES

The urban property price example is taken from:

Casti, J., and H. Swain, "Catastrophe Theory and Urban Processes," International Institute for Applied Systems Analysis, Laxenberg, Austria RM-75-14, April 1975 (also in *Proceedings of the IFIP Conference on Optimization*, Nice, France, 1975).

The lake pollution example is from:

Duckstein, L., J. Casti, and J. Kempf, "A Model of Phytoplankton Dieoff in Small Eutrophic Ponds Using Catastrophe Theory," *J. Water Resour. Res.* (in press).

Data are taken from:

Parks, R. W., *et al.*, *Phytoplankton and Water Quality in a Fertilized Fishpond*, Circular 224, Agricultural Experiment Station, Auburn University, Auburn, Alabama, 1975.

## PULSE AND VALUE STABILITY

For additional details on pulse processes and stability, see

Roberts, F., *Discrete Mathematical Models*, Prentice-Hall, Englewood Cliffs, New Jersey, 1976.

## RESILIENCE OF DYNAMICS PROCESSES

A qualitative discussion of resilience from the ecological point of view is:

Holling, C. S. "Resilience and Stability of Ecological Systems, "*Ann. Rev. Ecol. Syst.*, 4, (1973), 1–23.

## RESILIENCE AND CATASTROPHES

The stock market problem is adapted from:

Zeeman, E. C. "On the Unstable Behavior of Stock Exchanges," *J. Math. Econ.*, 1 (1974), 39–49.

## MORSE–SMALE SYSTEMS AND RESILIENCE

An introductory discussion of Morse–Smale systems and gradient dynamics is given in:

Hirsch, M., and S. Smale, *Differential Equations, Dynamical Systems and Linear Algebra*, Academic, New York, 1974.

See also:

Walters, P., "An Outline of Structural Stability Theory," in *Analysis and Computation of Equilibria and Regions of Stability*, H. Grümm, ed., CP-75-8, International Institute for Applied Systems Analysis, Laxenburg, Austria, 1975.
Grümm, H., "Definitions of Resilience," RR-76-5, International Institute for Applied Systems Analysis, Laxenburg, Austria, 1976.

## AN ECOLOGICAL EXAMPLE OF RESILIENCE: THE BUDWORM PROBLEM

The budworm model is taken from

Ludwig, D., D. Jones, and C. Holling, "Qualitative Analysis of Insect Outbreak Systems: The Spruce Budworm and the Forest," *J. Anim. Ecol.*, 47 (1978), 315–332.

STABILITY, CONTROL, AND FEEDBACK DECISIONS; LYAPUNOV STABILITY AND POLE
SHIFTING

More details on feedback control and stability are given in:

Casti, J., *Dynamical Systems and Their Applications*, Academic, New York, 1977.

For a proof of the pole-shifting result see the above book, as well as the original result:

Wonham, W. M., "On Pole Assignment in Multi-input Controllable Linear Systems," *IEEE Trans. Autom. Control*, AC-12 (1967), 660–665.

The example on group interaction is taken from:

Simon, H. "The Construction of Social Science Models," in *Mathematics and Psychology*, G. Miller, ed., Wiley, New York, 1964.

BIFURCATION CONTROL

More details on the linkup between traditional control theory and qualitative stability is given in the paper:

Mehra, R. "Catastrophe Theory, Nonlinear System Identification and Bifurcation Control," *Joint Automatic Control Conference*, San Francisco, June 1977.

CONTROLLED RESILIENCE

The analytic results and economic example are taken from:

Leitmann, G., "Guaranteed Asymptotic Stability for Some Linear Systems with Bounded Uncertainties," *J. Dynam. Syst. Meas. Control* (in press).
Leitmann, G., and H. Wan, "Macroeconomic Stabilization Policy for an Uncertain Dynamic Economy," in *New Trends in Dynamic System Theory and Economics*, Springer, Vienna, 1977.
Gutman, S., and G. Leitmann, "Stabilizing Feedback Control for Dynamical Systems with Bounded Uncertainty," *Proceedings of the IEEE Conference on Decision and Control*, Florida, 1976.

OBSERVATIONS

The question of determining the "best" estimate of the system state from observed data has been approached from many different viewpoints, depending upon the assumptions made concerning the data. A representative sample of the work for linear systems is:

Luenberger, D. "Observing the State of a Linear System," *IEEE Trans. Mil. Electron.*, MIL-8 (1964), 74–80.
Luenberger, D. "Observers for Multivariable Systems," *IEEE Trans. Autom. Control*. AC-11 (1966), 190–197.
Kalman, R., and R. Bucy, "New Results in Linear Prediction and Filtering," *J. Basic Eng.*, *Trans. ASME*, 93D (1961), 95–100.

In the context of stabilization, an important related question is the number of components of the state that *must* be measured in order to generate a stabilizing feedback control law. This is the question of "minimal control fields," which is studied in the papers:

Casti, J., and A. Letov, "Minimal Control Fields," *J. Math. Anal. Appl.*, 43 (1973), 15–25.
Casti, J., "Minimal Control Fields and Pole-Shifting by Linear Feedback," *Appl. Math. Comp.* 2 (1976), 19–28.

# Index

d'Alembert's principle, 13
Anosov system, 151

Barber paradox, 76
Behaviorist, 9
Bernoulli process, 103
Betti number, 59, 65, 68, 74
Bifurcation theory, 129
Binary choice, 4
Boundary, of chain, 62
Bounding cycle, 63, 73
Budworm, 178–181
Butterfly factor, 158

Catastrophe(s), 49
    cusp, 50, 162–163, 171
    fold, 153, 154
    map, 153
    theory, 129
        elementary, 50
Center, 47
Central place theory, 50
Chain group, 68
Chain of connection, 58
Chess, 18, 76,
    piece values, 77
Choice process, 113
Circle criterion, 135
Circuit, 10, 109
Coboundary, 69
Cochain, 68, 69
Cognitive school, 10
Cohomology group, 70

Complexity, 40
Complexity, axioms, 106
    computational, 105, 106
    control, 44, 100, 115
    design, 43, 115
    dynamic, 41, 102, 105
    evolution, 44, 110
    finite-state machines, 108
    function, 117, 118
    group, 108, 109
    measure, 107
    number, 111
    practical, 102
    static, 41, 98, 116
    topological, 107
Connective stability theorem, 142
Connectivity, 35, 37
    algebraic, 81, 82
Constraints, external, 27, 29, 30
    internal, 27, 28
Contact number, 111
Control, "bang-bang," 31
    bifurcation, 187, 188
    cybernetic, 25
    feedback, 181, 182
    open-loop, 182
    robust, 192
Coordinatization, 12
Cosimplex, 69
Culture function, 111, 112
Cycle, deviation-amplifying, 132
    deviation-counteracting, 132

201

202

Discriminant function, 121
Domain of attraction, 48, 52, 129, 170
Dynamics, free, 23
  controlled, 23
  societal, 86
  water reservoir, 2

Eccentricity, 39, 61, 72–73
Entropy, functional, 12, 13
  structural, 14
Equilibrium, stable, 46
  unstable, 46
Euler-Lagrange equations, 13
Evolution principle, 14, 110

Feedback, 25, 127
Fermat's principle, 13
Finite-state machine, 91
Focus, 47
Food web, 36

Global implicit function theorem, 187
Graph, 35, 36
  directed (digraph), 36, 131
  weighted digraph, 132
Group interaction, 185

Hamiltonian, 33
Hamilton's principle, 13, 33
Harmonic oscillator, 174, 175
Hicks condition, 144
Holist, 32, 33, 35
Homology group, 64, 74
Homology theory, 61
Homotopy, 40
Hopf bifurcation, 129, 130, 144–146
Hyperbolic closed orbit, 149

Identification, system, 25
Information theory, 120
  relativistic, 14
Insect pest control, 165

Jacob–Monod gene model, 44
Jordan–Hölder theorem, 90

Kalman filter, 193
Krasovskii's theorem, 140
Krener's theorem, 92, 120
Krohn–Rhodes theorem, 12, 88, 90, 108
$k$th coordinate action, 89

Lake pollution, 158
Law of requisite variety, 100, 101
Lienard's equation, 146, 147
Logistic equation, 162
Logistical growth, 26
Lorentz transformation, 14, 15
Lotka–Volterra system, 49, 150–151
Luenberger observer, 193
Lyapunov functions, 137, 138, 139, 140
Lyapunov stability theorem, 138

Macroeconomics, 2
Macroeconomy stabilization, 190
Matrix, adjacency, 37, 163
  Hicks, 142
  incidence, 17, 37
  interconnection, 130, 141
  Metzler, 138
  rational, 82
  transfer function, 83, 85, 118
Morse–Smala systems, 173, 175

Negentropy, 13
Nile delta, 24
Node, 47
Nonwandering point, 176

Optimization, 31
  criterion, 30

Parametric excitation, 140
Passivity theorem, 135
Pattern, 20, 39
  connective, 99
  graded, 20
$p$-chain, 62
$p$-cycle, 63
Permutation group, 90
Pharmacokinetics, 28
p-Hole, 66
Poincaré–Lyapunov theorem, 139, 186
Poincaré map, 149
Pole-shifting theorem, 184
Polyhedral dynamics, 116
Potential function, 12, 152
Predator–prey, antisymmetric, 48
  problems, 143
  relations, 3, 70
  system, 20

Prime decomposition, 91
Prime group, 91
Pulse process, 132, 133
Pulse process theorem, 163
Pulse stability theorem, 165

$q$-Analysis, 59
$q$-Connection, 39
$q$-Connectivity, 39, 58, 59

Reachability, 184
Realization, 8
    finite-dimensional, 26
Realization problem, 26
Realization theorem, 83
Reductionist, 32, 33
Relation(s), binary, 17, 37
    conjugate, 18
Resilience, 49, 52, 115, 131
    and catastrophes, 169
    controlled, 189
    of dynamical processes, 166
    minimal, 177
    speed, 178
    volume, 178
Routh–Hurwicz criterion, 136, 137

Search rule, 113
Semigroup, combinatorial, 108, 109
    division, 90
    "flip-flop", 91
    of transformations, 88, 89
Sets, 17
Set cover, 74
Set partition, 75
Sevastyanov–Kotelyanskii    condition,
    142
Shakespearean drama, 76
Similar phenomena, 120
Simplices, 18
Simplicial complex, 18, 37, 58
Singularity, 148
Hyperbolic, 149
Small-gain theorem, 134
Stability, asymptotic, 128
    bounded-input/bounded-output,
        127, 134

classical, 45
connective, 130, 141
input–output, 133
Lyapunov, 128, 136
pulse, 133, 163
structural, 46, 129, 147–148
value, 133, 163
Stochastic effects, 30
Stock market, 171
Structural stability theorem, 149
Structure vector, 59, 72–73
Subsystem, 41
System, canonical, 84, 86
    complex, 40, 41, 97
    hierarchical, 74
    indecomposable, 93
    linear, 82, 118
    "stiff," 105
    structure, 84
System description, entropy, 14
    external, 8, 127
    finite-state, 10
    input–output, 25, 57
    internal, 6, 10, 25, 127–129

Theory of types, 75
Thom–Zeeman theorem, 154
Tragedy of the commons, 115
Triangular action, 89
Torsion, 74
Torsion subgroup, 66, 67
Turing machine, 105

Urban property prices, 156

Value stability theorem, 165
Van der Pol equation, 41, 147, 174–
    175
Variety, 100
Vector field, 174
    structurally stable, 174
Vertices, 18

Watchmaker problem, 99
Wreath product, 88–90

## DATE DUE